HOME IS A LEARNING PLACE

A Parents' Guide to Learning Disabilities

HOME IS A

A Parents' Guide to

Martin S. Weiss

Illustrated by
Daniel Gildesgame

Little, Brown and Company

LEARNING PLACE

Learning Disabilities

Helen Ginandes Weiss

With a Foreword by Milton Brutten,
Clinical Director, The Vanguard School

Boston–Toronto

First edition

T 08/76

The authors are grateful to Remediation Associates, Inc., for permission to quote from "Educational Interpretation of the Wechsler Intelligence Scale for Children" by William E. Ferinden, Jr., and Sherman Jacobson. Copyright © 1969 by William E. Ferinden, Jr.

Library of Congress Cataloging in Publication Data

Weiss, Helen Ginandes.
  Home is a learning place.

  Bibliography: p. 256
1. Learning disabilities. 2. Child development.
I. Weiss, Martin S., joint author. II. Title.
LC4704.W44   371.9'14   76-17581
ISBN 0-316-92887-9

Designed by Janis Capone

*Published simultaneously in Canada
by Little Brown & Company (Canada) Limited*

Printed in the United States of America

To those who taught us how to begin to be parents:

To Elias Ginandes, who showed us how to give of ourselves to others . . .

To Esther Ginandes, who taught us how to try to understand the problems of others . . .

To Nat Weiss, who still shows us how to stick to our guns in spite of our doubts . . .

To Anna Weiss, who showed us how to be unselfish and forgiving . . .

To Mae Weiss, who has grandmothered our boys and took up where the others left off . . .

To Richie, Ira, Eric, Jerry and Alan Weiss, who have taught us how to laugh and cry simultaneously . . .

To Deedee, who has brought us the pleasure of having a daughter after so long.

ACKNOWLEDGMENTS

We wish to thank many people for the help that they gave in the writing of this book. To Dick McDonough, without whom it might never have been written; to Debbie Salem, Gale Waldron, Allison Selfridge and Nancy Ellis at Little, Brown, who attended to all the important details that we forgot.

To our "vast" secretarial staff, Delores Soalt, Charlotte Bernard, Karen Bernard, Kathleen Fergusen, Claudia Gimbel, Jane Crowe and Diane King, who typed this manuscript with tender loving care; and to Jacqueline Paltis Gildesgame, who gave of her wisdom.

Thanks also must be said to our children, Richie, Ira, Jerry, Eric, Alan, and to DeeDee, who kept the home fires burning, paid our bills, tended our home and fed our stomachs periodically so that we could closet ourselves off for days to write this manuscript.

Last but certainly not least to all the wonderful youngsters we have had the privilege of helping through the years, with special thanks to Josh Levy, Alan Owens and Peter Taffae for their special contributions, and Danny Gildesgame for his delightful artwork. Thanks!

FOREWORD

What have Helen and Martin Weiss brought us in *Home Is a Learning Place*? Nothing less than a small miracle of wisdom and compassion. Every parent is at times uncertain, even perplexed. But the learning-disabled child creates particular uneasiness and poses a threat to the parents' sense of adequacy. The child's needs are diverse and pressing and parents are often at a loss. They often fall back upon accustomed child-rearing practices, their heritage of conventional wisdom, and habitual modes. Too often the approaches that have proven successful in their rearing of the average child are exercises in futility with the learning-disabled, or even intensify and complicate the problem.

Helen and Martin Weiss have been there. As parents of two children with learning problems, they have been tormented by doubt and experienced strains almost beyond endurance, but they have revealed their growth in tolerance and love that has permitted them to cope effectively with every situation that has arisen. Now their experience as parents, and subsequently as educational consultants, has been distilled in this vastly useful book. They show how to be wise, tolerant and temperate. They show how to acknowledge and deal effectively with each child's unique manner of being, his learning style and his pattern of strengths and deficits. They bring a message of hopefulness and strength and especially of rare "common sense." The parent, they note, can be his child's most devoted teacher, and the home the special place where effective instruction and behavioral management can take place. The parent need not feel bewildered and hopeless. He can take positive and constructive action to help each child up the ladder of development through the kind of home program that Helen and Martin set forth. It is hoped that parents everywhere will avail themselves of the insight, techniques and the special qualities of ingenuity, warmth and love that Helen and Martin undeniably exemplify.

Milton Brutten, Ph.D.
Clinical Director
The Vanguard School
Paoli, Pennsylvania

CONTENTS

ONE

THE END

Or is it the beginning?

"Things were O.K. in school until I started first grade. From there on it was downhill all the way!"

Ira: age fourteen

"They taught me that 'All men were created equal.' It's just that some are more equal than others."

From an author
whose name we'd like to know

1

INTRODUCTION
Why Did We Write This?

FOR PARENTS

When a parent faces the fact that his (her) child is not succeeding in school and not learning at the same rate as others seem to learn, it causes great anxiety. When told a child has become a "problem" to himself and others, the parent is likely to feel sad, guilty, or angry. We have experienced all of these emotions ourselves. We have also learned that none of these feelings will help the child, the parent, or the teacher.

What our experience taught us is that all children have their own personal learning style. With few exceptions they all CAN LEARN. Given patience, love, and appropriate tools, they can succeed. A parent must be aware that he or she is the one teacher who will remain with his child throughout the twelve years of school. *If I am to be of assistance to my child, I need to have the tools available to direct my energy toward practical day-to-day activities that will help my child to learn in his own learning style.*

The purpose of this book: to give parents an insight into the handling of their learning-disabled children. We hope to assist parents in determining if, in fact, their child has a problem in learning; and if such a problem exists, to acquaint them with the kinds of problems that may be confronted and their meaning, testing methods, and treatment.

We further aim to provide parents with some practical activities that can be carried on in the home to assist their children in developing habits positive to learning, via games and play activities at home.

Learning lags, despite their origin, do not go away. Most learning-disabled youngsters carry some lags into young adulthood despite the kind of assistance they are given through the years. No one family can afford the kind of intensive one-to-one follow-up and remediation that the child with special needs requires. The parents must be ready, willing and able to fill in throughout the twelve years of school in the capacity of supporter, comforter, and tutor.

FOR TEACHERS

When a teacher faces a child day after day and feels that he is not teaching the child as successfully as he can teach others, he feels frustrated. Most children can learn what he teachers, so why not this child? He may see the child as being inattentive, careless, and not meeting day-to-day responsibilities. The child who senses his own failure may become sad and withdrawn. He may become anxious, or even hostile. The vicious cycle of failure spirals downward in an ever-widening circle. No "one" is to blame, neither the child nor the teacher. The pressures of time and class size make it impossible for most teachers to give a child the time he might require in one-to-one or small group settings when his learning style is unique.

To whom shall a teacher turn? The principal? The psychologist? The reading specialist? A tutor? Each of these is a possibility, but it is often an expensive, long-term situation. Or can parents be made an integral part of the learning environment? We feel that parents *can* be home teachers (in an informal way), once they have the guidelines and materials with which to work.

MY CHILD HAS A LEARNING DISABILITY!

We've heard this said often by parents, describing the special needs of their child. What does this mean to a parent when we translate it into feelings and gut reactions? As parents living in the world of the Horatio Alger myth, we have grown up in a world of "winners," championship athletes, students, performers. We bring each child into the world hoping that he or she will be the flawless combination of two parental personalities, blended so well that he can outstrip his loving parents. The all-time "winner," our son or daughter!

Suddenly, this delightful, charming child appears to deviate from the so-called normal. This child with the "invisible handicap" is yours and mine. He *can* learn, but appears to learn differently from others. He can perform, but it appears to be a spotty, patchy, somewhat inconsistent performance. He can be managed, but his misbehavior often troubles you, his parents. His behavior makes you feel guilty. It appears that he has been mishandled, spoiled, or neglected and all who deal with him may become frustrated or irritated.

He is often labeled as "immature," "lazy," "underachieving," "manipulative," and/or "emotionally disturbed." He may even be labeled "retarded" because of his inability to cope with learning in a traditional classroom situation.

Who is he?

He is the child with special needs. This book is written to help us tell his story.

2

My Child Has a Learning Disability. What Does That Mean?

Is it a learning disability or a teaching disability!
It's all a question of definition.

— A local administrator

The term "learning disability" is an umbrella covering a multitude of learning problems. As far as a precise definition is concerned, even the "experts" cannot agree. When the term was defined in Public Law 91-230, the disagreement persisted. The NINDS Monograph[1] found it necessary to include eight additional definitions from other expert members of the panel writing the report. (See page 14.)

Certainly the bases of these disabilities are important to understand. (These will be discussed in detail in Chapter 3.)

What the parent will first observe will often be a behavior problem, which when properly understood and diagnosed may be known by any number of fancy terms. The number of terms used by specialists are at times overwhelming to a professional or a lay person. The New York State organization — NYABIC — Association for Children with Learning Disabilities — went to the trouble of sending its members a listing of fifty-eight descriptions used interchangeably to describe learning-disabled children. The listing noted further that these children do not necessarily display any visible handicap.

As parents and professionals we feel that such jargon only causes enormous confusion among those of us who would try to read and understand educational reports. It seems as if each specialist feels the creative need to design his own personal language and code. Such codes only act as a barrier between the professional and the parent in what must be a joint effort on behalf of the child.

Through our own children and our students, their failures and their successes, their happiness and their heartbreak, let us explore some of the behavior of learning-disabled kids.

Billy was a youngster of irresistible charm. His sparkling blue eyes, rosy cheeks, laughing smile and cheerful disposition made him the darling of visitors to the J. household. Mr. and Mrs. J., however, were constantly wondering why their successful management of other members of the family seemed to break down when it came to Billy's behavior.

Billy was awake at the crack of dawn. His bustling and commotion awakened the rest of the family. Despite the charm he held for others, he did not appear lovable and affable at 5:30 a.m. to his weary parents.

"You might have thought Billy would at least be tired at 8:00 p.m. after a fifteen-hour day of constant activity," said his mother, when she brought him to our office.

"He wakes us up in the morning, and he puts us to sleep at night," she explained. "He outruns us, outwalks his brothers, and wears us all out."

Billy was a wiry, well-coordinated seven-year-old, who rested in a chair for short moments, then found his way around our office going from game to game, inquiring, "What's this?" "What's that for?" "Can I touch it?" (Sometimes *after* he touched it!)

He appeared to need to be in touch with everything that caught his eye, and flitted from one activity to the next, never alighting on any one thing long enough to follow through. By the time our interview with his mother was concluded, the waiting room appeared to take on the look of a zone visited by a small tornado.

Blocks were piled on the floor in one corner of the room, adjacent to a small tower that he had constructed.

Number tubes for math were strewn across the floor, books were spread about, and the magazine table appeared to have survived the foraging of hungry mice.

Billy's mother apologized profusely for the mess. She said, "You see, he does this at home all the time. I no sooner clean it up than he's at it again. Billy, pick all that stuff up and put those blocks back!"

She knelt on hands and knees and started to pick up the number tubes. Billy looked at his mother periodically as she tidied up, but he did little or nothing to contribute to the mopping up operations.

Billy was one of those youngsters whose excessive drive for un-directed activity created management problems for his family, his teachers, and himself. Billy was a *hyperactive* child and his pedia-trician told his mother that Billy was hyperkinetic.

Hyperkinesis is characteristic of some 2 to 3 percent of our school-age population. Many other youngsters, however, exhibit what we might call overactivity patterns that require special modifi-cations of teaching techniques to allow for learning by movement.

Teachers, when questioned as to the behavior patterns that inter-fere in a learning situation, rank *hyperactivity* and *short span of attention* as the most difficult patterns of behavior to manage in the classroom!

Youngsters who are in motion when they should be learning lose much of what is being learned, and are a distraction for themselves as well as others in a classroom group. They distract themselves from the subject at hand by losing thought continuity and recall in their constant shifts of activity.

As parents of a "hyperactive" child, we have lived for over twenty years with the problem of behavior management and impulse con-trol. Such a symptom is often associated with other characteristic behavior patterns that call for special attention in teaching. It is important, however, to emphasize that the hyperactive child does not necessarily exhibit other symptoms of learning lags. Conversely, children exhibiting other special needs educationally are not always hyperactive.

Hyperactive behavior within the range of normal must be differ-entiated from true hyperkinetic behavior. True "hyperkinetic be-havior disorder was identified about thirty years ago. The children cannot concentrate effectively, are distractible, and usually pay little lasting attention to correction or punishment. It is paradoxical that the administration of stimulant drugs such as dexedrine, methylphenidate, or ritalin are of such benefit in treating them." [2,3]

Our observations of children with whom we work as educational therapists and tutors have led us to believe that hyperactive children can be categorized in two main groups.

First, those youngsters who exhibit a kind of driven, or hyperkinetic, behavior. The need for constant motion is so excessive that they cannot attend to sedentary tasks for even a short period of time, despite their high motivation or interest in the task.

Second, those youngsters who exhibit a kind of excessive activity level, or hyperactivity, but who are able to get involved with a challenging task for extended periods of time, if the task can be one with high interest and personal value to them.

While Billy appeared to fit into the first category of driven behavior, Jack, age eight, was able to get involved in any challenging gross motor activities in which he could release body tension.

Jack would become completely involved in games in which he could move about the floor while learning, hop from square to square, or jump from box to box. For Jack, the need for movement seemed to be an integral part of his learning style, and once movement was included in a learning activity, Jack showed marked improvement in his ability to stay attentive to a task.

We repeat, Jack learned by movement — it seemed his learning style. He was not random or driven in his behavior once involved in an activity. We felt that Jack could not be accurately labeled as a hyperactive child, rather just a very active child who learned best by moving and becoming physically involved.

Often in the past, calling a child hyperactive was a direct result of unrealistic teacher expectation of prolonged sedentary activity (seat work or pencil-paper tasks, etc.). Even Jack's parents forgot his learning needs periodically and enforced sitting in the car, strapped to his seat, or sitting at the dinner table, only to find that Jack became unmanageable.

On the other hand, Jack exhibited other patterns long considered symptomatic of a learning disability. He would become confused when told to move in any direction involving right and left orientation. Jack would hold up his right hand when asked to do so. He could identify his left hand as well. When given a series of things to do involving a decision to move in a right or left direction, he became confused and usually reversed his direction in space.

For example, we played "Simon Says" with Jack quite frequently. He was asked to do as "Simon Says" but only when Simon gave the command.

We would say:

"Simon Says, hold your right hand to your left ear."

"Simon Says, take three steps to the right."

Jack became confused and invariably he brought his left hand to his right ear, or took three steps to the left.

For Jack, the world was a troubling place where things did not seem to stay in the same place for very long. It must have appeared to him that the left and right changed places, leaving him to decide which way to go from moment to moment.

Jack's directional confusion carried over into his work with letters and numbers at school. Not only did left and right directions appear inconsistent to him, but the loop that was attached to a straight vertical line to make **b-p-d-q**'s seemed to move about as well. He was never sure that he had seen it in the proper place. One day after experiencing a good deal of difficulty in working out his letter confusion, Jack turned to us and asked sadly:

"Why can't the parts of the letter stay in the same place so I can remember them?"

Numbers as well became confused when Jack tried to copy them from the blackboard to a piece of paper. His written letters and numbers were poorly spaced and of uneven size. He could not write them evenly on a horizontal line and they curved gently down his page. The total effect of this kind of work made him very angry at himself, and then he would throw the pencil and paper down in frustration at his inability to copy what he saw or to remember shapes and forms. Without assistance, his disappointment in himself might have led him to avoid written work completely.

By the time Jack was referred to us for educational help, he was totally unwilling to write anything on paper when the teacher requested it. He had built up a whole variety of excuses to explain this, but in reality he was so afraid of failure that he no longer had the courage to try at all. (See also page 23.)

While Jack's difficulty had overt symptoms of hyperactivity, it seemed especially severe in directionality and in fine motor control involved in writing. On the other hand, for Mary, also eight years old, the area of greatest need seemed to be in spatial judgment of distance and in the visual process of tracking smoothly across a line of printing in a left-right direction. Without any structure to assist her visual tracking, she became confused, lost her place, and her interest as well.

Mary was referred to us for severe reading problems. When we tested Mary, we found that she was experiencing much more than a reading problem. She could not catch a large ball or throw it accurately. She appeared clumsy and awkward when walking through any room filled with furniture, such as desks, tables, or chairs. She would bump into things, trip over them, and appear to be unmindful of mother's precious objects at home. When she held something fragile, it would often drop and break. Her writing was poor and copying of forms even poorer. She seemed to have no awareness of things with three dimensions when she tried to draw them on paper.

Mary was a poor reader; she lost her place when reading, and regressed and reread in order to understand what she had read. She used her fingers to follow the reading line by line but still became confused.

Mary was extremely verbal. She had a good vocabulary for her age and certainly could not be considered a slow-learning child.

For Mary, the amount of work required to follow a line across a page correctly was an enormous effort. She became nervous and did not want to read aloud at all, fearing confusion and humiliation. Mary avoided reading, yet appeared so bright and alert verbally that her teachers could not understand her obstinate refusal to try. Her mother and father encouraged her, but this only produced tears and temper tantrums.

Both Mary and Jack had gone to psychologists for counseling before being referred for educational therapy. In both situations, the psychologists felt that the children were responding to obstacles in the educational environment with which they were unable to cope. Rather than risk constant defeats, both were building a safety zone around themselves by defensively refusing to work in areas in which they felt they could not perform. For Mary and Jack, the psychologists saw an educational problem as the primary causal factor. Both youngsters were experiencing difficulties in dealing with space, coordination, and direction.

On the other hand, another of our students, Joey, had a minor problem in fine motor coordination, but his overreaction to physically based problems made him appear to be an "emotionally disturbed youngster." True, he did exhibit difficulties in dealing with his problem that might be called emotional, but let's see how we can restructure that scene and retrace Joey's steps up to the period of explosive behavior.

Joey, age ten, had a short temper and would become angry when frustrated. He could not handle tasks that required fine motor skills. When asked to do any job requiring such skills, his "clumsy fingers" might cause the project to be destroyed and Joey would fly into what seemed like an uncontrollable rage, breaking whatever he was working on beyond repair. His parents saw his angry outburst as the primary problem and did not notice the repeated pattern of circumstances that would cause Joey to act "out-of-bounds."

For example, Joey had dropped his younger brother Sam's toy car and the wheels and axles had fallen off. His parents insisted that he either repair the car or spend his next allowance on a new one. This was a perfectly reasonable request and the promise of justice eased little Sam's crying.

What his parents did not recognize was that the fine motor manipulation required to place a tiny axle and two rubber wheels in a small plastic groove was of comparable difficulty to Joey as replacing a watch movement would be for his dad. His chubby, poorly coordinated fingers were not ready for such a task. A slight bit of pressure to attach the parts was all that was necessary. However, for this little boy, who was not capable of the fine degree of effort required, the job was impossible.

The outcome was predictable, of course. Joey squeezed too hard, the axle snapped, wheels rolled away, and the car was destroyed. Joey was angry at his "stupid old fingers" for breaking it. But the toy was cheap anyway, so why should he be required to replace a cheap old car that was so fragile? His frustration mounted. What followed was a scene that occurred frequently in his young life. Little brother Sam cried; Mother arrived and sympathized with helpless Sam; Father heard the anger in Mother's voice and Joey's fresh back talk, and he entered the scene to order Joey to his room without any supper.

Joey felt totally betrayed by all, especially by the demands that made all the simplest activities of life such a trial and tribulation for him.

He knew it was his own fault, but stubbornly refused to apologize because he would not be forced to admit once more that his fingers were "dropping fingers," "clumsy hands," or "useless paws."

Joey's story illustrates how often we can be misguided into thinking that a child's overt behavior is the basic cause of his problem. Certainly, Joey overreacted emotionally to what seemed a relatively unimportant event. However, Joey had a cumulative record of failure. What he touched often broke; what he did often failed. He defended himself against defeat with outbursts of temper.

What did Joey's behavior really mean?

Was Joey responding to a world that pressured him too much? Making too many demands upon him? Joey dealt with environment in the best way that he was able. He was asking for help as all youngsters with learning disabilities ask for help. However, they don't simply request that help in a direct manner, they may ask for it indirectly.

We must often "listen with a third ear"[4] to what a child is saying. Such awareness is a product of practice and observation. We may have to observe with a "third eye" as well, and look beyond overt signs to find out what is really happening. Sometimes just "counting to ten"[5] restrains our initial response of negativism until we have taken stock of what is really happening.

Most important, as parents we must be tuned in to our child's learning style and his weak points. If Joey's mother had recognized his lack of fine motor coordination, she might not have been put in the situation we described. She might have eased the demands upon him, helped him, before he lost his temper.

In order to be aware of such strengths and weaknesses, a parent needs to understand what constitutes a learning disability and how to deal with these handicaps when they arise.

What kind of message can be gained from stories such as these? Hyperactivity, problems of fine motor manipulation, spatial relationships, coordination, and direction are just a few of the problems that may be diagnosed and seated under the umbrella of "learning disabilities." What is most important to note in all of this is that we must be aware that behavior as radical as Joey's tantrums can be a result of a primary learning disability rather than a primary emotional problem.

A learning disability is not primarily a problem of emotional disturbance, despite the numerous emotional side effects that we may see. Some learning skills may be retarded in development, but such a child is not retarded. Both the emotional defenses and the retardation of skills may be apparent when we deal with these children, but they are often the effect and not the *cause* of the difficulty.

WHAT THEN IS A LEARNING DISABILITY?

Learning disability has been defined in many ways; the multiplicity of definitions indicates that few experts agree upon the exact definition of the problem. According to the United States Department of Health, Education and Welfare the following primary definition is accepted: "the term 'children with specific learning disabilities' means those children who have disorders in one or more of the basic psychological processes involved in understanding or in using language, spoken or written, which disorder may manifest itself in imperfect ability to listen, think, speak, read, write, spell, or do mathematical calculations. Such disorders include such conditions as perceptual handicaps, brain injury, minimal brain dysfunction, dyslexia, and developmental aphasia. Such term does not include children who have learning problems which are primarily the result of visual, hearing, or motor handicaps, or mental retardation, or emotional disturbance, or of environmental disadvantages." However, there was such lack of agreement among the expert panel that an appendix was inserted including additional definitions.

The Massachusetts Association for Learning-Disabled Children uses the following definition in its monthly *Specific Learning Disabilities Gazette*:

> A perceptually handicapped or learning-disabled child is one whose intelligence is often average or better but whose learning is impaired because his method of learning some things is different from that of the majority of children. Dyslexia and aphasia are but two commonly known examples of specific learning disability. Prognosis for most learning-disabled children is excellent if they are given the educational tools they need to help themselves.

Accepting the two definitions as equally valid, we attempt to restate them here in terms of the things observed by parents in the daily life of any child.

The child with a learning disability may appear to be out of "synch" with the expected timetable of development of the so-called average child. Psychologists have observed children through the years and found that certain levels of activity are predictable. Most children are able to attain certain goals at predictable times and age levels. Any child who deviates more than six months from the expected level of attainment can be considered to have a slight developmental lag. The longer it takes that child to learn how to perform the expected activities, the greater is the developmental lag.

Such lags usually show up in performing a constellation of activities. For example, when our little friend Joey was age six, he could not tie his shoes. In kindergarten and first grade he was not able to perform other activities that required considerable fine motor dexterity, such as buttoning buttons, stringing beads, and sewing on a lacing card. He seemed to have a problem in fine motor control. After conferring with his mother, we found that there were many fine motor activities in which he showed poor skills. Her feeling that he was simply refusing to learn in order to gain attention away from his younger brother Sam was not necessarily true. Joey exhibited a number of problems in this area, and when it was no longer treated as obstinate behavior, Joey could drop some of the defensive behaviors he had learned and relate to others.

3

Symptoms and Causes

"I've got a yearning disability! — My teacher said so!"
— Jeff: age seven

"I know what my problem is — my tongue is too big for my mouth and it gets tangled when I talk."
— Richie: age ten

"Is he a late bloomer or an early failure?"
— A parent

What are some of the labels found in school reports that attempt to categorize the "learning disabled"? One of the most popular is dyslexia, or specific language disability.

These terms refer to children who exhibit partial word-blindness. Despite normal visual acuity, they have extreme difficulty in learning to recognize words from the letters that form the words. This appears to be a result of a developmental lag in recalling and sequencing letter and number symbols.

It first becomes evident as a child reaches kindergarten or the first grade. Following are some symptoms that appear both at home and at school:

a) There is some confusion about days, months, seasons, relative time, or one's body position in space. (These children seem to be late for everything, do not know what day it is, are always forgetful of sneakers, lunches, assignments, etc.)

b) Fine motor coordination is likely to be poor or below normal for age level. (These children receive school reports repeatedly criticizing any written performance as "sloppy," "careless," etc.) Such problems are more likely to be associated with difficulty in copying forms during the early years.

c) Such children are more likely to have male relatives with a history of having similar difficulties. Background investigation might indicate that they were premature, or survived a medical complication occurring during pregnancy. There is sometimes evidence of high fever during infancy or early childhood or injury due to an accident.

d) They will often have normal auditory acuity when tested; however, they may have poor auditory discrimination of similar sounds and this may not show up on a normal hearing test. (They may say "pissquetti" for spaghetti.)

e) They do not necessarily show any gross defects on a neurological examination or appear markedly immature on a pediatric examination.

f) Psychologically, they are likely to have an extremely poor self-image. This will intensify as the child grows older and the disability remains undiagnosed. They often express feelings of inadequacy, stupidity, or guilt, because of repeated failure in academic areas.

The pattern seems to be more prevalent in boys; this is complicated by the fact that boys mature at a slower rate than girls in most developmental areas. We apply the same social and behavioral standards to boys as to the faster maturing girls and subject them to further tension by limiting their activity levels. Thus, the average classroom situation is always more frustrating to boys than to girls of the same age.

The primary characteristics of the disability become more apparent when the child is exposed to reading instruction.

If they have an adequate visual memory, they will learn to recognize some words of differing shape (sight words).

However, they may have difficulty in associating sounds with the visual symbols. The greatest degree of confusion will occur when sounds are similar, as for example:

"Ow" as in bow-wow is pronounced as an "ou" — or "ow" as in bow and arrow. Vowels differ due to the position of the mouth. Notice the position when you say lad-led-lid-lod-lud. Now add to this difficulty several consonant sounds and you have a picture of complete confusion for such a child.

In the common classroom situation, when a child is asked to read aloud, he is expected to relate certain sounds and letters "automatically," and to blend those letters into words. This is difficult for dyslexic or language-disabled children. They tend to ignore the details within words and to base word recognition on the familiar initial letter, the length of the word, its configuration, etc. They may omit letters, insert letters, make substitutions of similar letters within words. They exhibit spatial confusion. They seem unable to differentiate between reverse images such as **b d p 6 9.** This disability then carries over into the handling of space-oriented activities such as map work. Moreover, we see this confusion in the inability to transfer a horizontal math example to the vertical form: $3 + 3 + 4 = 10$ to 3

$$
\begin{array}{r}
3 \\
+4 \\
\hline
10
\end{array}
$$

The same disability which affects the handling of sounds will also interfere with the handling of two-step or multi-step processes. For example, the child can multiply and divide. He is then given a word problem that requires the two processes. He cannot shift from one process to the next and see the need for both tasks unless it is broken down into a step-by-step sequence and he is led patiently from one step to the next.

For example: "If eggs are 90¢ a dozen, how much will 36 eggs cost?" The first problem to solve is determining how many eggs are in a dozen. Having solved this, the student then must know that he needs to divide the number in a dozen (12) into 36. Having gotten the solution to this problem (3 dozen) he now must know that it is necessary to multiply 3 times 90¢ to get the solution; $2.70. Let us review steps in simplifying this problem.

1) how many eggs are there in a dozen?   ans. 12
2) what must I do now?   ans. divide
3) what numbers must I divide?   ans. 12 into 36
4) what is the answer?   ans. 3
5) what must I do next?   ans. multiply
6) what numbers must I multiply?   ans. $.90 × 3

7) what is the answer when I multiply?   ans. $2.70
    (This step assumes knowledge of
    working with decimals.)

Many of these characteristics are often seen in children just beginning to read. However, they are overcome quickly, without the need for special help. In the language-disabled child, the tendency still persists.

Generally, we can say that the child seems almost massively unready for reading or dealing with abstract symbols. The process of maturation seems to lag behind age-mates'. Often the child will show other symptoms of lag, socially, emotionally, and physically (we have noticed the late replacement of baby teeth by adult teeth). Despite educational support, the child may lag to some degree behind age-mates in language arts. He may reach grade eight with a level of grade five in reading but continue to make what appears to be simple, repetitive errors, and continue to reverse letters, transpose syllables, use incorrect words, or omit parts of words.

Recommendations are made on pages 89 and 90 to encourage learning strengths while deemphasizing weaker learning modes. In these ways, a child with such problems can be encouraged, supported, and directed toward adopting a more positive attitude in his relationships and performance at school and at home.

Included, later on, are some suggestions of specific kinds of materials and approaches available to teachers. These materials offer one way to bypass difficulties while intensive remediation is undertaken. Thus, we can take the pressure off such "learning insufficient" youngsters while we attempt to remediate their learning difficulties.

The need for support, encouragement, and "sense of self" — because they always get "the short end of the stick" — is the basic underlying need expressed most often by teenagers. They want and need adults to have faith in them so that they may have faith in themselves.

We believe that one teacher can "light one candle" and spark a flame in the mind of such a student by making him feel important and valued as a person, and that this can "turn on" a winner. We have frequently seen this happen.

So — our aim is to increase the awareness that there are many

---

styles of learning which we must encourage despite our traditional attitudes. In many specific cases where we have been able to track down the pattern of strengths, use alternate materials, make different demands, give support, encouragement, and a sense of being valued, we have seen the so-called loser start to become a winner!

CAUSES

The causes of learning-disability symptoms appear to be multiple. It is often difficult to ascertain what has caused such a problem without the assistance of an expert who can test the child extensively. Despite the desirability of such testing, it is often not available to the average parent.

It is important for a parent to be aware of some of the factors that seem to predispose his child to learning difficulties. The major categories considered as causal factors are:

a) Physiological causation
   (1) Neurological dysfunction
   (2) Biochemical disorders
b) Developmental lags
c) Environmental deprivation
d) Emotional deprivation or poor adjustment to environment
e) Inappropriate teaching methods

PHYSIOLOGICAL CAUSATION

A) Neurological Dysfunction

Recently, researchers have suggested that primary dyslexia afflicts approximately 5 percent of school-age children. Dyslexia has long been thought to be some minimal form of brain dysfunction interfering with the brain's circuitry. Two researchers have theorized that it was a result of "something wrong in the pathway or circuitry between the cerebellum and the inner ear, resulting in a mild form of permanent motion sickness." [1] Drs. Jan Frank and Harold Levinson suggest in their research on two hundred children in a New York City study that these children have been found to be experiencing this inner-ear disturbance, and have symptoms of primary dyslexia. However, Drs. Frank and Levinson found what appears to be no evidence of damage to the cortex of the brain per se.

Previous to these findings, other experts have held that dyslexia is a "brain damage problem in the cortical area of the brain." [2]

It has also been suggested that such problems develop directly as a result of faulty development of the left side of the brain in predominant right-handers, that is, some slight deviation that confuses the pattern of predominant right-handedness, footedness, etc.[3]

> ... Suppose reading ability were measured in terms of comprehension. Then it seems to me that the novice readers also would profit from cerebral dominance. The relations between cerebral dominance and reading consequently will depend not only on the stage of the learning to read process but also on the way reading is measured.

This suggestion is made by Dr. Dirk Bakker. He goes on to say: ". . . I have tried to show some ways in which there is a relation between the reading ability and cerebral dominance. This relation appears to be stage-dependent; early reading seems to be hampered by dominance, fluent reading on the other hand seems to profit by it. . . ." [4]

Some explanations pose the possibility that our understanding and recall of things we see and experience is based upon our ability to recall the information that we store in our memory bank. If there is no synthesis or organization of such stored information, there will be a large discrepancy between input of information and output. That is, what comes in may not be what we produce in written or verbal performance.

What does all of this mean?

How can I apply it to my child in a learning situation?

What a teacher or parent might see, for example, as an "emotional problem" or a "personality disorder" may, in fact, have originated in a learning disability in earlier years.

Parents need background information concerning the causes of learning disabilities and the types of tests that can be employed by special service personnel or regular teachers to determine if such subtle learning disability patterns do in fact exist. Such problems seem more widespread than most parents and educators realize.

We must break down our categories so that we understand that children experience various types of problems, and the severity of these problems depends upon how many other complications interfere with the child's adjustment.

The child's response to his problems may or may not have additional side effects, and may or may not be complicated by parents' responses in the form of denial, guilt, overprotection or overt hostility.

It has been suggested that nearly 30 percent of all children referred to active teaching hospitals suffer from either neurologic disease or nervous system involvement. The researchers note that some specific delays in maturation are normal; however, many signify an underlying nervous system disorder.[5]

Dr. Annamarie Weil, noted psychiatrist, suggests that there is need to distinguish between those dysfunctions that are congenital (inherited) and those that are acquired. She considers developmental lags as inherited, and those specific disabilities resulting from prenatal illness, post-birth damage, prematurity, lack of oxygen at birth, or high fevers as acquired disabilities.[6]

Moreover, dysfunction is also suggested by what neurologists refer to as "soft signs," such as mixed dominance or the inability to establish right or left preference in the choice of eye, hand, foot, etc. There also may be some degree of motor impairment in the ability to learn and acquire such skills as hopping, running, skipping, and some differences in reflex response from right to left side of the body may appear.

Dr. Critchley suggests that the youngster experiencing developmental dyslexia has a specific language-related problem. He is most often a male child, experiences some degree of hyperactivity during his early years in school, and had a delayed development preference or choice of sidedness. Dr. Critchley sees this as a lag or delay in development rather than the lack of such development. There is often evidence of a male relative such as older brother, father, uncle, or cousin who has experienced a similar set of symptoms.[7] The prognosis for such youngsters to succeed in academic activities is favorable if they receive appropriate remedial training early enough. However, characteristic learning behaviors often continue through adolescence long after many remedial programs have run out! [8]

Often the kinds of remedial input needed by such youngsters are mechanical techniques in a structured language-retraining program. They need specific help in learning the coding (writing) and decoding (reading) processes. In many cases, early recognition and preventive teaching can prevent the emotional frustrations and resultant side effects so often produced.

The above two groups of children must be separated from those experiencing serious limitations in their mental ability to handle higher level thinking, for they may need completely different approaches to learning.

B) Biochemical Disorders

One biochemical difficulty that has been the focus of a great deal of interest in recent years is that of hyperactivity in learning-disabled children. Although many youngsters are extremely active or might be termed "overactive," few can be truly categorized as medically hyperkinetic.

Hyperactivity in children is hard to define, but as Keogh has said, "hyperactivity is like pornography. It is hard to define, but you know it when you see it." [9]

The hyperkinetic child appears to be moving constantly and seems to have a habit for selecting the wrong time and the wrong place to be in constant motion.

A whole constellation of behavioral symptoms seem to cluster around the hyperkinetic child. His high level of activity, inability to stick to one activity, and chronic state of excitement appear to be symptomatic of an underlying physical cause. This may be a result of minimal neurological problems or have biochemical cause.

The hyperkinetic child may be sensitive to many things in the environment. Food additives can produce food allergy types of hyperactive responses in many youngsters, according to F. Speer.[10] (See also page 8.) Dr. Speer suggests that hyperkinetic children have a "low threshold for activation of the sympathetic division of the autonomic nervous system." To a parent or teacher this means that these youngsters appear to be unable to get involved enough in anything to sustain their attention to a task. Their attention wanders from job to job without their completing anything.

Dr. Ben Feingold of the Kaiser-Permanente Medical Center in California demonstrated that food additives were a significant causal factor in the hyperactivity of twenty-five youngsters with whom he worked. Fifteen of these children showed marked improvements when food additives were removed from their diets.[11] Their hyperkinetic behavior ceased to be as much of a problem for their parents and teachers, and for themselves.

In addition to this we have increasing evidence that allergic responses also affect certain behavioral patterns in some patients. Dr. K. E. Moyer[12] contends that "the behavioral disturbances are only one of many possible allergic reactions" . . . although not all individuals experiencing allergies may show such difficulties.

He describes a symptom pattern that is characteristic of many individuals described as "minimally brain dysfunctioning." In addition to chronic "irritability," the affected person, particularly if a child, is "hyperactive." Dr. Moyer describes such allergy-prone children as tending to be "overtalkative," "restless," "inattentive," and having "difficulty learning basic skills." He reminds us that the medications used to control the behavior of the hyperkinetic child are often those used as medications for allergy.

This whole area of research, i.e., allergy-induced behavioral problems, must be brought to the attention of parents and school administrative personnel. Little is certain and much more information and research is necessary. However, this study holds a clue to the frequently high correlations of allergy symptoms and the learning disability syndrome in children. If children are not to be blamed for behavior beyond their control and be given proper therapeutic help, then we must know much more about their medical condition.

For many a teenage youngster who has severe allergy problems, the challenge from an administrator may be: "Are you taking drugs or smoking pot before coming to school?"

This was the experience of one of our sons and a number of our students. The red-eyed, teary, running-nose condition that plagued these youngsters, and their inattention, lethargy, and excessive fatigue when plagued with such symptoms are often confused by those who are not aware of their medical histories. The humiliation, frustration, and anger that follows such an accusation can only harm an already tenuous educational situation.

Nothing that the child can do will change the establishment's view of him after such an attack. And as one of our students so dramatically vented: "Why don't assistant principals apologize when they find out that they are wrong about you? Don't they have to be polite like other people when they make a mistake?"

How is the hyperkinetic child to be managed and handled in the confines of a school setting? If a medical condition is diagnosed, then medication is suggested and utilized with limited effectiveness. Despite the fact that medication seems to keep the children's activity level down or decrease their high and low tension-fatigue pattern, there seems to be no long-run effect. Dr. Herbert Rie found that youngsters medicated on Ritalin and other drugs were found to score no better on standardized testing after the treatments than before.

Dr. Rie, a professor of pediatrics at Ohio State Medical School, suggests that these children cause less trouble to the adults around during medication, but that their overall learning does not improve.[13]

Other studies suggest that hyperactive children appear to have a different learning style. They deal with learning in a different way than more reflective analytical children: Perhaps teaching to this style is the behavior management necessary to such youngsters.

When asked to select from several alternatives, the hyperactive child is more likely to respond impulsively without analyzing the various choices to be made. Such children appear to have their greatest learning difficulty in separating the center figure from a confusing background, either visually or auditorily. For example, they cannot distinguish the central picture from a group of pictures, find a specific word in a textbook page of print, or hear a single voice against the background of peripheral noise.

Such youngsters appear to be unaware of the fact that they are answering a question incorrectly and therefore they don't really seem to be listening to their own mistakes.

They have difficulty in monitoring their own immature behavior, so they appear totally unaware of what they have done wrong. They cannot shift gears to act more maturely because they don't really understand how one acts "his age."

The hyperactive child is often much less accurate in his responses when dealing with material that must be learned automatically. One example of such rote learning is the memorization of math facts. They respond impulsively without thinking, e.g., they blurt out a poor guess. They forget facts because their short attention span interferes with concentration on such rote learning.

Medication appeared to have improved the ability to delay answering and therefore give more thoughtful responses. The need to blurt out the first answer that comes to mind seems to diminish with children on medication.

As parents of five boys, we have lived through these various stages of development with our eldest son, who is truly hyperkinetic. When Richard was a toddler, he could dismantle a game, shelf, closet, or box of small objects quicker than we could observe the disaster. Having little or no idea of causal factors, we believed that we were not managing him with sufficient discipline.

There seemed to be a widespread attitude among school personnel that placed blame upon parents for all of the behavioral characteristics of youngsters that were unpleasant. We were called to school continually on questions of discipline, control, and "impulsive behavior." On one occasion, it was suggested that we might not be treating him the same way as his younger brothers because he was an "adopted" child!

On another occasion, it was suggested that we were not spending enough time with him and should be giving him more one-to-one attention! He might be suffering the competition of a younger brother, and therefore be anxious, tense, and emotionally upset.

It was a number of years later that we realized that all of these fine-sounding platitudes were true of almost any child and that such generalizations might be made within any family grouping. As our awareness of the problem progressed, we observed how many times we heard comments in professional meetings suggesting that "he is the oldest child in the family, that is why he has a problem."

"He is the youngest of three, he feels left out, babied; that is why he demands so much attention and is so overactive."

"He is the middle child of five and doesn't know whether he is fish or fowl."

"He is the oldest child born to young marrieds then only in their teens. They probably have spoiled him and allowed him to do anything he wants."

"He is the late child, born long after his brothers and sisters are grown. His parents just don't have the time and patience to handle him consistently."

Certainly all of these descriptions fit many children we have seen. But these youngsters exhibit patterns of hyperactive, impulsive, disorganized, immature behavior apart from their placement in the family, or conditions of their environment alone. They are the products of their own biochemical makeup and they respond to the world around them from their very first day on earth in accordance with behavioral rules that develop from their own temperament.

Certainly, they affect the people around them and are affected by them in return. We all respond differently to the cuddly, passive, huggable baby who coos back at us and responds to our loving care. We react with less patience to the wiry, active, nervous baby who cries all night, eats inconsistently, has frequent outbursts of temper, and leaps from our arms as if staying there represents a threat to him.

All children interact with their world. Most studies of children assume a "normal" baby in a "typical" environment. Perhaps the temperamental, hyperactive, volatile child who appears to be neurologically different creates around him a different set of factors that alter his environment's response to him.

We may consider this child's behavior "deviant"; however, in fact it may be rather normal when considered in terms of his personal organic factors and the environment around him.

Such children lack any control over the environment in which they grow. When things go wrong, as they frequently do, they blame themselves and consider themselves as "born losers." Despite the fact that they may be involved in something over which they have no control, or may be acting in a manner that they cannot control, they feel that they are always responsible for their acts and blame themselves.

Among the organic factors that may be beyond their control is their body's reaction to the intake of carbohydrates (sugar and starch). Research into hypoglycemia, a medical condition in which the patient's body does not properly utilize carbohydrates, has indicated that there are a large number of undiagnosed hypoglycemics. The reaction pattern seems to be as follows:[14]

1) The intake of sugar in any form leads to a drop in blood sugar. This happens because the intake of sugar triggers off a rush of insulin from the pancreas.

2) The effect of low blood sugar that is produced worsens the original symptoms; that is, these youngsters may exhibit severe discipline problems.

Often the pattern is a self-reinforcing one. When we feel anxious, moody and irritable we may reach for something to eat, to give us the momentary energy to handle the problem of the moment. For hypoglycemics, the pattern is often to crave sweets and to reach for more sugar in the form of a soda, ice cream, or a candy bar. They produce in themselves a reinforcement of the previous symptoms, a more anxious, hostile, and negative mood that is more "low blood sugar" brought on by eating sugar-content food.[15] The whole pattern, therefore, is reinforcing and the hypoglycemic student is the victim, and often he doesn't know why!

Among the symptoms of hypoglycemia appropriate to school and home behavior are fatigue, depression, nervousness, forgetfulness, confusion, anxiety, hostility, belligerence, antisocial behavior, indecisiveness, lack of concentration, and underachievement at school.[16]

Recent research reports some correlation between diagnosed

hypoglycemia in newborn infants and central nervous system disorders. Such difficulties are found most frequently "in infants of low birthweight, infants born of toxemic or diabetic mothers and twins. It is often associated with other neonatal disorders such as asphyxia, hemolytic disease or cerebral damage." [17] It also occurs in "normal" newborns not included in the high risk group.

> We can see that nutrition as well can play an important role in brain cell development. It has long been known that specific nutritional sources can seriously disrupt brain processes. . . . Since glucose is the brain's only fuel, hypoglycemia, low blood sugar, serves as a vivid example of the mind-body continuum in disease.[18]

What of the poorly nourished child, inadequately fed and chronically neglected? What of the poorly nourished middle-class adolescent, who chooses to eat high carbohydrate meals tastily served up in school cafeterias? He may avoid all protein food offered and fill himself with the snack foods so readily available. Often school menus will be extremely high in carbohydrates due to the high cost of protein foods. Parents need to go in and fight for better school lunch programs as well as better school remedial programs. Most parents would be shocked at the amount of sugar foods available daily to their children.

This is not intended to be an attack upon school nutrition personnel, but rather a compliment to most of them that they can do as well as they do with the funding of state and local support programs in which they must work.

However, until parents realize that the food intake at school may in fact be a contributing factor in some learning problems and behavioral difficulties, they will not come out and fight for better foods as well as better learning-disability programs. We spend so much money to undo the problems that we cause by saving on nutrition.

DEVELOPMENTAL LAG AS A CAUSE OF LEARNING DISABILITY

If we accept the fact that certain physical factors can cause a child to exhibit learning-disability problems, what are we describing when we refer to the child with a developmental lag?

In order to better understand what children can and cannot do at certain age levels, educators often compare a child's performance to certain expected norms for his age group.

These so-called norms are set up after many years of clinical observation of children of varying socioeconomic levels, differing temperaments and cross-cultural patterns. Thus we should be able to say that Navajo children on a reservation in Arizona can do as well on these expected tasks as children from the high-rise apartment houses of Chicago. The sharecropper's preschooler in a cabin in Mississippi should be able to perform as well as the preschooler in Boston from a white middle-class suburb.

Thus certain expected levels of development are estimated for a number of tasks basic to school success. The inability to perform these tasks at the expected age would be considered a developmental lag. The greater the number of tasks that cannot be performed when expected, the greater is the difficulty a child can be expected to experience in school.

Let us assume that you have a five-year-old child of normal intelligence and physical development. It would be expected that this child would be able to perform certain tasks with ease, such as crawling, walking, hopping, running, skipping, etc. He or she would be expected to be able to repeat a hand-clapping game like a drumbeat (three to four beats), to locate and name his body parts, to distinguish his left and right body parts.

Your five-year-old would be expected to be able to:

a) match colors of cutout felt pieces;
b) see likeness and differences in colors and name them;
c) recognize the constancy of shapes no matter how they are arranged;
d) express himself in full sentences and follow simple directions;
e) bounce and catch a large ball;
f) have established a right- or left-hand preference for holding eating utensils, pencil, crayon, etc.

Now let us suppose your five-year-old cannot do a number of these tasks. This does not mean he is not intelligent. This does not suggest a medical problem. It does suggest that he is experiencing a lag in development and needs more time and assistance to learn how to do these tasks.

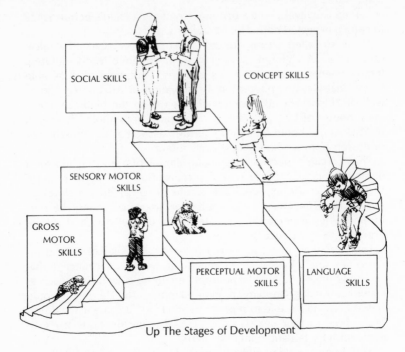

Up The Stages of Development

What happens if your youngster moves on in school without having learned to perform these tasks? Experience has shown us that many of these are readiness tasks preparing him for the more demanding lessons at school.

Psychologists tell us that the child must always pass through a successful stage one in order to move on to stage two of each learning operation. For example:

He must crawl in order to walk.

He must listen and hear accurately in order to understand.

He must recognize letter shapes and forms, similarities and differences in order to read.

He must babble in order to learn to talk.

He must have many kinds of experiences in order to learn how to conceptualize about things.

He must become aware of himself as a person and aware of others in order to develop some social maturity.

He must develop skills in at least six major areas of learning in order to move from the earliest primitive levels to the highest levels of thinking. Let us look at how the child should move up the ladder of development.

GROSS MOTOR SKILLS

Large-muscle development, like rolling, sitting, crawling, require some muscle tone and strength.

SENSORY MOTOR SKILLS

Child begins to integrate fine motor muscles and large muscles, gains balance and rhythm; becomes aware of direction out from body and body in space. Begins to develop right- or left-sidedness.

PERCEPTUAL MOTOR SKILLS

Child is now learning basic listening, looking, and writing skills; recalls sequences and has ability to make meaningful associations with spoken words and letters that he sees.

LANGUAGE SKILLS

Are dependent upon prior listening and speaking skills. Words must be associated with things as we think and communicate with words.

CONCEPT SKILLS

The ability to generalize from what we have learned in order to solve problems, make meaningful judgments, understand and classify information in math and reading.

SOCIAL SKILLS

Skills involved in relating to people and acting appropriately.

Human beings are extremely complex animals. We move through predictable stages of development but we tend to forget that we

---

move at inconsistent and variable rates of speed. Some of us move through all stages slowly. Some of us move through them more quickly. Some of us move at different rates of speed depending upon the skill required.

For example: I may be well able to learn anything that I hear spoken, such as sounds, rhymes, stories. However, I may be slow to remember the shapes of letters and therefore words. I may have difficulty in learning how to read because I am unable to hold onto a visual picture of the words that I need to remember. I may have delayed development in learning the similarity and differences among letters that look alike (**b-d-p-q**). I may have advanced development in remembering difficult words and information that people tell me.

Each of us develops according to the "drumbeat" of our own pattern. By expecting all children to move from stage to stage in learning, we are trying to make them fit into preconceived levels that were not designed for individuals. No individual child will develop just as the so-called average child does, but when a child exhibits marked immaturity in the step-by-step developmental patterns, he can be said to have a developmental lag.

We might ask why some of us seem to develop at a faster rate than others of similar background and intelligence even when offered similar educational opportunities.

Previously we mentioned that Dr. Annamarie Weil had classified developmental problems in the category of genetic, that is, inherited, patterns.

Biochemical research promises to give us much information on the "maturation of the brain" according to Dr. MacDonald Critchley. He suggests that there are complicated biochemical developmental processes that go on within the brain that ready us for each successive learning level. These factors seem to be affected by genetic makeup, says Critchley, agreeing with Dr. Weil. This would suggest familial patterns existing in such lags. Dr. Critchley stated that future research holds the "key to delayed cerebral maturation" and he looks forward to reversing the deficiencies of the brain via future research.

The promise of the future will not be available to Johnny and Jimmy or Terry and Sam. They must be helped now. Their parents need practical information to help them become aware of the kinds of lags that make school-associated activities difficult for these children.

Parents need to determine how their children learn best, that is, their perceptual strengths and weaknesses and learning styles. We would not give a blind child a non-Braille book to read, nor would we give a deaf child traditional music lessons, for failure would necessarily result. If we know what is expected of children at each stage in school, and how they best learn, we can help them absorb the kinds of learning necessary in their own way.

ENVIRONMENTAL DEPRIVATION

It is commonly believed that exposure to learning plays an important part in the development of curiosity and interest. The infant who receives limited personal attention or is physically confined to crib or playpen for prolonged periods gets little stimulus from the outside world.

If no one lovingly responds to the young child's first attempts at words or assists him in developing speech, he has little or no opportunity to practice a new skill. Physical confinement to a playpen beyond a certain stage restricts the toddler's exploration of his world. He must learn to walk, talk, and master complicated tasks through observation and trial and error. Without the clumsy first attempts at turning knobs, hammering nails, fitting things together, crayoning, cutting, and drawing, the preschooler is deprived of practice and learning and "how to" is delayed. He comes to school ill-prepared to handle some of the tasks expected of the kindergarten-age child.

The move to establish preschool "Head Start" programs represented the government's recognition of the need to supplement preschool education in areas where youngsters were deprived of such opportunities. This was especially apparent among children of the lower socioeconomic groups.

Contemporary critics of our early educational opportunities have gone so far as to develop "Head Head Start" programs. As Maya Pines describes in her recent article for the New York Times Magazine (10/26/75), "A major educational experiment is designed to show that early home education is the key to preventing many problems and training parents to compensate for early diagnosable difficulties."

It takes more than just love to produce a good learner in the school years. The Brookline Early Education Project (BEEP) program "operates on the theory that a child's future intelligence, social competence and general ability to learn are all largely determined before the age of two." If we accept this premise, then a loving but unaware parent, who is in fact the one who must perform the major educational job, will unwittingly cause problems by not providing a stimulating environment.

Dr. Burton White, of Harvard's Graduate School of Education Pre-School project, feels that the most critical period of education is between the eighth and eighteenth months of life, long before any formal educational program might be considered.

White says: "Babies generally manage to get to the crawling stage reasonably intact from an educational point of view. It is very difficult to stamp out pure basic curiosity. . . . It is, unfortunately, not that difficult to stamp it out in the next year or two, or force it into peculiar, aberrant patterns."

We often equate poorly planned home situations with economic deprivation, forgetting that the middle-class child may be equally deprived.

Unfortunately, educationally poor situations often go unnoticed when they occur in the middle class. A child whose father travels frequently and is rarely home, whose mother is always too "busy" to get involved, may in fact be equally deprived of the stimulus and structure for learning that grows from ongoing conversation, and direct physical involvement. His language and learning may show a similar delay born of unconscious neglect.

Although these factors may be secondary rather than primary causes of learning difficulties, the effect may be the same. Scars caused by such handicaps can present obstacles to skill development that last throughout school careers.

EMOTIONAL DEPRIVATION OR POOR ADJUSTMENT TO THE ENVIRONMENT

Children are often most unlovable at the time when they most need our love. The child who is characteristically moody, impulsive, difficult to manage, and least responsive to our loving overtures as parents is often the child who needs our acceptance and patience more than others. He is his own worst enemy but he is the last one to know it!

For the parent, the role becomes cloudy and most difficult. We must learn to reject our child's unacceptable behavior without rejecting the child. If he feels rejected he will spend a good deal of his time worrying and compensating for these feelings of deprivation.

Often a hard-to-manage five-year-old arrives at kindergarten sensing that his mother can't wait to get him out of the house in the morning and that she is equally displeased at his return home. Certainly he is difficult, but he doesn't understand why he can't sit still, or respond the way his mother might wish him to. He may be worrying when he is away from home, as he is concerned about what is happening there. Will his mother come to meet him at the bus and be *late again?* Will his cute little baby brother get more than his share of attention while he is away? What will happen to cause a scene when he gets home?

Put yourself in his place. Are you able to concentrate and do your job well when you are worried and concerned about a sick child, an ailing parent, business affairs, paying the mortgage, or some other personal problem? Perhaps the worry about being loved looms just as large for the "difficult" child who doesn't meet the standards of behavior we set for him.

Sometimes the problems are caused by things within the child's personality and physical makeup that are hard for a parent to understand. Other times the problems are caused by unreal expectations of parents for this child, or for themselves. Whatever the cause may be, the child will not be able to go about the business of learning until his fears are calmed. In order to take risks, solve problems, and remember things, we need to feel secure in both our home and school environment.

Frequently parents and children get locked into a pattern of fixed responses to each other as a result of poor communication or previous misunderstanding.

Joey expected his father to be angry at him because he was often annoyed. Joey was always armed for a fight when talking to his dad. Since anger feeds on anger their conversations often erupted into hostility, and neither one ever really heard or understood what the other one was saying.

Susie knew that her mother was especially sensitive to her carelessness and to her messy room. She used this device to get her mother's attention. If she couldn't get approval she'd get "a rise out of her" somehow. A fight followed and it became a reinforced pattern.

Within any family grouping, we may become so preoccupied with our personal needs that we do not recognize our effect upon the others and their effect upon us. Thus we can lose sight of what is really meant by the words that are said. Often we can benefit from the intervention of an objective outside observer who is trained to help us understand what is happening and why it is happening. Once we have some guidance to understand why a child behaves the way he does and why we seem to respond to that child with more anger, frustration, rejection, etc., we can better accept the child's needs and our own in a more open and honest way.

When the learning-disabled child responds to our encouragement with the comment "I am stupid," he may upset us more than any other random comment. Perhaps he is only asking for continual reassurance that we all *feel* stupid sometimes and we can do stupid things but this does not make us stupid. Often an example of something that occurred in his parent's life that made him/her feel just as inadequate will help to ease the pain. Parents will find that youngsters who perseverate (repeat themselves) will often ask for the same reassuring story to be told over and over again to help them handle an emotional hurdle or feelings of anger and frustration. Just the need to repeat this story over again may anger a parent who does not understand that this child needs the repetition and is prone to repeating himself unintentionally.

When one of our adopted children repeatedly baited us with the comment "You don't really love me, you're not my real mother," it was hard for a mother to handle. However, when we realized that this was his way of asking for reassurance that his adoptive mother was his "real mother," that no anger on his part would change that, his comment no longer threatened, and once it was no longer effective, it was dropped like so many other angry words of childhood.

INAPPROPRIATE TEACHING METHODS

A teacher may teach but that does not mean that a student must learn. If I expect too much from my students then they may not understand what I am teaching and of course they will not learn.

To risk using a colloquialism: "You can lead a horse to water but you cannot make him drink!" If you have seen to it that he is thirsty, he will drink. If you sweeten the water, he will drink. If you can make the water more refreshing, chill it, warm it, flavor it, he will drink! But if he has been drinking the same water, at the same temperature, for five or six hours per day, two hundred days per year, for up to twelve years, you cannot make him drink!

So it is with teaching ... you can offer information but the child will only learn what is interesting, relevant, and appropriate. It must be sweetened, refreshing, at the right temperature, and flavored to his taste. He must be thirsty in order to drink.

For many youngsters education is akin to "serving time." Must it be this way? The use of the same techniques, excessive and punitive discipline, and lack of enthusiasm all contribute to making it a lackluster experience.

More important to the learning-disabled youngster, the use of inappropriate techniques that do not match his learning style will cause him frustration and anger, and will result in failure. The failure may be the teacher's but the one who will feel it most will be the child.

We cannot teach the alphabet to youngsters with poor recall-of-form constancy by giving them a book of letters and a pencil. Rather, we must give them something that has shape and form, that they can feel in order to learn.

Throughout the 1960s mathematicians were promoting curriculum reorganization called modern mathematics or "the new math." Schools retooled and educators brushed up on their math terminology, and presently some 85 percent of our schools are using these programs of "new math." Now some fifteen years later we find that math scores as measured by standardized achievement tests have not gone up but rather are sagging and dropping off. We have taken time to review the so-called modern math programs after educating our present college and young adult population of children in such programs, and we find that much criticism is forthcoming.

Morris Kline has suggested that much in the new math is too difficult and meaningless to the student in such programs. In his book *Why Johnny Can't Add* he suggests that such instruction is divorced from reality. Others suggest that 90 percent of schoolchildren will never need mathematics beyond elementary school computational skills and that even these are not necessarily well-taught through such a program.

Thus the argument goes on and meanwhile many youngsters continue to be forced to "chase a curriculum" that is totally inappropriate for them.

Much of what psychologists like Piaget tell us of the way children learn is lost when curriculum is the rule in school. A teacher who is bound to a fixed curriculum and not permitted to deviate on behalf of any group of students is caught in such a trap. Teaching to the curriculum may meet the needs of many . . . but what of those whose needs are missed? We see them as the young adult high-school dropouts who were lost along the way through inappropriate teaching. We need not go to the extreme of talking about those who have dropped out physically. Just look at the faces in a high-school classroom where a long verbal lecture is in session and observe how many blank expressionless "dropouts" are there as well. Truly some of our youngsters are a product of "curriculum-induced learning disabilities."

It is ironic when we realize that the original Latin meaning for the word "curriculum" is "racetrack." The analogy is clear: such youngsters who must chase the curriculum are caught on a treadmill, in a "race" to nowhere.

Is that the definition of education?

4

The World of the Formerly Learning Disabled

"The dropped stitches of early childhood become the gaping holes in skill development during adolescence."
— Dr. Barbara Diamond,
Coordinator of Special Services,
South Shore Learning Center.
From a speech at the Orton Society,
March 1975

He is the teenager who at present shows none of the classic symptoms of learning disability. If his total history and previous evaluations are not known, he would appear to be a sometimes sullen, often inattentive, acting-out adolescent with what some administrators might call a "skills lag."

Nothing could be further from the truth!

The years of struggling to keep his head above water can't provide him with the fill for the gaping holes in learning. The problem of keeping him "going to school" has taken its toll of the patience and energy of his parents. The attempt to interest and involve him in work at school has exhausted his teacher's patience.

The "dropped stitches" of the earlier years have turned into "gaping holes" in the fabric of his education. The past history can't just be brushed under the carpet. There is no way to automatically equip him and then be able to say, "Now that you are in high school you should perform as if you belong there!"

His earlier lag in reading, writing, math, and spelling was based upon difficulties in the basic perception of symbols and slowed down the process of reading. The lag in maturity slowed the process of writing. The poor memory for sequences and facts slowed down the learning of math and spelling. The perceptual process is normal now. The other skills, however, lag far behind his peers'. The attitude that has been derived from eight years of failure is ever present and must be dealt with realistically.

We see such lags in skill development as an ongoing problem characteristic of all youngsters who exhibit learning disabilities. These children are lagging in their readiness for what is required or demanded of them at each stage. When they are ready for social interaction with their peers and learning to join in group games, others are ready to learn letter and number forms, others are already learning words and phrases. When they are ready to retain words and phrases, their peers are ready for sentences. When they are reading sentences, their classmates are learning paragraphs and stories. When they have reached the level of readiness to read paragraphs, their schoolmates are ready to handle longer stories. Thus the pattern persists, the frustration is constant. Progress is made each year with many youngsters, but they may never feel that they have "caught up" because no one ever stops to wait for them.

The frustrations that develop as a result of such ongoing lag often lead to acting-out behavior. In addition to this, it is often characteristic of learning-disabled youngsters to exhibit temperaments that are described as moody, impulsive, and volatile. This is especially true of teenagers with learning problems. It is normal and predictable for adolescents to exhibit such behavior and to overreact and have swift, exaggerated changes of mood.[1]

For our son Richie, this was particularly characteristic. We had seen an overall improvement in such mood swings since earlier days and better control developed as time went on. However, teachers only saw him as he was today. He appeared more volatile and moody than his peers. He did not seem to be able to anticipate the reactions of others to his moods and appeared to have immature social judgment concerning expectations of behavior.

Inappropriate judgment, impulsiveness, and poor control often get adolescents into situations that make them appear to be antisocial in behavior. Richie was constantly being extricated from situations that were a direct result of such actions without awareness of response. Any one of these acts would be insignificant taken by itself; however, when they become a part of a total educational report, they may be detrimental to his future, both educationally and vocationally.

Taken with all of this was the fact that Richie only learned by doing and experiencing. If we told him what was acceptable behavior, he heard us politely. However, he never really understood why it was acceptable to others until he had personally experienced the repercussions of his poor judgment. Then each situation became a true learning experience. Unfortunately, all parents and school personnel simply do not exhibit the patience required to allow these kids the right to make mistakes, and learn from their own experiences!

The parent is placed in a position of having an "antisocial" child; the school is placed in the position of having a child who is constantly testing the rules and authority. The total effect of this situation is often total rejection on the part of adults for this child. The child is then placed in the impossible situation of being rejected for making errors in judgment in situations that he truly did not understand. Because he is unable to predict the outcome of his acts and foresee the consequences, he is now the victim of his own problems.[2]

It often takes a kind of patience on the part of parents that may mark them as socially unacceptable also, to their friends and neighbors as well. The child may become a kind of neighborhood outcast, and the family will feel the brunt of such attitudes.

We have known many such youngsters and they cope with these problems in a variety of ways. They may continue to act out to call attention to their needs in an obvious way. Unfortunately, this only aggravates the situation even more.

We have seen fifteen-year-old teenagers leave home because of the inability to communicate with their parents. We have seen them float in a kind of "limbo" for prolonged periods of time, and miss vital periods of family contact and relationship.

We have seen many such youngsters drop out of school due to their inability to deal with school regulations and cope with educational demands. The dropout is on the road to nowhere. In times of economic recession, his problem is especially acute. He is trained for nothing, has a poor self-image, and often cannot get along with others due to his poor impulse control and immature judgment. He needs two or three years of school beyond the legal dropout age rather than a shortcutting of his educational growth. How many schools have programs that attempt to follow up the needs of the learning-disabled dropout? Emotionally, we can well understand why. Educationally, we can't accept the apparent lack of concern.

The learning-disabled dropout is often the youngster who has annoyed and bothered everyone at school and at home due to his lack of concern for rules and regulations. He tests everyone's patience. He cuts classes, forgets work, avoids responsibility, tests discipline, and seems to plague the administration. Why shouldn't the natural reaction be "Good riddance to bad rubbish!"

At home, his behavior is often much the same kind of pattern. He is not responsive to family demands and creates constant crises. He causes his parents to wear a path to the schoolhouse door. Having had two such youngsters with varying problems, we well understand the thinly worn patience of a parent. Such a child invades one's privacy and becomes the cause of family dissension. He can cause disagreement between the parents and within the family group. How natural is our impulse to fantasize our problems away. We can dream him away, or send him away. Often this is the case. It takes a kind of extra measure of patience to tolerate his actions without accepting them. In tolerating his acts, we grant him the right to make mistakes. However, in accepting his acts, we would place our approval upon them. Therefore we can only tolerate, but *never* accept.[3]

In order to tolerate these acts, however, we must drop some of our inflexible preconceived ideas about what our child should be, and what we wish him to be. He may never live up to our expectations unless we are realistic. Try to forget the gossiping neighbors and their disapproval, the school and its oft-implied criticism of us as parents. They do not live with our child! We do! His frustrations become our frustrations. We are responsible for him during his twelve years in school. No one else bears that full-time responsibility!

Perhaps a portrait of the "formerly learning-disabled child" should hang in each guidance or administrative office at the secondary level. If we could paint such a portrait with words, it would spare much sadness and pain.

The situation of the learning-disabled adolescent has been summarized in this way by DeHirsch, Jansky, and Langford: "In summary, the over-all performance of the older child, the so-called dyslexics, seem to point to a profound and basic maturational deficit, a deficit so severe that one might speculate that it is rooted in the biological matrix and constitutes a type of cerebral dysfunction." [4]

For practical purposes his behavior appears somewhat different and suggests emotional disturbance to those who work with him.

He's always had a record of cutting classes intermittently through the years. Though this gave the appearance of disinterest, it really was a way to avoid frustration in the academic situation. He just couldn't step up and meet the teacher's demands and do something for authority's sake alone. You just can't say, "Do it or else!" to this youngster. If there is no personal motivation that connects with his interests, he just won't get involved.

He appears to test the limits of authority to the furthest point, stretching the principal's patience taut as an overstretched rubber band!

The constant calls and reminders from school authorities torture his parents. They have many mixed feelings about him. Is he just a discipline problem to whom you must say, "Shape up or ship out"? [5]

Or is he trying to say something about the kind of inappropriate classes he must sit through day after day, like "serving time" for twelve years, spiced with short periods of high interest and motivation brought about by an especially interesting project, or a dynamic, creative teacher.

As time goes on he becomes the central figure in the dissension within a complicated family. . . . "Our other children performed academically, but why can't he . . . why won't he? He had had the benefit of tutoring, remedial reading, and seems well able to understand the work presented to him."

Father says that "Mother is too soft on this kid." He needed discipline and she coddled him throughout the years. Mother wonders why she is being blamed for treating this child the same way that she treated her other children. He experienced the same mothering, the same fathering, the same loving energy and nutrition, and more attention than the others.

Mother feels guilty. Perhaps there is something within her that has made this child different. She must have done wrong; everyone suggests that she has not been strong enough, harsh enough, or disciplined him enough.

Mother reads information on the subject and finds that more and more experts find that the vulnerable child who is hard to nurture and has difficulty as an infant will continue to be vulnerable as a toddler. He will be troubled in school and, despite the kinds of attention he receives, he may in fact be more difficult to raise throughout his growing years.

Dr. Stella Chess suggests that his learning style has not changed much. If we had observed him closely, we would notice that he is much the same kind of a child that he was as a young infant in temperament, attention span, and behavior.[6]

School tells us: "He's lazy and isn't trying." But the same child who will not write reports in seventh grade social studies will voluntarily cut a cord of wood for his family fireplace, or mow lawns all day and enjoy it. He will ride his bicycle for miles, hike up a mountain, ski for eight hours at a stretch, or build a workshed, spending his weekend time without flinching. He will get involved when he can perform, in the way that he *can* perform! He will avoid the things which he cannot do well, by acting out, copping out, or striking out.

He takes on the appearance of an undisciplined, somewhat lackadaisical teenager unable to set "real goals." He can't delay today's impulses and wants everything now, appearing unable to delay anything until later.

He is the formerly learning-disabled child who appears to have grown out of his problems. However, there are scars as a result of failure. The scars are often involved in the area of motivation, directly related to the amount of failure he had felt so often. "If I do well once, then everyone will be on my back to do it again. If I don't appear to care, then it won't hurt me when I fail!" These remarks came from a fifteen-year-old young man who told us that he deliberately avoids doing well on tests even when he can do what is asked. "I know I can't always do well, so why have more fights?" Telling such a boy how "bright" he really is can work in reverse. "Knowing how smart you are makes you feel that you are responsible for all the stupid things you say and do," he said.

Kids are great believers in magic. Learning-disabled kids are the greatest believers of all. They await success like Charlie Brown awaiting the arrival of the "Great Pumpkin" on Halloween eve.[7]

They approach each new problem as if they will fail just as they have in the past. Life appears to be an uphill climb, two steps forward and one step back. Just when you think you have begun to see a marked improvement in personal attitude and cooperation, there is backsliding in another area. If schoolwork improves, personal problems are manifested. Progress is uneven, inconsistent, and unpredictable. Living with such a teenager is like living on a roller coaster. Each climb gets a little bit higher, but drops off once more at the peak.

It is so easy for parents and teachers to lose their patience with such a teenager. He never brings us the predictable kind of satisfaction that other performing youngsters do. When he does perform, he can only sustain it for short intervals, fall back, and disappoint us again. His own success frightens him. He feels it is undeserved.

We were at a local high school at a conference concerning our son. One of the teachers had given him the first grade of a B+ that he had ever received in high school social studies. Naïvely we all assumed that he would be delighted at receiving this first good mark. His comment to the teacher when faced with this first successful written report was, "I thought you felt sorry for me, and that's why you gave me a B+!"

Such is the strength of the personal feelings of failure experienced by these youngsters. They deny their own successes for fear of future expectations. They deny their own success in fear of fraud. They personify the "loser's loser." To turn that feeling around is an awesome job, requiring home and school working together as a team. Neither the parent nor the resource teacher at a school can do this alone.

Being a "winner" is one step on the ladder of personal success. Once it occurs in little ways, a youngster can become comfortable with the role. To perform just one small "hero's deed" is the issue. We must find the door marked *hero* for these children.

How can one be a hero if he is not even acceptable in his own home; if he must act a part he cannot play? If his friends are unacceptable at home, then he must also feel unacceptable. He cannot be what his parents might wish. He knows this but they do not.

"If I brought any of my friends home to visit, you'd probably give them an I.Q. test," said Jerry, an angry sixteen-year-old who had stayed aloof from any contact with his family during the last two years. Jerry was expressing his awareness of his parents' non-acceptance of his friends.

He had been seeing what his mother considered an unhealthy, nonacademically oriented "fringe group" of kids in and out of school. The image of these long-haired, blue-jeaned youngsters who punctuated their school experience with avoidance, non-involvement, and some minor acting out was not exactly the one Jerry's mother wanted for her own son.

Jerry's dad had been an athlete who made the varsity basketball team in high-school days. Despite his own minor educational problems he had been able to get through high school with a 75 percent average. He dealt with his educational lag through some maturing in the army and returned to college with a more serious attitude and better-planned life goals. He had forgotten how frustrating those days in school had been when his own reading problems had kept him from the successes he might have had.

Jerry's parents were sincerely concerned about their son and they felt that he would be "known" by his group of friends. They felt that he might have a series of more sophisticated experiences and be exposed to rounds of drinking, pot-smoking and sexual encounters by traveling with what they considered to be a "fast-moving crowd." By forbidding Jerry to bring his friends into the house, the parents gave Jerry only one option — to choose between their rules and his accepting, status-giving friends.

Jerry chose to see his friends outside of the house, and this cut off most of the communication at home.

Jerry resented the constant round of speeches and the invasions of his privacy when his mother went through his belongings to see if there was any evidence of pot-smoking or drinking. Jerry resented the fact that his friends had been labeled as "losers" without a fair trial. Jerry stopped talking to his parents because they wanted to know too much about him, his friends, activities, and interests. They seemed to be spying on him and he resented this.

Jules Henry, noted sociologist, has called our attention to the fact that resistance on the part of children is greatest when parents intervene in a child's life, when they stop him from getting what he wants, when he feels degraded by their acts, or he sees no advantage to giving in to their demands. The child will further resist when he has little to lose by resisting, or when he feels that his parents' rules are made for their benefit rather than for his. Dr.

Henry goes on to say that such resistance seems to increase "in cultures where mutuality of adult-child interest is being lost and children have come to distrust adults." [8]

To bypass this block in communication with our learning-disabled teenagers, we must fully understand the age and stage at which they are performing. If we are aware of the need for independence in adolescents, we will be less likely to create roadblocks which might increase their resistance to our ordinary and daily demands.

Information is available in the school's permanent record files showing evidence of learning difficulties and behavioral problems that already have been clearly recognized by teachers. These persistant difficulties are bound to result in the cycle of failure, frustration, and "chip on the shoulder" reaction.

Many students who find their way into special programs at secondary level can no longer be easily categorized by their clear-cut disability pattern, but fall into a rather heterogeneous group with a wide range of disabilities and problems.

They exhibit a marked discrepancy between their level of ability and their educational achievement. There is often wide variation in achievement from subject to subject.

Said Alan Owens, now an executive trainee in a corporate management program, "When I was in high school I knew the reading and writing did not show my intelligence, because if how I function was shown by how I read and wrote, then I would be some kind of vegetable!"

They are often characterized by an attitude of disinterest and low motivation for academic tasks.

Alan went on to say: "I've been thrown out of class before, because I got so frustrated with the work. I just gave up trying. Teachers would get mad because I wasn't doing the work the way they wanted me to, but it really was because I couldn't do the work!"

Their overall record generally shows consistent failure despite average to superior intelligence.

Alan told us, "When I was younger I found my mind would wander and I would stop concentrating. At one particular time a teacher was holding up cards with letters, vowels and consonants. The teacher would explain one letter daily; she would go on for about an hour on one letter. Eventually, I would just forget she was even holding the letter. I lost interest. If I were teaching, I wouldn't harp on one thing too long!"

In Alan's case, and certainly in many others', the school experience has totally failed to meet their needs. While school programs may meet certain basic educational needs and requirements, they often fail to motivate these students and without motivation little ongoing progress will be forthcoming.

Alan concluded, "My experience was that some teachers seemed to have 'all the power' and I was *afraid* to say I didn't understand something even if I didn't know it."

Careful observation of the way teenagers discuss their specific difficulties will lead to the awareness of a number of possibilities in improving parent-child and teacher-child communication.

Alan, whom we have quoted, was aware of his disability, though he was unable to communicate this to his teachers and parents. He was embarrassed and humiliated by the quality of his written performance and would not want anyone to evaluate him this way.

He felt that his attempts at performance were misunderstood and interpreted as "carelessness" and he angered teachers because he threatened them. He responded to the teacher's overteaching by losing interest. This suggests that the method being used by the teacher was inappropriate to his learning style. No amount of repetition could cause him to learn if the teacher was using the wrong methodology.

He felt impotent and powerless in the hands of some teachers. Fear is no basis for real learning. Alan recognized that this was a powerful destructive emotion.

Haim Ginott has offered us some helpful suggestions for communication in his *Between Parent and Teenager*.[9] These are:

1) that we avoid threats and sermons when talking to adolescents;
2) that we abbreviate our speeches, simplify our statements;
3) and that we avoid bitterness and sarcasm in our conversations.

Such biting comments act as the red flag of danger for teenagers. Sarcasm begets sarcasm.

He suggests that we do as the Hebrew sages do to gain wisdom: "The beginning of wisdom is silence; the second stage is listening"; that we tolerate much, but sanction little, in dealing with teenagers. Parents of learning-disabled adolescents may have to tolerate even more and sanction little, giving patient, objective direction to the young.

As you can see, the aforementioned situations can all be interpreted and reinterpreted in different ways depending upon the particular bias of the one interpreting them. We strongly believe that frequently what passes for emotional instability is in fact the inability to see the world as a stable, unchanging, predictable place. This is especially true for the normally disharmonious stage of adolescence. As Anna Freud has stated it:

> There are at least two pronouncements which may prove useful. . . . That adolescence by its nature is an interruption of peaceful growth, and that the upholding of an equilibrium during adolescence is in itself abnormal.
> I take it that it is normal for an adolescent to behave for a considerable length of time in an inconsistent and unpredictable manner, to fight his impulses and to accept them; to ward them off successfully and to be overrun by them; to love his parents and to hate them; to revolt against them and to be dependent upon them; and to be deeply ashamed to acknowledge his mother before others and unexpectedly, to desire heart-to-heart talks with her; to thrive on imitation of and identification with others while searching unceasingly for his own identity; to be more idealistic, artistic, generous, and unselfish than he will ever be again, but also the opposite; to be self-centered, egotistic, calculating. Such fluctuations between extreme opposites would be deemed highly abnormal at any other time. . . .

Add to disharmony of a "normal" adolescence the complicating factors of living with constant questions about his basic intelligence, self-worth, peer-group status, and stability and you have a far more vulnerable emotional state in the learning disabled student.

He — won't help himself, or so it appears;
    — will seem to take what others offer but not give of himself;
    — does not usually take the initiative in learning tasks;
    — seems dependent upon others for strength and direction;
    — appears shortchanged on perseverence and follow-through;
    — seems to lack confidence in himself;
    — often tests authority;
    — acts somewhat less mature than his age group;
    — learns to survive by manipulating others;
    — refuses to try;
"IF YOU DON'T TRY, YOU CAN'T FAIL" appears to be his motto.

Meanwhile, back at the drawing board, we may question the options and alternatives that face the learning-disabled adolescent who has not developed basic literacy skills. The facts are that we are sending approximately 25 percent of our young people out into the world without their having completed their high school education, according to an article in the *New York Times* on August 24, 1975. A sizable percentage of the youngsters who do complete grade twelve are emerging from school poorly prepared to perform the basic tasks necessary to earning a living or making a meaningful contribution to our society.

The statistics give mounting evidence that a large proportion of those teenagers and young adults who find their way into penal institutions show evidence of severe learning disabilities in two or more academic areas.[10]

The message seems clear: many kids are coming out of school lacking the basic rudiments of an education that would give them the training to cope with the real world. Survival skills is the name of the game and we must prepare all kids with them, but most of all, our vulnerable youngsters, the formerly learning-disabled.

We had better be certain that the high-school students we are sending into the working world have some of the basic skills of survival as well as ninth grade algebra or tenth grade geometry...

1) They need to be able to select appropriate reading material for themselves.

2) They must have an awareness of sources of information, and a basic know-how concerning where you find what you are looking for.

3) They must be familiar with the use of reference materials. This ranges from Sears Roebuck catalogues to phone books, from newspaper indexes to encyclopedias.

We would like to suggest that some other areas of learning concerning our high school students be examined:

1) Can they administer first aid to someone who is choking, drowning, or bleeding? (Many so-called normal students who have no academic difficulties have stood by helpless for lack of basic information on how to act in an emergency.)

2) Can they perform the basic functions of measurement, using a ruler, yardstick or metric ruler?

3) Can they handle measurement of liquids, solids, area, perimeter? Skills such as painting, carpentry, lawn tending, etc., all involve being able to approximate area and get correct measurement

before buying materials or making estimates. It is much more important to understand what goes into the computation than to memorize meaningless facts. If the required operation is understood, then the facts can be gained through the use of a small computer or adding machine. A 10 × 10 multiplication table can be used as well if no mechanical aids are available.

4) Can they handle a checkbook efficiently? We know a brilliant psychiatrist who claims that his Ivy League college did not prepare him to manage a checking account or balance a checkbook. They never prepared him for the skills that would be required in filling out an income tax form or bookkeeping. He learned by trial and error and by marrying a girl who could handle his money adequately. Pity the poor soul who can't find such a mate . . . !

5) Do they understand credit and money — which truly has become a survival task in the modern world? That is, the understanding of how credit is computed when one needs to borrow money to buy a car, a washing machine, or simply to borrow. Without understanding what credit costs, a car appears to cost $100 per month. What does $100 per month mean in real terms? How much interest is he really paying to borrow the money? How much would he save by saving the money in an interest account and then paying the money out when he makes the purchase? The situation with regard to personal credit indicates that all school graduates need a course in how interest is computed. The youngster with difficulties in math computation, compounded by immature judgment, may saddle himself with an enormous debt burden if he really does not understand what such luxuries are costing him.

6) Does the young adult know what he is signing when he signs a contract for a house, business, or apartment? If he does not understand and cannot read the contract, he may be cheated of his savings with no protection. We are remiss when we send young adults out into the world after twelve years of education — unable to understand what they are signing when they put their name on the dotted line.

Basic to our life-styles in the modern day are many other related survival skills. We must be able to pass a driver's test if we need a license to go from home to job in most nonurban areas. Many states are unaware of the need for extra reading time when taking such a test. The slower reader needs to be prepared to handle the questions that come up, as well as the motor performance and driving segment of the test.

Despite these days of adding machines and calculators, one must be able to make change with ease when buying things in a store. Pity John, one seventeen-year-old youngster we knew, who had not yet learned how to handle the job of making change for purchases under $10.00. He tried to get a job in our local stationery store and made so many errors that he could not keep the job. He was too humiliated and embarrassed to tell his employer that this was a skill he had missed along the way!

So it goes on and on, the need for survival skills in our schools. It is incumbent upon us as parents to see to it that our secondary schools prepare our kids for living in the real world before we send them out to survive. We can't always count on our schools to do the job. We must often do it ourselves. Arguing over whose responsibility such education is is like the old joke about the man who asked a passing waiter for the time. The waiter replied: "I'm sorry sir, but you're not sitting at my table."

If our learning-disabled youngsters are to survive in our increasingly complex world, they must be told the time — no matter whose table it is!

We are speaking of the basic responsibility of education, and accountability as well. Truly, it is one of the jobs that must become the focus of our educational system. How many youngsters must be sacrificed before our schools recognize this and are held accountable?

5

Perception

"My right eye is left-handed."

— Jerry: age eight

OR

"Is the glass half full or half empty?"

— Anonymous

"Mr. and Mrs. Weiss, your son just can't seem to learn the way other youngsters do in a large group. He can't remember the letters of the alphabet... he needs a lot of review at home. He just can't remember number facts." These words were to haunt us for many years until our search for information disclosed the reasons for our son's different style of learning.

Thirteen years later, from the vantage point of having observed him in many learning situations, we can see more clearly that he could remember these numbers and letters.

We know now that he was exhibiting the classic symptoms of a perceptual problem, so common among youngsters experiencing difficulty in school. Such problems do not mean that a child does not see clearly. He may have normal visual acuity and test out at 20/20 vision in the doctor's office. However, he may not interpret what he sees *consistently* and may recognize the same letter **b** as a **p** or a **d**. He may recognize letters having similar shapes with only a slight variation as the same letter. For example, the **p, b,** or **d** may be recognized as **b.**

The way we perceive objects is often based upon the way our prior learning experiences affect us.

Jerome Brunner stated it quite well when he said, "Normal adult human beings not only use the minimal cues provided by split second presentation of stimuli, but use them as a platform to leap to highly predictable conclusions. Much of perception involves going beyond the information given through a reliance on a model of the world of events that makes possible interpretation, extrapolation and prediction." [1]

To illustrate what is meant by visual perception, we borrow an idea from Dr. Cecelia Pollack of College of the City of New York. Dr. Pollack demonstrates as follows:

She holds up a pipe, bowl to the right of stem, and traces the outline **b, d,** with her finger along the edge of the pipe.

Then she asks, "What is this?"

The response is, "It is a pipe."

She then rotates a pipe in space so that the bowl is on top and the stem is at the bottom.

She asks, "What is this?"

The response is, "It is also a pipe."

She then turns the bowl of the pipe to the other side so that it is now to the left of the stem.

She asks, "Now what is this?"

The response as before, "It is still a pipe."

No matter how she turns the pipe, she indicates that it is always a pipe. However, when we rotate letters in space, such as the letter **b** or **p** or **d** or **q,** they change their *name* and their basic sounds. When the sounds change, they alter the words we can make and the meaning of those words. When the meanings of the words change, the context of what we are reading is also altered. The pipe remains constant as a concrete meaningful object with the name "pipe" no matter how we turn it or alter its position in space. However, the letters of the alphabet and many of the numbers change in their basic qualities when we rotate them in space.

How confusing this can be for the child who cannot remember

the position of these letters and numbers in space! Yesterday the book said "dad" but today it seems to say "bad."

When we turn to the listening modality, or auditory learning, even greater confusion may occur for the perceptually impaired child. His hearing may be accurate when measured on an audiometer test, yet he may not be able to discriminate among sounds and words; consequently he may not comprehend what he hears.

The child with *auditory perceptual problems* may have difficulty in learning reading through phonics. For Richard the discrimination of different sounds was an extremely frustrating task. He had great difficulty at age four in hearing certain sounds and was constantly confusing them with others. For example, *doggie* was said as *"goggle,"* Uncle **D**ick was called "Uncle **G**ick." This kind of early confusion is often a strong indicator of difficulty in discriminating among sounds coming in through the auditory channel. The so-called baby talk of the toddler stage may in fact be the faulty discrimination and processing of sounds heard.

Throughout his early years we were constantly aware of his need to have instructions repeated a number of times before they appeared to be understood. In addition to that, we often had to break things down from complex to short, simple statements so that he could handle the incoming information.

If I said, "Richie, go upstairs and brush your teeth and get ready for bed. . . . Don't forget to wash your hands and face," the result would be the reappearance of a shiny, bright-eyed boy who had washed hands but omitted the washing of his face. He had completely forgotten the rest of the instructions by the time he reached the top of the stairs.

Most often he would remember only the last thing that we had said to him and forget the other instructions. We had to learn to break down our instructions and information into small step-by-step procedures. He would return to us after completing each step for a pat on the back and the next installment.

What was most frustrating was his frequent difficulty in recalling what we had said from room to room. One day I asked him to get a box of biscuits for his younger brother's snack time. Ten minutes later he still had not come back from the kitchen, so I went to find out what had happened. I found him standing in front of the refrigerator staring at the contents, the door standing open on a ninety-degree day!

"Where have you been!" I demanded impatiently.

He stared back, looking totally puzzled at the source of my irritation. "I gotta do sompun, but I don't know what!" he replied!

Before we were made aware of the pattern such learning problems take in children, we made him cry over such scenes a number of times. Like most parents we assumed he was not listening, or paying no attention to what we said.

It saddens us now to think of the number of unhappy youngsters who are experiencing such difficulties, for whom success is blocked each time someone becomes angry with them for things they cannot help. When we lead parent workshops and courses in home management for such youngsters, we find that the parent who is not aware of the learning patterns and the frustration that constant criticism can cause will only create more problems for the youngster with learning disabilities. More and more schools must assume the responsibility of helping parents to become more aware of their children's special needs and how to support them in the home situation.

For us it was necessary to explain the problem to Richard so that he might be helped to develop his own compensations. We used a concrete example so that he might be able to keep a visual image in his mind and understand his difficulties. We suggested to him that the way he heard information was like a giant switchboard in the telephone company. His ears were picking up all kinds of messages from the outside world. When a message came through the switchboard a button was turned down. If two messages came in at the same time, he became a little confused. However, if three messages came in simultaneously, he was really "mixed up" and he really couldn't remember any one message properly.

We explained that when there is a short circuit in a phone wire, you often hear another voice coming in on your line in addition to the person to whom you are speaking. The problem Richie was experiencing was likened to such a short circuit, making it difficult for him to listen to his own "phone call" as well as he might want to.

This explanation has helped many of our students to understand why they are experiencing so much difficulty. When they can understand their problem they don't worry about being "stupid or retarded," and they can handle the questions and comments made by their schoolmates.

With older children or adult groups we have found that auditory perception is best explained by introducing them to hearing an unknown foreign language. If I hear Chinese spoken and I have no experience with the language, then I have no basis upon which to translate the information. I hear what appears to be jumbled sounds that have no meaning. However, if I understand the language, it has meaning for me. Then it makes sense. Perception is only meaningful if we have previous information upon which to base our understanding of a subject, and that information remains constant.

The child with an auditory perceptual problem may have much confusion in understanding the world. What he hears may not always be what it seems. We work with many such youngsters.

Richie was such a child. He spent a good deal of his day dealing with confusions that upset him. He did not perceive things accurately and would express himself verbally with some difficulty. Words seemed to "tie up his tongue."

As Richie himself had said, "I think my tongue is too big for my mouth and it gets tangled when I talk."

Richie would come home from school daily with bundles of misinformation about the world. When the sixth grade social studies class was working on some of the cities of the ancient world, Richie went directly to the map and searched it for a while. He then pointed to the continent of Asia and said, "I think it was here!"

"What?" was our response.

"You know, that city that was buried under the ashes from a volcano," he responded.

It took a detective's skill to confirm that our suspicions were correct. Richie had confused the city of Bombay with the city of Pompeii. He was convinced that the story was *The Last Days of Bombay,* rather than *The Last Days of Pompeii.* He was searching on the wrong continent for the wrong city and was totally disoriented. Auditory misperceptions invaded all areas of his life and caused him much frustration.

For those of us who live and work with Richie and others like him, the story is always the same. We must find ways of predicting the kinds of errors that these children will make. We must observe the quizzical look on their faces that indicates the haze of misunderstanding.

We must try to find visual clues and images to help them retain what may be confusing information when they first hear it. We must keep those visual clues around long enough for them to absorb and retain a visual image when they try to recall auditory information. So it was with Terry, a twelve-year-old student of ours.

It just isn't enough to talk about Paul Revere's ride without picturing the event for Terry. The equator may appear as "a menagery lion" rather than "an imaginary line" around the center of the earth. We can take nothing for granted when dealing with these youngsters. What they appear to understand may be pigeonholed in the wrong time and place and retained as misinformation.

Since perception invades all the sensory processes by which we learn and know about our world, it is affected by every aspect of human organization. A child's development, his learning style, his ability to think concretely or abstractly, his creativity, his personality, and the ability to relate to others will be directly affected by how he perceives the world. If the world appears accepting of him, consistent, predictable, and stable, he will feel free to take chances, risk error, and not be destroyed by his own inconsistency.

If, on the other hand, it appears an unstable, inconsistent, unpredictable world, Terry will be far less able to risk error. He may appear to be far less creative, more rigid in thinking, less well able to relate to others, and more governed by the need for security and safety in his personality development.

The more clues and aids we can give him to make his educational world a stable, unchanging place the more consistency we are building into his life.

If $3 \times 7 = 21$ on Monday, what does it equal on Tuesday? Does the answer appear to be the same from day to day? Is $\begin{array}{r} 7 \\ \times 3 \\ \hline \end{array}$ the same problem? If he has a 10×10 multiplication square in his pocket, or on his desk, then 3×7 will always equal the same number, 21, and the square will visually reinforce it.

Terry is a child with a normal healthy body, but he cannot always get his body to respond as he would like it to. His ears hear, but he becomes "mixed-up" at what he hears. His eyes see, but they also seem to play tricks on him when he tries to remember the sounds that letters make. He is increasingly aware of his difficulties and the differences between him and the others in his class. He becomes angry at himself, but projects it onto his classmates and becomes both a bully and a scapegoat for their irritations. So grows a behavioral problem that can only result in failure for Terry.

6

Parents Have Feelings Too!

"Children — the ultimate status symbol"
> — *"Something Is Wrong with
> My Child,"* Brutten, Richardson
> and Mangel

The growth of realistic handling and acceptance of a learning-disabled child's limitations is a slow and steady growth situation through which a parent passes. The stages of this developmental pattern are not clear-cut, nor do we all pass through them at the same rate, or within the same time span. However, we must all change and grow just as the butterfly must emerge from his cocoon.

Initially, we can recall the sense of shock through which we passed when we first became aware of our own child's difficulty in learning according to predictable norms. We, at first, denied his problem, because to us he appeared so alert, vivacious, and normal in his ability to interact with us.

We felt shame, humiliation, and guilt at being so inexperienced and untrained as parents and possibly having "caused" this problem in our child. When one is alone and isolated, all things become magnified out of proportion to reality. Had we known that other parents were experiencing the same frustrations, we might have been better able to understand our own feelings.

With hindsight, we see the tremendous service that parent groups and parent counseling play in helping us deal with this problem. As parents, we tend to blame ourselves, feel inadequate, and become depressed.

When one is feeling inadequate and represses anger, all kinds of fantasies become a factor. We have lived with them all. Mrs. S., the mother of one of our students (mother of five boys, two of whom experienced learning problems), said:

"I became angry at myself for having made these mistakes that caused my child to have problems at school. Anger that is turned inward can only be self-destructive. I nearly developed a case of full-blown ulcers, and suffered intestinal discomfort continually.

"I became angry at school personnel for not understanding my problems and only recommending outside psychological help on how to manage my child more effectively. The school seemed a remote, impersonal place, where I felt defensive and guilty and most uncomfortable. The more frequent my trips to the school to deal with my child's problems, the less willing I was to go there, and the more traumatic became each visit.

"I was not made aware of other parents with similar problems. No parents' groups were available in our community to extend a friendly understanding hand. Each family kept to itself, fearful of discovery. We each were closeted with our own nightmares, ambivalence, and inability to communicate our fears and plan our children's educational future. The experience has reinforced my strong belief that schools should acquaint parents with sources of information to help them deal with their problems. It just isn't enough to recommend a psychiatrist or psychologist who may or may not be the appropriate person to help you and your child. It is necessary to refer parents to books on the subject, to local professional meetings and informational gatherings. This should all be part of the school's service route to parents of children with special needs."

We have seen parents move through stages of awareness in dealing with their child's special needs. For those of us who have arrived at what we hope is a realistic appraisal of our problem, the stages seem to occur in a predictable order.

In stage one, we are likely to blame our child's problem on the previous school that he attended. If it was a traditional school, we feel that the methods utilized there were not appropriate to his needs. They just didn't understand his need for ongoing concrete learning materials and he just couldn't learn any other way.

We may shift schools or place our child in what seems a more appropriate program, but if it still doesn't do the job we expect, we may feel that the teacher the previous year was absent too much, didn't understand hyperactive little boys, or had personal problems herself that year. Despite the fact that all of this may be true, our child is still not learning, he is feeling frustration, and this is making us increasingly unhappy.

In stage two we may shift to the stage of recognizing our family's role in the problem. For example, each parent may blame their child's difficulties on the management techniques of the other one.

Mothers often tell us that we need to explain the learning problem to Father, because he just thinks that "the boy is careless and lazy and that he is a product of poor discipline on my part." Fathers may tell us that they had problems in school when they were younger but were able to make their way in the world and "pull themselves up by their own bootstraps." Therefore, why can't their child?

Management of the child with special needs may create problems of consistency when dealing with all children in a family group. If the child with special needs is allowed to take advantage of his needs and manipulate others, he places special demands upon the whole family. Such special needs create increased stresses on a marriage. If mother and father are not solidly supportive between them, that can split a vulnerable marriage.

Therefore, the final stage is the acceptance of reality. At this point parents can stop blaming and start managing their child and dealing with their problem.

Mrs. T. described herself as a full-time mother who spent her whole day caring for an extremely hyperactive, impulsive, aggressive child as well as three other youngsters. "I can remember feeling captive in situations that never gave me any pleasure or feelings of competency."

She described how she became angry at her husband's freedom to come and go and his ability to remain somewhat more objective about the child's problems. She often felt guilty and responsible, but she could not get away from the problem, nor could she feel like a successful mother.

Fortunately, out of these emotions, grew a communication between husband and wife that helped her master her feelings, and helped him to understand the enormous demands that were made upon both of them. Here too, no help came from educational personnel to help her manage the frustrations, or the communications gap that they might be experiencing.

When a school assumes a narrowly defined role of teaching READING, WRITING, AND ARITHMETIC, who shall teach parents REALITY, AWARENESS, and problems of MANAGEMENT with such children? Without help and counsel, parents may be working at cross-purposes with the school without realizing the conflict of aims and goals. The success of any educational program for special children is directly related to the amount of follow-up, behavior management, and counseling that is nurtured after school hours within the home and with others.[1]

Such parent counseling, when it becomes a regular part of any program, leads a parent directly to a realistic acceptance of the problem. It helps parents understand the child, his special needs, and his interaction with his environment. It leads a parent to the realization that there are things about his child that he can support, interfere with, and alter, but that he cannot change. This awareness of learning style helps a parent to find practical, enjoyable activities to support school learning.

What are some of the ways that we, as parents, can deal realistically with our child's special need? This question is often asked of us and, of course, the answer is not a simple one.

A parent must first become aware of his child's learning style, that is, how his child learns to understand things best. For example: Johnny B. could look at certain letter forms, ten times or a hundred times, but could not recall the positioning the **l ɔ** and the **c l** that differentiated a **b d p q g.** He made persistent errors of rotation of letter forms, and appeared to have memory problems in learning such information.

Imagine the frustration of a child like Johnny when he realized that he was making those "baby mistakes" in the third grade, long past the time that everyone seemed to be able to remember the forms of the letters of the alphabet!

When Johnny's mother came to us, she was made aware of the need to examine his learning style when helping him with schoolwork. She was told to observe his leisure-time activities. What did he choose to do in his spare time?

She observed that he liked to work with block building, making roadways, mechanical toys like little matchbox cars, and would only play with puzzles, or put models together via trial and error. John would not take the time to try to read the instructions in any game before he attempted to play it. When she sat on the couch beside him to read to him, he would become squirmy and restless in a short time, interrupt, and frustrate her in the attempt to help him with his reading.

In our parent counseling meeting, she suggested that she had determined that he was a "hands-on learner." He seemed to learn by experience rather than through preplanning or instructions. His free-time activities were always those that involved a lot of body movement. The need to sit still for long periods of time was too much of a demand on Johnny. He needed opportunities to combine learning with moving.

Johnny's mother could only assist her son without frustrating him if she understood the way he learned best, his span of attention, the kind of successful feedback he needed, and the reasons why he was experiencing difficulty. Without this kind of information a parent's well-intentioned aid may prove more of a hindrance than a help.

7

Home Is a Haven...
or Is It?

Let's Talk of Consistency and Communication
or
Conflict and Clutter

Try to encourage a positive atmosphere in your work time with your child.

An angry, sullen, unhappy or frightened child cannot learn, and punishment for nonlearning causes resentment. A child should feel that his efforts are what counts, even though these efforts may not always be successful.

It isn't always easy to maintain a strong and supportive attitude in dealing with your child's frustrations, negative feelings, and sense of inadequacy. If he has no place to show his feelings at school, he will often vent them in an exaggerated form at home. Home is where one should be able to kick and scream and rant and rave and still be accepted and loved. Such behaviors are often a manipulative technique used to gain attention in any way possible. Your child may have learned to survive by being what Dr. Larry Silver[1] has called a "plunger." A plunger is a child who can cause constant crises by getting another person to react. He judges others' weaknesses and seems acutely aware of their Achilles' heel (vulnerability). He creates a situation as a spider spins a web, catching his victim in the complex web from which he cannot remove himself. The victim or "exploder" then reacts or overreacts and bedlam follows.

If your child is a "plunger" and you are the "exploder," you had better rewrite the script before beginning to do any work with him. Otherwise, you will find that he is able to blow the whistle on you and cause havoc. Your ulcer will begin to react.

If you are a firm believer in scheduling, your "plunger" may take delight in testing you by coming home late for dinner, missing appointments, or dawdling on his way home from school. He obviously gets a bigger payoff through your reaction than he does through the positive effects of being on time!

To change his behavior in this respect, you must try to rearrange the situation so that his emotional payoff increases when he does arrive home on time, and meets responsibilities on schedule.

The first prerequisite to changing behavior is in the parent's reaction pattern. Our second son, Ira, was just such a "plunger" in his dealings with us. Marty did not react as easily as I did. I was constantly finding myself in the position of giving lectures to what were probably deaf ears.

Ira was late for lunch, late home from school, late for dinner. He was late for school, late to classes, and generally tested everyone by his apparent inability to maintain any sort of time schedule.

The first improvement in his attention to time came when I consciously stopped giving long-winded lectures on the subject.

If he arrived late for lunch, Marty and I agreed that there was to be absolutely no discussion. He was told that he could not have anything to eat until supper! The kitchen was closed and off limits to him.

The same procedure occurred when he was late for supper! It took a superhuman effort to keep me from letting loose a verbal barrage whenever this happened. It took unbelievable self-control for me to stick to my guns and maintain consistency in handling him. He sensed this, I'm sure, and perhaps my very inconsistency had been one of the factors in sustaining this behavior for so long.

I realized how far we had come when he responded to my terse "No dinner tonight — you're late" with a silent wide-eyed look.

"Aren't you gonna say anything else?"

I gritted my teeth — "Nope!"

He waited around a bit, looking for some way to start a verbal contest. I simply nodded or said "Huh!," a most uncharacteristic response for me.

Somewhere along the way, I had become a classic "Jewish mother." I had confused loving with feeding and it seemed especially difficult for me to deny food. However, my rights were being tested. I would not "explode." That was the quicker, easier and more satisfying response but it did not change his attitude or behavior.

Basically, these changes in my attitude helped bring about changes in his attitude, and gradually, over time, we began to see a shift in his patterns of manipulative behavior. I don't mean to suggest that this is any easy process. Children change quickly but adults do not. I was far slower to learn than he was. What I probably mastered was the ability to cover up my feelings of anger, hurt, and disappointment so that my weaknesses could not be manipulated. Without such changes in the relationship, we could not have worked with our boys without untold emotional cost.

When a parent says that he or she can't work with his or her child, we must ask, "Why? What feelings in you does he provoke and how do you respond?"

We have them keep a record of their child's "plunging" activities or manipulative behaviors. We ask them to list their exact immediate response to such behaviors. We explore other ways in which they might have responded. What other things they might have said and done. We try to find out what child's behavior really meant after learning to "listen with the third ear."

Practice in this kind of communication helps us tune into what is being meant rather than just what is being said. When Richie often said that he could not go back to school, we took it to mean that he needed help in reentry. He had gotten himself into a difficult situation and rather than openly admit that to us, he refused to return to school. Borrowing a bit of advice from Haim Ginott, we would try to sympathize and offer assistance, but would insist upon his meeting his obligations, tough as he thought they were.

When Ira refused to communicate verbally concerning his difficulties, we felt that it was an inability to deal with the realities of
his educational situation. We read it as avoidance and often had to
provoke discussion by making him angry before he could express
himself. As the teenagers might say, "letting it all hang out" is often
a very healthy therapy for all. However, parents must be pretty sure
that they can handle what is going to be said before they encourage
any teenager to do this. Otherwise a very difficult situation will result, in which the troubled youngster expresses his real thoughts
and feelings and the parent becomes quite angry and hurt at facing
the depth of these emotions.

Often the way we react to our children, and especially to our
learning-disabled children, is directly related to the way we are
feeling about ourselves. If we feel strong, independent and secure
in our decisions, then our need to administer consistent discipline
does not cause us any mixed emotions. We feel that we have rights,
our child is violating those rights, and he must be called to task
for this. No guilt, anxiety, or ambivalent feelings need to muddy
the waters of our relationships. However, if we are at a time of
emotional stress ourselves, and are under business or professional
strains, our reaction can be quite different. At times like these, it
might be helpful to delay action or punishment of a child and discuss what has happened with someone who can be a bit more
objective at this moment. Overflow anger from one crisis can creep
into another situation causing us to react with far more anger than
the situation requires.

Some psychologists believe that adults go through precisely the
same kind of developmental stages as children. Crises occurring at
different stages will result in different kinds of responses, depending
upon the amount of conflict within the adult. Thus, the minor crises
that come with day-to-day dealing with the learning-disabled youngster are often profoundly affected by the stage of development of
his parents and their reactions to his antics.

Let us examine those stages to see how we might react to our
own stresses rather than the real problems of our children. Between
the ages of eighteen and twenty-two, we seem to be quite ambivalent in our feelings toward our parents. We love them and hate
them, need them and wish to be rid of them. We are anxious to be
free of them. This seems to guide our behavior.

From about twenty-two to twenty-eight years of age, we continue this breaking away and become competent in some skill or area. We work to build a life, business, or profession. These years have been referred to as those of the "now generation."

In terms of dealing with problems that face us, it can easily be seen that dealing with the problems of one's children during these years might be less threatening than in other stages. We are basically secure in our feelings, we focus upon the positive aspects of life. We are no longer dependent and anxious about ourselves, thus allowing us to handle someone else's dependence upon us with strength and some objectivity.

The period from about twenty-eight to thirty-five years of age seems to be one of questioning and reflection for the young adult. He or she begins to inquire into the meaning of life, relationships, and the role of provider or parent. The problems of a learning-disabled child pose further questions at a time of introspection. They may be more stressful for the parent if he is not able to handle his own personal conflicts. Thus the same difficulties that did not bother us at age twenty-seven might cause us much emotional conflict at age thirty-three!

At around age thirty-five, we become aware of the finite number of years we have to satisfy our personal and professional drives. We become more urgently involved in satisfying our basic personal and professional needs. No longer do we foresee an endless period of time left during which we can work, enjoy, grow, and prosper. This is our period of drive to achieve. Success is an important part of this period of adulthood. The demands of a passive, dependent, apathetic learning-disabled adolescent when we are at a period like this can give us a greater anxiety.

We may feel threatened far more seriously by a learning-disabled adolescent's lack of desire to succeed, lack of goal orientation, inability to deal with real problems and avoidance of them. Without realizing it, we may in fact be projecting our own emotional needs upon him and asking of him the same urgency for success and prosperity that we have. We know that there is a limited amount of time left for us. He does not know that there is a limited amount of time left for him. He sees parenthood and adulthood as a magical stage of privileges and comforts, easily won. Our urgency conflicts with his stage of moratorium, one in which he is trying alternatives, delaying commitments, and attempting to set goals. Although he may be considered an adult in the eyes of the law, he is very much an immature adolescent in the eyes of society.

The learning-disabled adolescent, who often exhibits developmental lags in all areas of educational and social experience, is running on a schedule two to three years behind in this as well. He arrives at each stage well behind his peers. He may have the mental age of a twenty-year-old, the chronological age of a seventeen-year-old and the developmental level of a fourteen-year-old!

We must accommodate to this developmental level rather than his true chronological age, or our expectations for him will be unrealistic. We must also understand how our own stresses may result in "overreacting or overkill" in dealing with such an adolescent.

At about the age of forty-five, we become far less urgent in our own personal drives and relax in a stage of equilibrium once more. At this time in life, adults are better able to deal with children as independent people, rather than extensions of their own drives and needs. We are better able to let go of them and allow them to rise or fall as they may.

This period of equilibrium allows our relationships with our children to flourish. We grant them the right to succeed or fail as independent young adults. We stand by as supporter and advisor but not as parties in the performance.

Our personal experiences have given us a different perspective on our learning-disabled adolescents. They were easier to handle at different times because of their growth stages and our own. We have reached the period of "letting go" now, just at the time when they have reached the developmental stage of independence and anxiety. Wish us luck!

During these periods of growth, the need for consistent handling is extremely important. Without such consistency, no child is sure of his limits. For parents it is harder to maintain consistency when they are under increased stress.

Consistency means that Father and Mother must agree on how a youngster is to be handled. If Dad says: "No supper, you are late again!" Mom cannot interfere. If Mom says, "Jim, you can go out and play," Dad had better not contradict her statement!

Sometimes children become sensitive to differences in their parents' attitudes and handling. They know that they can "mooch" money from Mother but Father stands firm on the limits of budgeting the allowance. Care must be taken not to allow kids to get between their parents and create dissension and anger.

The "plunger" wins when he creates a crisis and leaves the victims to fight in his place.

Jim could cause the family arguments, but his mother and father always went on to finish them. Jim silently slipped away, having left Mom and Dad to fight it out. He felt pleased to have saved his skin, but guilty for having created the scene.

Furthermore, constant conflict may develop into a more profound disagreement between Mother and Father. If they recognize what has been happening, they become angry at Jim. Jim responds with further manipulation, and so goes the vicious cycle of family confusion. No one can win in this situation. Everyone is bound to lose!

It is helpful to get a learning-disabled child out of the home frequently and expose him to activities of all kinds. There may be many athletic activities in which he can succeed in some small way. Any kind of experience that contributes to learning and enhancing the feeling of success is good. Success can result from a task as simple as sweeping the floor or as complex as a course in basic calisthenics.

Kids need to succeed! They don't necessarily need that success in academic areas.

Art, music, sports, scouting, volunteer service, and others are activities that involve doing, not just seeing and hearing.

We would give one word of caution before we move on. Try to avoid placing a learning-disabled child in situations that are too demanding. This will cause more stress and anxiety. The poorly coordinated child can be enrolled in calisthenics, but the group he is with must not be so good that he can't feel any success at all.

Unfortunately, we can't give any formula for setting up realistic expectations. Such decisions depend on basic common sense and intuition. If you have ideas, but question their appropriateness, check with the school learning-disability specialist, psychologist, or guidance counselor before you make plans.

Overscheduling can be as disastrous as boredom for the learning-disabled child. We have worked with youngsters who say that their only free playtime is while waiting for the bus in the morning! Their week is filled with a daily round of lessons in music, sports, religion, or Little League, swimming, gymnastics, and more. What initiative and independent resources can a child develop if he is being ferried daily to a round of planned activities?

Parents can fall into the trap of pushing their children into all the school activities, because their friends' children are involved.

One nine-year-old youngster told us, "I'm always taking lessons. No matter how good I get, I'll never be good enough." When activities become busywork they may hinder more than they help.

Sometimes, in our desire to help our child, we can overburden him with demands. To help him too much can smother feelings of initiative and independence.

8

Managing Behavior and Tensional Levels

"Sometimes I feel like I'm too jumpy to stay in my own skin."

— Richie: age thirteen

Learning-disabled children seem to produce more tension in a family than the so-called average child. A child who has been frustrated often develops a whole set of defenses that can cause his family to respond to him in a predictable way. As parents of such children, we learned that we had to constantly handle such tensions. The tensions, however, were both in our children and in ourselves, and in the interaction among us all. Without this kind of adjustment on an ongoing basis, we were vulnerable to overreaction and they would only respond in a similar fashion, creating a poor situation at home.

Since there is much in the learning-disabled child's tensional buildup that is a function of his own body chemistry, we could not change many of Richie's impulsive, explosive responses. We could, however, learn to deal with them without becoming involved in his personal tensions. Our calm response often helped him to gain control of himself. If, on the other hand, we became embroiled in his frustrations and responded in anger, we only fed into his problems and made them worse. We found that our response acted as the "plunger" or the "pacifier" in feeding his poorly controlled emotions. We could virtually turn him on or off depending upon our responses.

As an overall group, we have found that parents of such kids are generally more sensitive to the presence of increasing levels of tension of their children. However, what of the increasing tension within ourselves? Each of us must learn to find appropriate tensional releases that avoid emotional clashes that do harm to others.

The process of dealing with one's personal tensional buildup is a very real problem in daily living. We found that our learning-disabled boys seemed to need periods of relaxation from primarily scholastic activities. As long as we kept in touch with their timetable, we could work at home in short time intervals without their balking at that work. For example, Richard lost interest after fifteen minutes. We could not have even tied him down at that point! He had to move and "run off" his energy. We wouldn't even go to dinner at a local restaurant without affording him the opportunity to run off his energy midway during the meal. We took turns at this often annoying but necessary job. Gradually, as his attention span increased, we lengthened his work periods, but often had to backtrack to our fifteen-minute rule on a bad day. A "bad" day was any day that was warm, humid, snowy, or when he was sick. A bad day might also be one on which the other boys were all home, interrupting, playing, invading his attention and distracting him.

We had to develop the flexibility to be in touch with his time clock; without this the whole working period turned into a major fiasco, with our irritation and his temper tantrum becoming the focus.

With Ira, the tensional buildup showed itself in yawning spells. After any difficult work was partially accomplished, he might break out in a series of yawns, one or so per minute. We had one student, Jack, a boy of eight, who could yawn thirty-one times in twenty-nine minutes, a feat that we often considered a kind of national record!

For both Ira and Jack, we found that moving around and doing some fast play exercise seemed to counteract this habit. Jack liked to do jumping jacks or hopping around the room, so that was helpful for him. Ira seemed more lethargic and the only activity he warmed up to at this time was a bowling game that we made with paper tubes and a beanbag. Getting up, throwing the beanbag, and moving around the room seemed to relieve his need for activity.

We believe that parents as well as teachers have to build in certain accommodations in their lives to accept their child's individual learning and living style. If your child works best during a ten-minute interval, then space out a few ten-minute work intervals during the day. It may be more convenient for you to work for thirty minutes at one time, but it is a serious mistake to try it. You will have to force the child to attend, and stress and hostility will build up. The end result will be failure of any attempts to work at home.

If his best work time is in the early morning, try to plan some time before he leaves for school. We often played phonics and letter-identification games at breakfast time with magnetic letters on the refrigerator. This became a morning habit that was not broken. We now leave shopping notes and information about chores on the refrigerator door in just such a way.

It is critical to keep expectations on a realistic level. Learning-disabled youngsters have many gaps in their ability to handle educational and social problems. These are often further complicated by emotional gaps that make them act in a way that is far less mature than that of their peers.

Progress in all areas is often uneven. It is as if the amount of effort required to mature in any one area of development is so enormous that they can move forward in only that area. For example, we observed that our own boys grew educationally but seemed to regress at the same time in their handling of personal responsibilities. It was as if the one area of progress demanded so much of them that the other areas were sacrificed. The following year, we might see growth in their sense of responsibility, follow-through on tasks, performing chores, etc. However, that year there might be little or no academic progress. This was extremely frustrating for us. Each time we felt that we were coming out of the woods in one area, we were disappointed in another.

It is as if they can take two steps forward and one step back in the growth and maturity. Just when a parent has become accustomed to the advance to a new stage there often appears to be a regression. This can be most disappointing for us and if our disappointment is communicated to our children, they may become extremely angry at themselves.

When we talk about keeping expectations realistic, we are talking about our expectations for the child. What of our expectations for ourselves as parents? Those must be kept realistic as well. In this world of superathletes, of "winners," we often come to expect that we can do more than we really can to help our children solve their problems.

Basically, the difficulty in learning is within the child. It is *his* homework, *his* reading, and *his* frustration! We can only give him a supportive, comforting environment that helps him to know that we are always there to assist him. We can go to school and talk to teachers and try to help them to see what we see in our child. But we cannot solve his problems, do his homework, or feel his feelings. He will have to go through these himself, with us by his side. He will need to feel free to express his feelings of anger, hostility, and frustration to us. He will not be allowed the freedom of expressing these in school where a code of group behavior must be maintained. He will benefit from knowing that we give him the right to let off steam, blow up, and be open and honest. This may be painful to us at times, but it becomes a very necessary role that parents must play in the life of any child.

9

TESTING–
Tool or Torture?

*"All they do is test me!
When are they gonna teach me!"*
— Richie: age twelve

*"Through these portals pass some of the most tested
students in the world."*
— Sign at the entrance to
Pine Ridge School, a
Secondary School for Learning-
Disabled Students:
Williston, Vermont

The date is May 26th. The phone rings and parents are asked to come to school for a conference concerning their child's problem. The parents have been told that their child has done so poorly on this year's achievement tests that the teacher feels that he should be retained in the same grade for the following year. The discussion might be that of summer school placement or tutoring during the vacation period.

We must ask if there has been evidence of difficulty previous to this time and often the answer is "no." Children don't begin having their difficulties on May 26th. Long before that time some evidence has appeared. Why were the parents told so late in the year?

Much of the timing is dependent upon the structure of the child's class, the intelligence of the child (and his ability to compensate for his problems) and the type of testing that has been done in school during the year.

Parents need to understand the types of testing that are carried on in their schools. They need to know reasons for this testing, its benefits and drawbacks. Often certain kinds of tests are not appropriate for use with learning-disabled youngsters. Without this kind of information, testing results are merely numbers and percentages that have little information for the parent and contribute little to assisting the child.

Testing has been called a "tyranny" by many contemporary educators. The publishers of tests represent a large and lucrative segment of the educational materials industry. Once established, a testing program can become a self-perpetuating bureaucracy, a "procrustean bed" that would cut off the feet of the child to make him fit its dimensions.

In the movie *Alice's Restaurant,* Arlo Guthrie is quoted as saying, "I've been inspected, detected, selected and rejected and they left no part untouched!" After reading some of the diagnostic histories of youngsters, including our own sons, we can agree that that may well be the way a youngster feels.

Basically, testing is of no value to us if it does not give us information that leads directly to concrete practical assistance for our children both in school and out. Testing is expensive. Test files build up dust and take up space. The terminology used within those files may have the effect of labeling a child for the rest of his educational life. Often those labels are applied by a specialist, only to be misinterpreted by the untrained layman. Labels are a strange thing; they assume the quality of permanence. They may become self-fulfilling prophesies if they are not reversed or removed.

In a keynote speech at the New York Orton Society presentation dinner at the Biltmore Hotel, March 1975, Dr. Lawrence Silver of Rutgers Medical School said that he can estimate the type of education and the graduate school attended by a specialist from the specific labels that specialist uses to describe a child's learning disability. He says that labels have changed so often that one specialist may be calling a child "minimally brain damaged," while another refers to him as having "a central processing problem," and a third may use the term "brain injury" for the same condition. Most doctors feel that youngsters diagnosed as learning disabled have what they term neurological "soft signs" but do not see as definite medical evidence of dysfunction.

Implicit in this reliance on labels is the danger that the specialist may be conveying to the person reading the report an impression that has a different impact from what was originally intended.

To give vague conditions specific names implies that there are clear-cut, discernible symptoms that are exact and scientific. Labeling often gives a medical name to what is basically an educational and management problem. With computerized information systems becoming an integral part of our lives, the learning-disabled youngster who has been labeled "brain injured" may carry such a label into his permanent employment records.

Much of this need to label comes from parents as well as professionals. In our tremendous need to understand the problems our children are facing, we find it difficult to deal with uncertainties. Parents ask such questions as: Will my child be able to finish high school? Will he be able to go on to college? Is his condition covered by medical insurance because tutoring him is so expensive? Is his problem a mental problem? Have I failed my child? Do I need a psychiatrist?

We are more troubled by something intangible and vague. We can't see it, feel it, touch it, or smell it.

"Trying to define a learning disability is like trying to catch the wind in a net."

Labels are comforting to us. They mean that we have found a particular condition to be the cause of the problem. To have a persistent headache is all the more troubling if one does not know why. If we are told we have a sinus infection, the pain remains but the uncertainty is gone.

Moreover, for many years the most popular label given youngsters who could not perform in school has been that of "emotionally disturbed". . . !

This represented an oversimplification on the part of educators. Often it appeared that they were not able to categorize a youngster's behavior in any other way. This was especially true when dealing with the diagnosis of teenagers with problems. They acted out their frustrations in highly emotional ways and therefore were often labeled "emotionally disturbed."

Many parents find this unacceptable, for it suggests that they have done something wrong to this child, possibly depriving him of his basic needs for love and nurture. Others feel guilty about their children's learning problems and feel threatened by the schools.

The recent evidence that children often exhibit problems apart from any wrongdoing on the part of their parents has taken some of the weight of guilt off parental shoulders. No longer do we put all learning problems in the emotional disturbance cubbyhole. Yet we are nervous with this vague new "umbrella" term. We long to make a specific cause-effect relationship out of stimulus and response.

In addition, the whole problem of who shall pay to aid these children with special needs plagues us. Is it the job of the parents to provide for their children's special needs or is the onus upon the schools? Several states have ruled that it is the job of the schools. Many have not yet faced this reality. Often the kind of label used directly determines who shall pay the cost of special needs. In New York State, a child designated as "handicapped" can get funding to get therapeutic educational help to meet his special requirements.

In order to clarify the issues, we have come to rely more and more upon testing and evaluations. However, our educational solutions to the problems are a direct result of our test findings. To get good test findings, we must give good tests that are appropriate for the needs of these specific children.

Once more we are placed in that gray area of uncertainty. There is no one way that has proved to be *the* way to test for a learning disability. Each expert has his personal bias that determines his choice of the materials he considers appropriate.

Fortunately, we can make some generalizations despite this clutter of conflicting information. Certain tests appear to be better predictors than others. Some testing has proved to be less useful for learning-disabled children.

There are two ways of testing: in a group, or individually. Most group testing per se tells us very little about the learning-disabled child except what we already know — that he cannot perform as others can. If he is given a group I.Q. or achievement test, his inability to read the test, follow directions, organize spatially, or write, and his rate of performance may give us extremely poor results. However, we really don't know whether he has information. We just know he can't perform on this kind of test within an arbitrary time limit.

On the other hand, a test performed individually will produce valid information if we use the appropriate testing. If the same tests given to groups are administered in a one-to-one situation, the same results may be obtained. The child still cannot perform the needed operations. He may be less distracted than he might have been in a group setting but results will not change. So the operative word here is *appropriate* testing.

Testing results are also colored by the relationship established between the child and the person doing the testing. If the rapport is not good, the results may be depressed. Results are also strongly influenced by a child's previous experiences in testing situations. No one who has felt failure enjoys being tested. Previous experience makes this a painful ordeal.

Basically, test batteries are those administered to gain some idea of a child's intelligence or general aptitude for academic tasks. It is extremely difficult to evaluate what intelligence really is. In academic terms, it is a measure of those skills required to perform school-associated types of tasks. However, there is no true measure of competence in other areas built into the testing. This does not evaluate a child's reaction to a social situation, his emotional stability, his competency in survival skills, etc.

Group intelligence tests may also provide us with another type of label that might be used to track a child into classes for "slow learners," but any child who is not reading on grade level may score poorly on group intelligence testing! Tracking a child may put him in an inappropriate grouping situation for the rest of his educational life. Labeling him may be detrimental.

Of course, there are many I.Q. tests, too numerous to mention here. The major drawback of such testing is that it is often inaccurate to base one's estimate of a child's potential upon a group testing. If the child reads poorly, cannot follow directions, becomes confused or frustrated, the scores may be misleading.

If your child's evaluation was based upon such testing, it is extremely important that you request individual testing for a more precise view of your child's strengths and weaknesses.

The Wechsler Intelligence Scale for Children (WISC)–Revised (WISC-R) is a composite of subtests that estimates a youngster's abilities in both verbal (language-associated) tasks and performance tasks that closely associate with nonverbal functioning. By use of various subtests, a broader picture of a youngster's competency is gained.

The interpretation booklet for the Wechsler Intelligence test describes the subtests this way:[1]

INFORMATION:

"This sub-test measures associative thinking and general comprehension of facts which are acquired both in the home and school." It is a measure of our reservoir of general information.

COMPREHENSION:

"The Comprehension sub-test measures the child's use of common sense, judgment, and reasoning. It measures judgment in practical situations." It would correlate with a child's pattern of awareness of how to act in social and educational situations.

ARITHMETIC:

"This test measures the child's ability to apply basic arithmetic processes in personal and social usage of problem solving . . . abstract concepts of number and numerical operations, overall numerical reasoning and abilities are involved." It correlates with attention, understanding of language concepts, and ability to perform math processes without concrete supports such as chips, counting frames, counting lines, etc.

SIMILARITIES:

"This sub-test measures both abstract and concrete reasoning abilities. It involves verbal concept formation, capacity for associative thinking and remote memory." Here a youngster must be aware of the subtleties of language, relate meanings of words, and be able to categorize information.

VOCABULARY:

"The Vocabulary sub-test measures the child's ability to understand words, and reflects his level of education and environment. This sub-test also measures the individual's accumulated verbal learning ability, range of ideas, fund of information, and qualitative levels of reasoning ability." This test also measures a child's ability to express such information verbally, how direct or tangential his thinking is, the level of concreteness or abstraction.

DIGIT SPAN:

"Ability to recall auditory information in proper sequence and detail is measured by this test. This test also demands of the child the ability to hold attention and the ability to synthesize and organize in a structured situation." In this test, the child is asked to repeat a series of numbers of increasing length, immediately after hearing them. Because the numbers have no meaning, it is a rote memory task.

PICTURE COMPLETION:

"This sub-test measures the ability to visualize essential from the non-essential detail and to identify familiar stimuli from one's environment (school and home)." The results of this subtest give us an idea of the way in which a youngster pays attention to visual clues in his environment, how observant he is of detail seen.

PICTURE ARRANGEMENT:

"This sub-test measures the ability to see a total situation based on visual comprehension and organization and environmental experiences (social intelligence)." Here a child must relate a series of pictures in a logical sequence so that they tell a meaningful story.

BLOCK DESIGN:

"The Block Design sub-test measures the ability to perceive, analyze, synthesize and reproduce abstract designs. This sub-test utilizes non-verbal concept formation, capacity for sustained effort, visual motor coordination, abstract and concrete thinking ability and overall ability to plan and organize." Here we see how a youngster can recall a design and relate the part of a design to the whole shape and form.

OBJECT ASSEMBLY:

"This sub-test measures a visual-motor coordination, simple assembly skills, the ability to see spatial relationships, and the ability to synthesize concrete parts into meaningful wholes." This is like a picture puzzle game that must be completed within a time limit.

CODING:

"This sub-test measures flexibility in new learning situations, ability to learn visual-motor skills from repetitive experiences, ability to absorb new material in an associative context and general over-all psycho-motor ability. It also measures visual-motor dexterity, pencil manipulation, speed and accuracy." Here a child must write a series of symbols from repetitive visual forms and perform it under pressure of time.

Let us look at a sample of an individual psychoeducational evaluation:

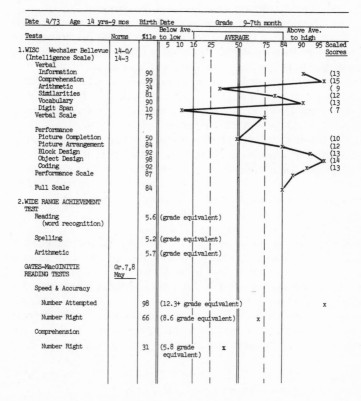

Date 4/73   Age 14 yrs-9 mos   Birth Date   Grade 9-7th month

Tests	Norms	%ile	Below Ave. to low	AVERAGE	Above Ave. to high	Scaled Scores
1.WISC Wechsler Bellevue (Intelligence Scale)	14-0/ 14-3					
Verbal						
Information		90			x	(13
Comprehension		99			x	(15
Arithmetic		34	x			(9
Similarities		81		x		(12
Vocabulary		90			x	(13
Digit Span		10	x			(7
Verbal Scale		75		x		
Performance						
Picture Completion		50		x		(10
Picture Arrangement		84		x		(12
Block Design		92			x	(13
Object Design		98			x	(14
Coding		92			x	(13
Performance Scale		87			x	
Full Scale		84		x		
2.WIDE RANGE ACHIEVEMENT TEST						
Reading (word recognition)		5.6	(grade equivalent)			
Spelling		5.2	(grade equivalent)			
Arithmetic		5.7	(grade equivalent)			
GATES-MacGINITIE READING TESTS	Gr.7,8 May					
Speed & Accuracy						
Number Attempted		98	(12.3+ grade equivalent)		x	
Number Right		66	(8.6 grade equivalent)	x		
Comprehension						
Number Right		31	(5.8 grade equivalent)	x		

In looking at the sample performance on the WISC, we see that it showed a great deal of strength on all performance subtests except the picture completion subtest. There the score was average for age range. That means the youngster did as well as fifty out of one hundred youngsters taking the test. He appears to be a hands-on performance-oriented youngster. He was able to indicate and express with his hands what he could not express with a pencil to paper. He was able to do block designs accurately, to assemble objects accurately, to code or write down forms quickly with a pencil; yet when it became necessary to put thoughts on paper, to process and think through meaningful sentences, his performance deteriorated despite a high level of vocabulary and comprehension.

The WISC-R, WAIS[2] and WPPSI[3] are individual I.Q. tests that are relied upon by psychologists. Other well-known ones are the Detroit Test of Learning Aptitude[4] and the Stanford Binet.[5]

The advantages of having your child tested with one of these are that you will gain a far more perceptive picture of his strengths and weaknesses than could be given on a group test. On the other hand, the time involved in testing and scoring all of these (from two to six hours) makes them an expense for school districts to administer. Schools will arrange for such testings when they deem it necessary. However, there will be some delay between a request for testing and the reporting of results.

The learning-disabled child is one who often exhibits symptoms of delayed or uneven development in many areas. It is very important to get some idea of development levels with respect to the handling of basic tasks. One of these basic tasks is writing. Since so much of schoolwork is dependent upon your child's skill in copying the forms he sees to paper, some level of writing or copy-forms test helps to determine his functional level.

If your child is to be tested by a school psychologist, guidance counselor or learning specialist, one of the tasks he may be asked to do is to copy forms that he is shown. This particular kind of testing is usually included in most test batteries administered by schools and clinics.

We call this particular testing an evaluation of the development of skill of visual-to-motor integration. Among the tests that may be utilized for this purpose are any one of the following:

1. Bender-Gestalt Test: Western Psychological Services. An individually administered test of copying designs.

2. Berry-Buktenica Developmental Test of Visual Motor Integration, Follett & Co., Chicago, Illinois. An individual or group-administered screening of copy forms.
3. Benton Visual Retention Test, Psychological Corporation, New York. An individually administered test of visual retention and memory.

These tests are designed to determine how your child sees forms visually, perceives them, and translates them into written performance. They are not visual tests, but rather a measure of the ability to see an object, understand its form, shape, and direction, and reproduce it on paper so that the copied form appears to be the same as the one seen.

The results of this kind of test correlate closely with the kind of written classroom performance that a child may produce. It is important to note that more than 75 percent of the work done in most classrooms involves the copying of visual symbols on paper. Writing letters, numbers, words, sentences are all tasks of visual to motor integration.

Some of this copying is done from the blackboard. This task requires the child to look at the board and then back to his paper repeatedly in order to make a group of forms similar to those he sees. This is called far-point copying.

Most copying is done from textbooks, workbooks and papers, and involves the child in a process of looking from book to paper or from one place on a page to another place on the same page. This is called near-point copying.

Your child's academic achievement correlates closely with the degree of accuracy with which he can perform these tasks.

Unfortunately, development of this skill does not proceed at a predictable rate for all children. There are large variations among children in their readiness for copying tasks. Most classrooms require a series of tasks that lean heavily upon copying and writing skills despite the fact that many children are not ready for this complex task.

When copying accurately from visual forms and shapes, a number of acts must occur simultaneously. The child must have the visual acuity at both near and far points to see the symbol accurately, judging its detail and spatial orientation.

Dr. G. Getman devised a model of development of the visual and motor systems and their interrelationships. Dr. Getman defines *sight* as the human being's simple responses to light; *visual acuity* as the clarity of the light pattern striking the retina; and *vision* as the child's ability to interpret his environment, and to understand things outside of oneself that are seen.[6]

Your child must understand what he is seeing and channel his visual information so that it can be written accurately.

If symbols are received correctly via the visual system, but garbled in transmission to the vocal expressive channel, a speech or language problem may result. If they are garbled in transmission to the writing channel of expression, the result may be a problem of poor writing, rotated letters and numbers, or size, space, and directional confusion.

Your child must have developed the level of fine-motor co-ordination required to be able to draw what he has seen and understood. He must be able to recall the parts of the whole form, relate them to each other, so that he can duplicate the form with parts that are roughly the same size.

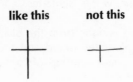

He must perceive that forms change direction at certain points and form angles:

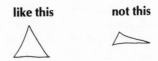

He must understand the direction of objects in space and be able to reproduce them correctly:

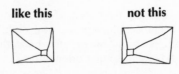

The same difficulties occur when he deals with letters and numbers.

He may be unable to duplicate forms with parts that are correctly sized and spaced in relation to each other:

like this   **not this**

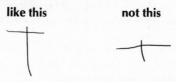

Or he cannot perceive that forms change direction and form circles or angles:

like this   **not this**   **or this**

Or cannot understand the direction of objects in space and rotates them:

like this   **not this**

Another important type of evaluation that helps us gain prescriptive teaching information concerning a child is the use of specific learning-disability testing. We have found these especially helpful.

These particular tests aim at finding out how a child performs in specific school-associated tasks:

For example: How will he do at

a) copying information from a book;

b) copying from a blackboard;

c) finding words that are similar or different;

d) remembering and identifying words (sight memory) that he sees;

e) remembering and writing (after short delay) symbols that he has been shown on a flash card;

f) identifying sounds heard at the beginning and the end of words (phonics);

g) remembering what he hears and identifying it (auditory memory);

h) remembering what he hears and writing it down;

i) repeating a series of syllables that he hears;

j) understanding and writing from dictation (auditory comprehension);

k) answering comprehension questions.[7]

This kind of testing can help a teacher focus upon a child's basic educational problems and direct him to specific remedial techniques that are most appropriate for that child.

Let us see what we can find out through one sample performance of one of these subjects. The one we have chosen is the one that requires listening to sentences and writing what one has heard. Paul, a sixteen-year-old, performed the given sentences as follows:

The following phrases were dictated to Paul: from the Malcomesius Screening Test, Subtest V119.[8]

1. throwing pebbles and blowing bubbles
2. stored bran in the barn
3. it goes from right to left
4. under the top and over the bottom
5. desiring and deserving better
6. vast foreign complication
7. fumbled with the throttle
8. permanent government situation
9. from the first girls' playground
10. dabbling with bubbling water
11. 6,936
12. 906
13. 24×538
14. $9,683 - 58$

Here we see that a breakdown occurs in the recall of word patterns. Paul was able to handle many single sounds, consonants, vowels, and blends correctly but could not ENCODE them when writing multisyllable words. Thus it can be inferred that the skill of handling the isolated patterns has been learned but the central processing of information breaks down when there are multistimuli (too many sounds and syllables to handle at once). Moreover, the performance exhibits phonetic respelling, transposition of sounds, omission of letters when writing from dictation.

1 - thoriurn pebbels and blow bubbles

2 - store barn in the barn

3 it gos form right to left

4 under the top and the botom

5 desuring and dessur beter

6 vast funer comtamtashen

7 fubeled with the thortel

8 pernemet gonevrmet sityuashen

9 form the frist girls palygraid.

10 dalebry with bubble wraster

11 - 63 9 6   13. 24 X 583

12   9 0 6   14 - 9, 6 93 - 85

For example: phonetic respelling   situation became sityuashen
transposition   left became letf
throttle became thortel
omission of letters   blowing became blow
fumbled became fubeled

Paul needs to learn how to deal with smaller demands that require less written work before he will be able to deal with longer, more complicated written tasks.

We found it helpful to take Paul back both to the syllable patterning, so he could relearn spelling, and to basic sentence structure, so that he could learn how to deal with words, phrases, and syntax.

We initiated his work by having him deal with a variety of interesting, colorful verb forms. He learned these verb forms and then was asked to add various kinds of subjects to the verb, then predicate phrases and object words. Finally he was asked to vary multiples of adjectives, thereby changing the context of the sentence. We built up Paul's work from the analysis and development of one sentence to writing two sentences, then three, four, and so on. We taught him how to build short paragraphs. Paul began to gain confidence in dealing with writing. He became aware of basic sentence form, and syntax. A twelve- or thirteen-page written assignment might prove too frustrating and cause him to avoid any performance. However, a more realistic assignment of two or three pages would prompt him to make a meaningful attempt.

The opposite is a sample of Paul's written work. Notice the quality of his ideas, despite the inaccuracies of spelling, punctuation and paragraph form.

Paul was a youngster who had something to say. When he was made to feel inadequate and self-conscious, he would not say it. However, when he felt accepted, supported and respected, he was willing to risk embarrassment and say what was on his mind. Paul put his pencil to paper and wrote after he felt accepted and respected. He was painfully aware of his primitive spelling and poor exposition. However, he was bright, sensitive and aware. He wanted help but could not get help in writing unless he wrote.

To learn a skill one must practice it. To practice a skill in which one is deficient, one must take risks. One will only take risks when one feels accepted. Acceptance means that those who are teaching will make constructive comments on one's work rather than destructive comments of a personal nature.

Adolescents like Paul must spend so much of their energy role-playing the part of a "devil-may-care," "don't give a damn" person that they have little time and energy left to recognize themselves as they really are. Let us see how Paul could write after he was convinced that his ideas were the primary concern and not his

TESTING — TOOL OR TORTURE?

Paul's Composition: as a reaction to a news article
(as he typed it)   concerning the futility of war

There is a sine you can buy to hang on your wall (a fipof)
xgx which says "the only difference between boys and men is the
pr␣ce of there toys" I think they could ad xxx nother line to
that sine xxx " and the games they play". When kids gxxxxxpxxkxx
play war games with the little soldgers and knock them down dead
with a flick of their finger they dont th␣nᴋof the toy soldger
as a person and in a way when they grow up they don't think of
a soldger or eany other person as a person t␣hey think in # 's and
other non personal things. So to order a was is not like killing
people its just #s, we killed43 and they killed 26 wex won but did
we,. I think we lost we were not able to comunacate, when my buother
and I boath want to use the stereo we will compromize mabe he will
get iᵴ for an houre ␣z each or play records we boath engoy. Know we
boath have to give in a bxᵢ bit but we know if we would fight it out
one of us might kxx get hurt xxp especialy me and we think of each
other as people. If two kids can settle a dispute there is no reason
why people runing huge nationsxx being backed buy very ent␣lightn
people cant say well we can make Veatnam one country with 2 s␣ᵥes
the nor␣h and the saouth the north would ␣e marxis and the south would
be demicradick and the people in the country would have freadom to
go from one state to another. But the governments chose to say kill
and wid␣le each other down to the point of toatle dizaster when
every body says help ␣ and ould agree to enaything. We can stay
ighnorent or use our brane the chose is ours,I think?

Paul's performance on a composition. Note the quality of ideas despite the poor
spelling. If we overcriticize performance in spelling and grammar, we dampen his
enthusiasm and turn off the flow of words.

We wish to thank Josh Levy for the above and other significant contributions
to our book.

TESTING — TOOL OR TORTURE?   91 spelling, punctuation, etc. (see page 91). When he felt confident he was willing to risk making errors without feeling threatened.

JIM: AN OVERALL EDUCATIONAL LAG

Often an adolescent appears unmotivated despite years of remedial assistance and tutoring. At age fourteen, Jim was just such a youngster. Jim seemed to have lost interest in academic areas. He appeared apathetic, did not join in classwork, did not seem to want to get involved with group discussions. His parents and teachers agreed that he needed to make himself join in and get involved in class.

The psychoeducational report comments:

"In general, Jim's present scholastic failures are a result of instructional gaps. With respect to his progress, the concerned adults involved with Jim must understand that his FAILURES have been long-standing ones. It will take many more years of efficient remedial work as well as therapy to bring active involvement in the educational process up to the level of his true intellectual ability. This not only involves motivation but training in reasoning and verbal conceptual thinking. He must also make up the great amount of lost ground in content just to keep up with current school demands. He faces a formidable task during which he will not be able to do without continued encouragement and recognition of small successes to build ego."

Let us look at the actual graph of Jim's performance in critical areas of achievement.

In order to measure Jim's overall achievement, we chose to use the Peabody Individual Achievement Test,[9] a wide-range, screening measure of achievement in mathematics, reading, spelling, and general information. In all but the reading subtests, the subject does not need to read the questions; thus the mathematics and general information subtests do not measure reading but rather acquired information and conceptual skills. In the spelling subtest, word identification rather than written spelling is required so that the findings are not confused by difficulties in writing. The following is Jim's performance on the Peabody (PIAT):

JIM: Age 14-5, Grade 9

Chrono-logical Age	Visual Motor Integra-tion	Math Grade Level	Reading Recog-nition	Reading Compre-hension	Spelling	General Informa-tion	Mental Age (WISC)
15	15	Grade 10	Grade 10	Grade 10	Grade 10	Grade 10	15
-	-	-	-	-	-		-
-	-	-	-	-	-	-	-
12	12	7	7	7	7	7	12
-	-	-	-	-	-	-	-
-	-	-	-	-	-	-	-
9	9	4	4	4	4	4	9
-	-	-	-	-	-	-	-
-	-	-	-	-	-	-	-
-	-	-	-	-	-		-

As can be seen by the graph of scores, Jim was fighting a severe handicap in basic skills. If he could not handle the recognition of new words at more than a grade six, seventh month level, he could not possibly read the textbooks that he was given in his traditional grade level–academic English, social studies, science or math classes.

The deficit in reading comprehension skills of more than three years means that Jim is handicapped both in word attack and meaningful comprehension skills when reading required material. Moreover, the reading comprehension subtest of the Peabody gives the youngster picture clues with which to gain context from the text he is to read. This means that he is not entirely dependent upon words to gain meaning. Even with this material Jim was not able to perform at better than grade six, seventh month level, indicating a severe handicap in dealing with reading tasks. For him every test or assignment was a frustration because he could not read it easily, understand it, or gain meaningful information from it. This certainly affected his performance in every subject which required reading . . . thus the severe educational lag of long standing.

Testing on the mathematics subtest suggested difficulties in many areas of math language and concepts. He was not always certain of the meaning of a math problem, due to the technical "foreign language" of mathematics jargon.

The teacher in junior or senior high school may see a student like Jim for only thirty or forty minutes per day. He or she only sees Jim at the present level of performance, not at the low point at which he started a number of years ago before intensive remediation was undertaken. At that time Jim was enthusiastic, anxious to improve, positive and hopeful.

During the past two years Jim has had to run fast, yet he still trails behind his classmates. He has had to work twice as hard to accomplish half as much. He has not yet had the satisfaction of seeing the "lag" made up. In fact this lag may continue throughout his school career, for no one stops to allow him to "catch up" with the class. Jim may never have the pleasure of winning at anything academic.

How long would *you* try to run a race if you continued to come in last?

How many times would *you* play baseball if you never made a hit when you were up at bat or a catch when you were out in the field?

How long would *you* keep trying in class when your best efforts always fell short of arbitrary standards?

That is the quandary that Jim finds himself in.

How would you respond if you found yourself in such a quandary?

Unfortunately, tests like the Peabody Individual Achievement Test are not used routinely to get achievement levels as with Jim. Such tests must be given individually and take approximately forty-five minutes to administer.

Most youngsters are given an annual battery of achievement tests that are group administered. *They are basically reading tests.* Although titled social studies, science, etc., all tests that require reading of language become reading tests although they may attempt to test a specific subject area. As a result of this, their results may be misleading. They may imply a lack of information rather than poor reading skills or a slow rate of reading.

The primary purpose of achievement testing and evaluation should be to tell us more about how well our child has been taught specific subject material. If he is of normal intelligence and has no primary physical or emotional handicaps, his failure to perform on such testing tells us that the testing is inappropriate for that child, or the subject has not been taught appropriately for that child. Just because teachers are teaching does not necessarily mean that children are learning.

When an observant parent or teacher notices a discrepancy between yearly achievement test scores and the child's verbal aptitudes, a thorough evaluation of learning style and possible learning dysfunction should be undertaken. This kind of testing is best accomplished individually, and the evaluation should be specifically designed to answer the following questions:

a) What does this evaluation tell me about my child and his strengths and weaknesses?

b) What does it tell me about how my child feels? Is he anxious and worried concerning his poor performance? Have these worries resulted in self-derogatory attitudes?

c) What does this information tell me about my child's true aptitudes and potential? Does the report help me to be more realistic concerning my child's educational needs?

d) Now that the school personnel have a more detailed picture of my child's needs, how are they planning to help him?

e) Now that I better understand my child's educational situation, how can I structure the home learning environment to assist my child?

f) Is the evaluation complete or should I seek further information via medical or psychological testing?

g) Can my child's school give him the assistance he requires through its present structure? If not, what modifications are planned to meet his needs?

h) Will I need to seek help outside the school in order to fill in the gaps and give my child full support? If so, who will bear the expense of such educational therapy or private schooling?

i) What laws exist in my state that give aid to parents of youngsters with learning disability problems? Is my child included in the provisions of aid under this law?

k) Are there any parent organizations to assist parents of youngsters with a learning disability in my community?

l) To whom can I go in my home school district for advice concerning aid for my child?

This is a challenging group of questions to be answered. How shall a parent know and understand the value of an evaluation if these questions are not answered? The value of any testing program is not in the numbers gained but in the implementation of findings. We test to determine how children are learning; if they are not learning, we alter our way of teaching until we find the correct technique for these children.

IF A CHILD CANNOT LEARN THE WAY WE TEACH HIM

WE'D BETTER TEACH HIM THE WAY HE LEARNS.[10]

Unfortunately, during the past twenty-five years testing and evaluation have become a political tool. Often they are used as a device to sell one particular educational philosophy over another. They are studied and compared like the numbers that make up the Dow-Jones average. Sometimes they are used to show that Ourtown, U.S.A., is a better place to educate kids than Theirtown.

We are not interested in your child's ranking in his class. We are not interested in his test scores per se. What we consider primary are his feelings of satisfaction about school as a learning place.

Home, too, is a learning place, just as life is a learning place, and all parents are teachers.

PARENTS OBSERVATIONAL CHECKLIST

PARENTS MUST FUNCTION AS TRAINED OBSERVERS

> *Jeff was an eight-year-old who came to our office twice weekly for educational therapy. One day Jeff arrived wearing only one shoe.*
> *"Lose one shoe, Jeff?" we said.*
> *"Nope, found one!" he said.*

The following is an observational checklist to help parents decide if their child is experiencing the symptoms of learning disability problems. Obviously, no observational checklist can be a precise tool of testing or measurement, since it is designed to be used in an informal manner by persons untrained for the work of specialized testing. However, we believe that parents are the only full-time observers available to the educational process. They are the only source of ongoing data for the twelve-year period of school attendance.

We caution anyone who is using this listing that it is extremely difficult to be objective concerning one's own children. However, certain learning habits and attitudes are quite obvious to the observer, especially to the aware parent.

The checklist should be used as follows:

If you feel that any statement correctly describes your child's pattern of learning, put a check in the column marked "Yes."

When you have completed each section on the checklist, total the number of checks at the bottom of the column. Now compare your totals with the checklist norms listed on each page. If the number of *yesses* is equal to or greater than the *norm* number, your child is probably *not* experiencing any marked difficulty in that subject area. His difficulties are probably more those of having a learning style that allows for certain normal weaknesses. Just as we all consider ourselves better in certain areas of performance, so too your child may have similar strengths and weaknesses.

On the other hand, if the number you get is *less* than the listed norm number, you should confer with the appropriate school personnel concerning further evaluation and testing as soon as possible.

Schools will differ in their response to parental involvement in the programming. Most schools are delighted to gain parental involvement.

A parent's reporting to the school, however, should not appear as an attack, or threat. Rather, the same information can be expressed in a constructive way if possible. *Not* "Miss Carmody, you've missed the boat. My son Jeff has a learning-disability problem and you haven't referred him for testing or help or anything."

Rather, express it this way:

"You know, Miss Carmody, I've noticed some things about the way Jeff works at home. I think that these things might be of some interest to you. I think that they may suggest a need for more testing. Do you?"

Parents and teachers are both working toward the same educational goals. We both aim at educating kids in the most appropriate manner. If we lock horns in disagreement, then no one hears the value of the other's message. If we work together and constructively, then our work can be mutually helpful and supportive.

Parents Observational Checklist

I. EVALUATION OF SPEECH

My child:	Yes
1) Talks clearly and understandably.	
2) Pronounces final sounds in words.	

3) Does not confuse words he hears when he tries to repeat them,
    e.g., profane becomes propane
          animal becomes aminal
          hospital becomes hostibull
          or other similar errors.	

4) Speaks slowly so that I can understand and follow what he says.	
5) Gives direct answers to questions; is not tangential in responses.	
6) Can find correct words when speaking without hesitating.	
7) Finishes what he is saying without becoming confused, distracted, or constantly changing the subject.	
TOTAL	*
Expected norm for speaking 5 or more yesses	Number of Yesses

Check here _____ My child may be experiencing difficulty
in speech and needs further evaluation.

* If the number of *yesses* is equal to or greater than the *norm* number,
your child is probably *not* experiencing any marked difficulty in that
subject area.

If the number you get is *less* than the listed norm number, you should
confer with the appropriate school personnel concerning further evaluation and testing as soon as possible.

II. LISTENING SKILLS

My child: Yes

1) Seems to understand instructions after they are
given to him.

2) Appears to be paying attention to what is happening
around him most of the time.

3) Has a good understanding of spoken language
although he can't always express what he understands well.

4) Can audit and understand what I say to him even
though he is not facing me.

5) Likes to listen to records rather than watch
television.

6) Does not appear to be bored or restless when he
is listening to conversation, at dinner, in car, at
school, etc.

	Yes
7) Never engaged in so-called baby talk when he was younger, e.g., said "aminal" for animal or "hostibull" for hospital.	

	Yes
TOTAL	*
Expected norm for listening 5 or more yesses	Number of Yesses

Check here _____ My child may be experiencing difficulty
                     in reading and needs further evaluation.

* If the number of *yesses* is equal to or greater than the *norm* number, your child is probably *not* experiencing any marked difficulty in that subject area.

If the number you get is *less* than the listed norm number, you should confer with the appropriate school personnel concerning further evaluation and testing as soon as possible.

III. READING

My child: Yes

1) (After grade 2–3) Reads with oral expression, accenting, and voice variation, not just monotone.	
2) Does not guess at words after sounding out only the first or second sounds; e.g., stamp becomes stop house becomes horse why becomes who	
3) Reads in phrases and thoughts (not word by word, giving each word the same stress).	

	Yes
4) Ignores mistakes and can understand the meaning anyway.	
5) Stops at each mistake to figure out the word, then goes on without forgetting what he has read.	
6) Is able to blend sounds together to decode words.	
7) Is able to read silently without moving his lips or whispering.	
8) Is able to understand what he has read after he finishes reading a paragraph or page.	
9) Is willing to read for pleasure. Reads at home without constant prodding.	
10) Is willing to read aloud to you (up to age 12).	
TOTAL	*
	Number of Yesses

Expected norm for reading   7

Check here _____ My child may be experiencing difficulty
                        in reading and needs further evaluation.

* If the number of *yesses* is equal to or greater than the *norm* number,
your child is probably *not* experiencing any marked difficulty in that
subject area.

If the number you get is *less* than the listed norm number, you should
confer with the appropriate school personnel concerning further evaluation and testing as soon as possible.

IV. WRITING SKILLS

My child: Yes

1) Can hold a pencil or pen correctly. The normal
   position is approximately ½ inch from the tip,
   gripping with thumb, pointer and index finger.
   (This is appropriate only after age of six.)

2) Can recognize the difference between letters that
   are directionally confusing:

   After grade 1   b----d

   u----n

   m----w

   t----f

   Total possible score (4 points)

3) Can write these letters from dictation when told
   the name of the letter:

   After grade 1   s----z

   t----f

   m----w

   g----q

   n----u

   b----p----d

   Total possible score (6 points)

	Yes

4) Can spell words without confusing the sequence of letters such as:

After grade 3	calm ---- clam	
	dirt ---- drit	
	girl ---- gril	
	was ---- saw	
	pots ---- stop	

Total possible score (5 points)

5) Can remember spelling patterns that are not phonetic (that is, do not get spelled the way they are heard), e.g., *ham* is phonetic. It looks exactly the way it sounds.

However	*their* is not phonetic	
After grade 3	*eight* is not phonetic	
After grade 4	*nation* is not phonetic	

6) Does not erase or cross out on papers too often ... papers appear neat, not messy.

7) Writes with neat form, spacing, and even placement on the paper. Words are not crowded into the corner, or begun on the right side rather than the left.

8) Can write the same way after a period of time and work does not deteriorate because there is a lot of writing to do.

	Yes
9) Work is placed and spaced well on the page. He can copy diagrams in science adequately, or keep math work in straight columns (after grade 4).	
10) Can do written work that is as good as his verbal performance in class (after grade 3).	
11) Can organize his ideas into meaningful paragraphs (after grade 5).	
12) Can punctuate correctly (after grade 6) when he must write a:	
sentence	
paragraph	
composition	
Total possible score (3 points)	
13) Can spell on or near grade level.	
14) Does not avoid all writing tasks, or make them so short that he is in fact avoiding the job.	
15) Can complete assignments that involve written work within the time allotted.	
TOTAL	*
	Number of Yesses

Expected norm for writing skills:
Grade 1: 10   Grade 4: 18
Grade 2: 12   Grade 5: 20
Grade 3: 15   Grade 6: 24

Check here _____ My child may be experiencing a difficulty
                        in writing skills and needs further evaluation.

* If the number of *yesses* is equal to or greater than the *norm* number, your child is probably *not* experiencing any marked difficulty in that subject area.

If the number you get is *less* than the listed norm number, you should confer with the appropriate school personnel concerning further evaluation and testing as soon as possible.

V. MATH SKILLS

My Child: Yes

1) After grade 1:
   Can recognize the shapes and forms of numbers
   when asked to identify them from their names.

2) After grade 1:
   Can write the numbers correctly when the names
   are dictated to him.

3) After grade 1:
   Can make a 1 : 1 correlation of objects and
   numbers. That is, when shown

   ....   Can count the dots (one-ten).

                  Can identify the number 2.

                  Can write the number 2.

   Total score (3)

4) After grade 2:
Can identify the word "two."
Understands that:

     5 is more than 3

     8 is more than 6

Total score (3)

---

5) After grade 2:
Can understand addition.

---

6) After grade 2:
Can understand subtraction.

---

7) Can he recall math facts automatically in:

After grade 2	Addition
After grade 2	Subtraction
After grade 3-4	Multiplication
After grade 3-4	Division
After grade 5	All computation above
Total score (5)	

---

8) Does not have difficulty in judging distance in space.

---

9) Seems to be able to do computation in math with ease.
Total possible score   17

10) Can understand what language problems in math are asking for and can solve these grade level problems (after grade 2).

11) Can understand borrowing and carrying in math (after grade 2).

	*
TOTAL	

Expected norms for math	Number
grade 1: 5 grade 4: 12	of
grade 2: 9 grade 5: 13	Yesses
grade 3: 10 grade 6: 15	

Check here _____ My child may be experiencing a difficulty in math and needs further evaluation.

* If the number of *yesses* is equal to or greater than the *norm* number, your child is probably *not* experiencing any marked difficulty in that subject area.

If the number you get is *less* than the listed norm number, you should confer with the appropriate school personnel concerning further evaluation and testing as soon as possible.

VI. ATTITUDE AND MOTIVATION

My Child: Yes

1) Follows through on most tasks and completes them.

2) Appears interested in school assignments, and enjoys accomplishments.

3) Performs equally well in all areas of achievement and is consistent in his attitude toward all classes in school.

	Yes
4) Seems to feel quite adequate, does not often put himself down.	
5) Gets along well with his peers. He plays well with youngsters his own age and makes friends easily.	
6) Does not act out or become explosive when frustrated.	
7) Seems to enjoy school.	
8) Is confident in new situations, socially, academically, athletically.	
9) Has an adequate attention span to complete most of his work. He seems to concentrate on one task for a period of time.	
10) Has managed to do adequately in school without any great need for help after school or remedial assistance.	
11) Does his work independently without needing constant prodding and reminder.	

Total possible score (11)	
_____Check here 7 or more yesses TOTAL	*
Expected norm for attitude and motivation 8	Number of Yesses

Check here _____ My child may be experiencing a difficulty
in motivation with regard to school tasks.
He may need further evaluation.

* If the number of *yesses* is equal to or greater than the *norm* number,
your child is probably *not* experiencing any marked difficulty in that
subject area.

If the number you get is *less* than the listed norm number, you should
confer with the appropriate school personnel concerning further evaluation and testing as soon as possible.

SCORE CHART	Place norms here	My child's scores	Check here if score is less than norm score
Expected norm for speaking			
Expected norm for listening skills			
Expected norm for reading			
Expected norm for writing skills			
Expected norm for math skills			
Expected norm for motivation			

Another word of caution. These are informal observations. They
are *not* a substitute for professional testing. They are intended for
use by parents to help them direct their energies toward helping
their children in specific areas of achievement. Many important
skills have been omitted for they are better examined in the specialist's office. Only basic skills are included. These are the skills
that can be observed in classroom written exercises, testing, homework, and overall attitude. Poor scores on this checklist should send
you to your school specialist for further direction and guidance.

10

What Every Parent Should Know About Learning Styles

"I can learn when I can do something"

— Richard

I hear and I forget —
I see and I remember —
I do and I understand.

— Chinese proverb

There are many styles of learning. It is important for the machinery of education to teach to them all. It is important to allow for all kinds of expression, not just the reading/writing techniques.

It follows, then, that there are also many alternative kinds of remedial techniques appropriate to the many individual cases. We suggest that there is no one simple answer to the problems of the underachieving, learning-disabled child.

Research into teachers' attitudes suggests that we all hold preconceived notions of the characteristics that make a successful student. This often represents an unconscious bias that can exclude bright alternate-style (nonbook) learners from honor rolls. These youngsters may be slow learners in the skills we traditionally emphasize for success, but they may be adequate or superior performers in alternate learning modes. We tend to overemphasize success in reading and writing, and to ignore successes in verbal areas, or "hands-on" performance activities. The child who can express himself better verbally than in writing can perform this way. We forget how much of our successful adult life is tied to the need to relate to people socially or professionally through our ability to communicate through speech.

The salesman is largely dependent upon his ability to sell his product verbally. The number of orders he gets is in no way related to the skill with which he writes up an order form. The nurse communicates through her verbal skills, her empathy with the patient, and her knowledge of the medical problem. The artist may never need to read another book after he leaves school. Unfortunately, the way formal education is geared, he may never even want to.

The plumber, carpenter, mason, and automobile mechanic may learn more by observation and experience than they will ever absorb through reading a technical manual. We measure them by the final product they create or repair and not by their reading speed in words per minute or their comprehension on a timed test.

Furthermore, we make contact with people via verbal communication in a social gathering. At a party no one introduces himself as a C+ person or an A— student! We take people on face value, their appearance, manner, and we accept them in this fashion.

Only in school do we make such arbitrary rules to measure achievement. The twelve-year full-time vocation of being a student is measured in impersonal letters and numbers. If we continue our bias against nonbook learning, we will "turn these kids off" through our unconscious attitudes and our classroom approaches.

Often youngsters need to be directed to concentrate their learning via modes in which they can succeed. The poor math student should not be made to feel he is failing because he is placed in business math at grade nine level, rather than thrown into algebra where he cannot succeed. He needs alternatives.

On the other hand, he may be a good athlete who gets his feeling of success through basketball or the swimming team and gains the confidence he needs.

We all have natural strengths. We need to foster a child's activities in these areas of strengths. For the child who may rarely gain success in academic areas of achievement, some successful feedback is important and it may never come through the traditional channels. Parents may have to rethink their expectations for a child.

In our parent counseling groups, we attempted to help parents arrive at realistic guidelines of behavior and goals for their young-sters. In order to avoid unrealistic expectations they needed to un-derstand their child's assets, limitations, and style of learning.

We helped them to find activities intended to discover the child's strongest mode of learning and weakest mode of learning so that they might "accentuate the positive and eliminate the negative" in dealing with these children. We directed them to concrete mate-rials, rather than abstract pencil-to-paper tasks, to tapes for the auditory learner, to pictures and drawings for the visual learner. Once given a mind set, the parents became creative in devising all kinds of techniques to help teach their children abstract concepts.

We used the parents' own analysis of their children's learning styles, and suggested ways in which they might be home tutors for their children without the kids' feeling that they were being taught. We suggested games and activities that incorporated a good deal of motor activity into the task of learning. We told them to be on the lookout for other ways that the child could learn by moving and they came up with a few ideas pertinent to their own life and in-terests.

All the parents in the group were asked to observe their children and come back with responses as to how they felt their chil-dren learn best. Based upon these responses, they were given sug-gestions of ways to make learning easier and more appropriate to their child's learning style.

There are guidelines that can be used in analyzing a child's learn-ing style:

He is probably a visual learner if:

— he likes to look at books, pictures and other visually ori-ented displays.
— he uses picture clues to give him meaning when reading in a book, depends upon pictures.
— he needs to be given written directions, or a list of things on paper when he is asked to do chores, homework, errands, shopping.
— he notices visual details, e.g., the new dress mother is wear-ing, a new object in the room, displays of pictures, ob-jects, etc.

— he needs to see things in order to better understand how they are put together or how they work. For example, telling him how to tie a knot or bow is not as effective as showing him.

He is probably an auditory learner if:

— he is able to follow your directions after listening to you once, and does not require things to be repeated again and again.
— he appears to choose musical activities, listening to songs, rhymes, radio, etc. He is less interested in drawing, art activities, looking at picture books, or reading.
— he enjoys telling you about his experiences rather than drawing a picture or showing you in a graphic way.
— you can maintain his attention by just his listening to you, without the need to be physically involved in an activity.

He is probably a tactile (hands-on) learner if:

— he seems to learn everything by experience, trial and error.
— he appears to be always touching things within reach, at home, in school, in someone's home, etc. He may often reach for objects and touch them inappropriately even if they are out of his reach.
— he appears to need to make physical contact with other children and adults. He wants to sit on teacher's lap, hug her, kiss her "good-bye." He is constantly nudging, pushing, shoving other children.

A child who is a visual learner will learn better with pictures, movies, sight-memory games. His stronger visual perceptual skills can be used as a teaching tool by constantly calling his attention to visual clues. He will learn better by being clued in on visual similarities, differences, details, and color clues.

The child who is a strong auditory learner might benefit more from his reading if he can hear the text on tape or records while he reads them himself. Using such auditory input, he can listen, read, and learn. He is the child who will benefit from hearing things explained verbally as he tries to do them.

On the other hand, the hands-on learner may need to experience things in order to retain them well. Trips, museum visits, trial-and-error learning may be his best teacher. However, never allow his learning to take place just by chance. Explain why the visit to Gettysburg or Washington, D.C., is important. Tell him about the dinosaurs as he visits the museum. Place things in the perspective of time and place rather than allowing things to float around unattached to his reservoir of information.

It does no good for such a child to be told how many inches are in a yard, or how many pints in a quart. He will recall this best by being given the opportunity to measure with ruler and yardstick, or pint and quart containers.

The child's innate learning style will persist throughout his school career and may extend into his choice of vocation or profession in later life. It is extremely important that as parents we do not project our own unreal expectations or expected learning style upon our children. This is especially important when dealing with the child with special needs. He is more vulnerable and tense and has a lower tolerance for frustration.

Moreover, a recent study by Dr. Stella Chess[1] suggests that there is strong evidence that the child's temperament and the kind of response it brings about from his parents, teachers and others can be a critical factor in his personality development.

It has been said that children with impulsive, volatile behavior so often characteristic of the special needs child are most "unlovable" when they need love the most. Such children respond to the way people closest to them feel about them. Though words may not be said, body language and tone of voice express our hostile or loving feelings as well as words.

Dr. Chess further states that children who are born "difficult" have difficulty in relating to others with whom they must live and work. Their negative ways, slowness to adapt, distractibility, dominant negative mood, withdrawal from new situations, difficulty in regularizing body functions (such as toilet training), etc., all feed into what may become "unhealthy dynamics" between parent and child or teacher and child.

Practically, the implications of Dr. Chess's study seem obvious. It is necessary for both the parent and the teacher to facilitate the development of the child's strengths while playing down the child's weaknesses. Parents must learn to analyze situations in advance to the best of their abilities. Thus they may become better able to foresee the inappropriate situations for their own child's temperament as well as learning style.

The nervous, fragmented, disorganized youngster will act as a negative force on the nervous, fragmented, disorganized teacher. Better to search out the more structured situation despite the teacher's good intentions toward your child. At home, the disorganized, fragmented parent will be more successful with such a child if he sets up a schedule for himself and for the child so that life will be more predictable, organized, and satisfying to both.

The slower-moving, anxious youngster will continue to exhibit such personality traits. If you are impatient, tend to work quickly, and rush from chore to chore, better let someone else manage this child. Pressure from you will only succeed in causing the child to withdraw and become more anxious and pressured. If you are such a parent, your child's slower-moving pace will irritate you and create situations that could be avoided.

Julie was just such a child. For Julie, life was a situation akin to "the faster I work the behinder I get." She spent much time worrying about not completing homework, avoiding facing obligations, and daydreaming. Of course, with a fast-paced, aggressive mother, who managed a small store in town, she became increasingly aware of her inability to compete as she became more mature. Her mother could work, manage the home, plan and cook meals, and appear neat and well dressed with little apparent effort. For Julie, a decision on what to wear to school, or getting out of the house on time seemed a full day's activity and often led to an argument. Julie's mother was a "tough act to follow" and Julie appeared lethargic, lazy, and apathetic. Their temperaments clashed constantly. Both would have to compromise, but Julie could not alter her pattern without her mother's understanding that her own level of drive acted as a causal factor in Julie's response. Basically both Julie and her mother would not change in temperament substantially; however, both would have to learn to accept the other and her pattern of temperament.

Unlike Julie, Barry was a hyperactive teenager. He had been through all the stages of development so characteristic to the hyperactive child. He had been medicated periodically, and responded well to the medical management until he reached age thirteen. At that point, his doctor suggested ending medication and substituting counseling to help him manage his own tension buildup and activity needs. At seventeen he was still excessively active, driving, and still hard both on himself and on fragile things. Barry's parents had helped him buy a car and they felt that this reward for better school performance was going to spur him on to further achievement. What they did not take into consideration was the fact that Barry handled the car just as he handled everything else, taking out his frustrations on this delicate piece of machinery. He might have made better use of a small truck, four-wheel-drive vehicle or heavy-duty van. A small, light-weight foreign car was better looking but not designed for Barry's temperament. In no time at all, damage had been done. The clutch was gone, the gears stripped, and the repair bill was extensive.

Barry felt terrible about the problem; it only reinforced his negative feelings about himself. "I break everything I touch," he told us.

Barry's father was furious, called him "careless and ungrateful," and threatened serious reprisal. All this could have been avoided if his temperament and behavior pattern had been realistically appraised. Barry was hard on things; anything that required special attention or care had better be kept out of his reach for a longer period of time. So many hostile, unnecessary words that were said could have been avoided had his parents considered this. What was intended to be a reward had turned into a punishment.

Steve was a tactile learner. Everything he did involved touching or handling. Unfortunately, if the object was fragile, invariably it broke. Steve lived in a home filled with fragile antiques from his mother's prized collection. For Steve, life was a series of "no-no's" from the first day he emerged from his playpen. Steve could crawl up within reach of anything, but his lack of fine motor control and clumsy little chubby fingers broke things as soon as they touched them. The constant "no's" were a self-reinforcing attention getter. If he couldn't get "yes-yes" responses, "no-no" responses were better than no response at all. He became negative and uncooperative and appeared to be continually testing authority at home and in school.

Steve became a behavior-management problem. He might have been spared this frustration if his parents had observed his learning style initially and removed their most fragile possessions to a safer place until he was old enough to understand why some things were no-no and some were yes-yes "touch me" objects.

Dr. Chess, whom we mentioned before, designed a research study that was based upon a twenty-year follow-up study of 135 youngsters, and traced them through their earlier years of development through the post–high school period. Her conclusions have strong implications for the parents of all children, but are most significant for the parents of children with difficult temperaments. We may foster certain strengths and play down certain weaknesses, but we will not basically change the temperament of such children. In a sense, we are suggesting that the parents of children with special needs will have to develop some of the skills of a learning or behavior therapist. They must be trained to identify the appropriate mode of learning through which the child will gain the most success. They must develop a battery of home-teacher techniques that help condition their child's learning attitudes, encourage successes and deemphasize failure.

What are the characteristics of the successful parent-therapist? According to Laura Schreibman and Robert J. Koegel,[2] parents were trained to be therapists for their own severely disturbed youngsters. The most successful of these parent-therapists exhibited the following characteristics:

They cared a great deal about their child's success and indicated their extreme happiness to their child at the occurrence of each specific achievement.

These parents did not appear to consider their children as ill. Thus, they did not act from pity or excuse various kinds of bizarre behavior as excusable symptoms of illness. They worked hard to increase normal behavior, without making excuses for setbacks.

They showed a willingness to commit their own personal time and physical efforts to help their child. They did this rather than rely on professionals to care for or train their child on a day-to-day basis. For middle-class parents who have resources available to them, it is often simpler to pay someone to perform such training therapy.

The great benefit seen in the training of such parent-therapists by these researchers is the fact that they alone can provide personal, continuous, twenty-four-hour support and follow-up programs for children with special needs.

Vital to such training of parents is setting specific target goals that are small-scale goals rather than the typical generalized goals we so often hear.

Terry's school report, grade five, read as follows:

"Terry seems to have a poor self-image. He is lacking in confidence, needs to take more interest in his work at school. He must learn that in order to perform in school, one must listen and concentrate."

Terry's poor self-image was not going to improve unless the things that feed into making one feel like a "loser" are altered or turned around to making him feel a "winner." Terry needed to be helped to read better, spell better, understand the association between sounds and symbols. Terry confused what he heard and often could not repeat what was said to him immediately after hearing it.

Unless something was done to improve all of these educational factors in eleven-year-old Terry's life, how could his poor self-image improve? No amount of talking to Terry would effect a change without altering his real instructional level, which was approximately two years below that of his classmates.

Therapists, parent and teacher alike, must ascertain the specific learning behaviors that go into making a child feel better, happier, and better accepted in his world. When these specific goals are set and mastered step by step, then better self-image, happiness and confidence will grow.

It is extremely important to get the child's full attention to the task. Proper instructional techniques, appropriate to a child's temperament and learning style, will be the key to success. If the child is a visual learner, use "show-me" techniques, such as pictures, objects, visual examples of what is being taught.

If the child is an auditory learner, listening and reading simultaneously, repeat material aloud so it may be heard as it is said, using tape cassettes when the parent can't provide the time to read or tell a story. All of these devices will assist such a child.

Finally, if the child is a tactile learner, hands-on learning must be provided whenever possible. This may mean the use of sandpaper letters for tracing, a sand- or saltbox for tracing, etc. Or it may require objects correlating with numbers 1:1 for addition, subtraction, and other math functions. Later it may require a 10 × 10 multiplication table to perform multiplication and division operations or cut-up paper pie plates for fractions.

Whatever the goals set, the proper instructional approach must be chosen to help the child maximize his learning effectiveness.

With a younger child, or one who experienced many negative responses associated with new learning tasks, some cues or hints may be required until he gains some confidence in his ability to give correct responses. As the child performs better, drop the cues.

Doctors Schreibman and Koegler[3] suggest that each successive step in such training must indicate performance better than the previous one. If the child is to be rewarded verbally or concretely for performance improvement, he must be expected to improve upon the previous stage. To expect less would be acceptance of lesser aims and goals for that child. They are also emphatic in their reminder to parents that they must not reward incorrect responses just because the child appears to have tried. Trying is not succeeding. Only trying harder will lead to success.

11

Task Analysis for Parents

"If I do not teach, then I alone shall excel."
— Leonardo da Vinci

"But what am I trying to teach?
And how do I go about the job of teaching it?"
— A parent

We must reexamine some of the things we ask children to do on a daily basis. Often we find upon reexamination that although we intend to teach one thing we have inadvertently taught another. Often the lesson is more negative than positive as in the case that follows.

Jimmy's mother was anxious to encourage Jim to use his newly learned reading skills during the summer vacation. She thought she had found the ideal opportunity to do this when she heard that the movie *Charlie and the Chocolate Factory* was coming to town. She suggested that they read the book, chapter by chapter, each night before the movie arrived. They devoted twenty to thirty minutes per night. The book, however, was really beyond instructional reading level for Jimmy, and despite his high interest this became especially frustrating for the ten-year-old at bedtime. Jimmy made an increasing number of errors, guessing at words, mispronouncing them, forgetting his place, and finally became so impatient that he blurted out:

"I won't do it . . . I hate reading!"

Mother responded with annoyance, "Just ten minutes more, Jim; you know you promised to read for at least twenty minutes every night."

Jimmy tried to read the next line but was so irritated and annoyed at himself that he was even more blocked than before. He closed the book, dropping it to the floor with anger. "I just don't care!" he said.

Mother responded, with rising tension in her voice, "If you don't read anymore I won't take you to see the movie at all."

That was the last straw. Jim howled in anger. He felt betrayed. He had tried to accomplish a task that really was beyond him and now he was being punished for his efforts.

"I hate that old book!" he said, "and I wouldn't go to the movies with you anyway." The rest of his words were covered by sobs and screams; another temper tantrum flared. He would have no supper, no television, and certainly no movie.

A confrontation that could have been avoided has now become a reality. Threats have been made that cannot be withdrawn. Unintentionally, mother has succeeded in making a chore of reading a delightful children's classic. Jimmy has had reinforcement of his feelings of inadequacy and reading has become frustrating work rather than a pleasurable experience.

If only mother had checked with the teacher to see if that particular book was within Jimmy's instructional level. If she could not talk to anyone at school during vacation, she might have checked with the librarian.

Once she observed that it was difficult for Jim and errors were increasing, she might have alternated reading pages with him or even read two pages to every one page he read independently.

She should not have set an unrealistic goal for Jim. He could not finish that book within the time allotted. She might have made an agreement to start the book and read as much as possible but not insist on its completion.

Once she threatened Jim with "no reading, no movie!" she was boxed in by her own statement. To backtrack and contradict this statement would be difficult, might be interpreted as inconsistent, and certainly all the other things done in anger could not be taken back anyway.

If she had preanalyzed the task, the whole story might have been different. She would have been able to think out what was required to accomplish the task.

— What am I trying to get Jimmy to do and what must he be able to do in order to accomplish this?
— Does Jimmy have the reading level to finish the book himself in the given amount of time?
— Since enjoyment of reading and a feeling of success is my primary goal, how can I help Jimmy to attain it?

HELPING YOUR CHILD STEP-BY-STEP: TASK ANALYSIS

All work must progress in a step-by-step manner. Try to demonstrate the simplest, most concrete operations before asking a child to understand the more complex ones. In order to set up such a developmental continuum, one must break down each complex task. This is the process by which the teacher analyzes the tasks that he is working on to determine the following:

1) What am I trying to teach this child?
2) What must he or she be able to do in order to learn the task?
3) What skills are required in order to help this child understand what I am trying to teach?
4) How many of the prerequisite skills does this child have?
5) Are there any specific physiological or developmental dysfunctions that pose specific problems for the child?
6) How can I measure whether or not the child can perform this task and evaluate the quality of his performance?

This process of task analysis may appear complicated, yet much of the information gained is based primarily upon observation and common sense rather than educational theory.

I observed that our son Richie could not follow a long list of complicated directions. I would try to analyze the task. What must he be able to do first, second, and third? For example, I found that he did not remember or organize the sequence of operations in written reports. I would write the steps down in a checklist form to help organize his working procedure.

If I am teaching a child something that requires a knowledge of alphabetization, he must be able to sequence the alphabet first so that he can find what he is looking for.

If Ira was looking for something in the Yellow Pages of the phone book, he needed to understand how to decide the category or grouping of the item he was looking for and how to find it. It is often easier and quicker to do these things ourselves. However, they are usually learned by doing, not by observing someone doing it.

Let's go back to basic skills at an early age and see how they can be analyzed down to their component parts to help a child to learn them in a simpler, less complicated way.

For example, tying one's shoes appears to be a relatively simple operation for a child to understand. However, for small, clumsy, poorly coordinated fingers, it may be a superhuman task. Let us change the ground rules now, and try to break this job down into its simplest component operations.

The child must be able to do the following before he can learn to tie his shoes:

1. He must be able to grasp the material that he is tying with one hand; therefore the material must be sufficiently easy to handle, grasp, and manipulate.
2. He must know how to fold one strand of material over another so that he can begin making a knot.
3. He must be able to tie a simple knot.
4. He must be able to make a loop and grasp it in one hand while he is holding the other strand of material firmly in the other hand.
5. He must be able then to pull one loop through another.

All of these fine motor operations may appear relatively simple, but they are all single learning operations independent of each other. They must be learned separately, then blended into a sequential step-by-step operation in order to learn how to tie the laces.

We can aid our child's learning process by replacing the laces with an apron's strings. These are more easily grasped and manipulated by the young child. The operation can be performed face-to-face rather than reversed in space. When we tie a shoe, we look out from our body forward. When we tie an apron's strings over the back of a chair, we are facing the materials and can do the job without reversing ourselves in space.

This principle of task analysis, or the breaking down of learning into step-by-step components, is something that should be applied to all learning when we are dealing with the learning-disabled child. For he is a child who cannot handle complexity. Much of learning is by its very nature a complex task, so we must simplify it for him. We are in fact doing for him what he is not yet able to do for himself, despite his high or normal intelligence.

This principle applies when dealing with all school tasks as well as home tasks. The hammering of nails into a piece of wood to make a shelf must be broken down by such a process; the following of a simple recipe to bake cookies, or the researching of any topic to write a term paper, each is much the same kind of task requiring proper sequences for success.

Often we are called upon to work with an older child who has severe difficulty in the process of writing an original written paragraph, essay, or paper.

Our sons had just such difficulties when they attended school. In order to assist them, we found that the procedures that seemed most helpful were those mentioned above. We had to sit down with them and analyze the task first, in order to help them to decide what steps to take, their order, and how to organize all of the suboperations into the whole job.

Too often, we have found that when youngsters like our own are given a task of writing, they will panic and avoid rather than face the emotional crisis that goes into even thinking about the task. When we ask such a child to write a paper, using his own ideas and words, we are asking him to put himself on the line. More than that, we are exposing all of his weaknesses for the eye to see. His defenses are attacked, for he may have been able to avoid writing by using his verbal skills thus far. He may be able to copy someone else's words but have great difficulty in deciding what words of his own are appropriate. He may be able to select the correct spelling of the word from a group of three or four misspellings but may not be able to spell it correctly when asked to write it. He may be able to write short copied sentences or paragraphs from a book or the blackboard, but may have so much difficulty writing that any short paragraph becomes a Herculean task.

He may lack many of the prerequisite skills required before one can do research and write effectively. Can he select appropriate reading material on the subject assigned to him? Does he pick books that are too difficult for him to read and comprehend? Here a parent can be of enormous assistance in helping a child select what he can read and choose material directly on the topic.

This may mean that he must be shown how to use the index at the back of the book. He may not have the skills to know where to look for the correct topics. We found our son looking in the table of contents and there he might never find the particular items that he sought. He was not aware of the index, nor did he handle the alphabetization problem effectively at first.

Let us assume that we have helped him to find a few reading books that contain material on the topic he has chosen. We have had him read a paragraph or two to see that he could read it adequately. Some youngsters will not be willing to read aloud to you. This is especially true of those youngsters who are ashamed of the way that they read and are aware of their errors of omission, substitution, phonetic mispronunciation, etc. Do not force your child to read aloud to you! This is especially important when reading with adolescents. According to Dr. Harry Lewis, author of Second Step Reading Program (for adolescents and young adults with poor reading skills), reading aloud only interferes with fluency and comprehension.

Dr. Lewis emphasizes utilization of skills already developed in the poor reader over thirteen years of age, such as vocabulary, ability to predict outcomes, reasoning, and judgment. He capitalizes on these skills that have already been developed, utilizing them as a starting point to move on to a second step to easy fluent reading.[1]

Let us return to aiding our child in the writing of a report. Give him one question to answer based upon one or two paragraphs of the book. If he can't answer your one question, he may not be able to handle that book by himself. Now you have a few decisions to make to help him. If there are other easier-to-read books on the subject, you can help him locate these. However, if he is an older student who feels that easier books would be a put-down, you can do as we did with Richard.

We took the more difficult books home with us. We either read them to him, helping him to decide what was most important to include in his paper, or we taped the reading material for him on a tape cassette. He then listened to the tape recorder while trying to read the book himself. This particular method is educationally sound and really preferable to reading *for* him. The use of simultaneous reading (seeing the text) and listening to the text is a good way to utilize a multisensory technique with older students.

When students see and hear material simultaneously, they are double-imprinting sounds and words. They do not have to stop, regress, and sound out words that they can't pronounce at the first reading. Such stopping and rereading is harmful to comprehension and inefficient for most readers. When listening to a tape, they hear words they can't identify by seeing. They can stop the tape and review pe iodically in order to understand better. They are not made to feel as dependent upon Mother or Father sitting by their side.

We tend to take for granted the existence of certain basic skills when we assign tasks to our children. Our teachers make similar assumptions. Let us just list the skills basic to the writing of a "simple" short research paper.

Richie was asked to write a paper on the life of Andrew Jackson as an eighth grade project. We decided to analyze the different jobs that were involved in the writing of such a paper. Aware of Richie's problems, the teacher had said not to worry about the length, so he felt sure that he could do the job.

We listed the jobs involved:

Selecting reading material that he could handle independently.

Using the library card catalogue to find these books.

Handling the library number system and locating the books.

Finding out whether or not he could read a book independently.

Research:

How to decide what is important to take notes from the text material.

What is important and why it is important.

How to write notes on a card.

How to keep track of the sources, for later use in a bibliography.

Taking notes:

Turning topics into questions, reading to answer questions, and writing notes.

Quotations and footnotes.

The mechanics of writing:

Making clear, readable letter forms and words.

Syntax and sentence structure.

How to organize a paragraph to have an introductory sentence, details, and a conclusion.

Organization of the paper.

Spelling.

Needless to say, acquiring the skills listed above could have occupied the whole term without any of the other required course work being done. In addition to this, however, there were ongoing assignments of reading in a textbook that he could not read independently. We were constantly taping the text onto a cassette so that he could work from the textbook on his own time.

Let us not forget that he had four other subjects as well, with reading, quizzes, and classroom preparations.

What we assume as routine work for the average to superior student may be a truly impossible set of demands for the youngster with learning problems. This has no relationship to his intelligence level or basic aptitude for academics, but rather to the developmental level that he has reached with regard to the daily performance required in school.

We felt that demands upon our son and others like him were totally unrealistic when his levels of skill development were taken into account. He suffered throughout his years at school. It was an ongoing daily erosion of feelings of self-worth. How could he feel worthy when all of the things required were things that he could not do?

The child feels frustration, but what of the adult? Teachers are trained to teach. How does a professional feel when he confronts a child who challenges his social values, professional theories, and personal security? As educational therapists as well as parents we have dealt with our share of threatening, hostile, acting-out kids; shy, withdrawn uncommunicative kids; hyperkinetic, scattered, distractible kids. They often caused us to feel defensive and insecure in our choice of methods. They appeared to be disinterested in what we wanted to teach, or uninvolved in the whole educational process. They protested that they didn't care. They dared us to teach them . . . we tried . . . and many times we had to try harder.

We ask of other parents and teachers only what we have tried to do ourselves. Try! Try harder! And if that fails, try again!

12

Home Structuring for Learning

"Hoping and praying should never be confused with studying."
— Lucy — from *Charlie Brown Datebook, 1975*
Schultz, United Features Syndicate, Inc.

We often seek complicated solutions to a problem when the answers are simpler than we might expect. This is especially true when providing for the child with an educational problem. Sometimes we set up a complicated educational tutoring program when a rethinking of the learning structure within the home may be a better approach to solving the problem.

We have seen this occur with many children, including our own. Parents tend to find solutions that are emotionally comfortable for them. However, sometimes these solutions are expensive and require paying heavily for the privilege. We found that we simply could not afford to pay someone for the amount of individual instructional time that was needed for Richie in the earlier grades.

We decided that we had no alternative but to provide such services ourselves.

We decided to try to be analytical concerning his learning style, timetable, and his relationship within the family. After much trial and error, we found that he was best able to concentrate on home learning tasks early in the morning, and immediately after dinner. We restructured our day to take advantage of his calmest, least distractible periods.

We could do twice as much educational work during those two time intervals than could be done in similar time periods at any other time of day.

We also observed that he learned best when allowed to engage physically in the learning process and do as much as possible on his own. The more we did for him, the less he learned from the activity. We had to concentrate on his need for independence from us and devise as many programmed, or preplanned, activities as possible. At that time we took advantage of programmed texts such as Sullivan Reading and Mathematics Programmed texts[1] and World Book Cyclo Teacher.[2] These materials allowed him the independence he desired, the constant repetition for overteaching, and the successful feedback of self-correcting.

As he matured, we noticed that the need for independence was still a strong trait. We have since noticed that many early adolescents, still needing assistance, require a similar structure that allows them to feel less pressured, less dependent upon adults, and more independent in their actions.

When difficult reading material became the major frustration we turned to taping materials, as mentioned before. The one major drawback of this approach is that Mother, Father, or friend must help by initially reading the text onto tape. This is a labor of love. Richard made it through ninth and tenth grade social studies with this technique. His readings and reports were read onto tape so that he could handle them by himself without feeling that he was completely dependent upon us for all his needs.

We have noticed that there seems to be less conflict between parents and children concerning this dependence when the parent does not have to take time from other jobs or siblings to sit with them and read to them.

Mother or Father is not captive nor is the child. The cassette tape is an independent "person" who can be called upon to help as needed and is never too busy or too tired.

We have seen the constant need for support backfire upon well-intentioned parents. The older learning-disabled youngster becomes angry at his constant need for someone to "hold his hand" so that he can make it in school. He feels that he is being policed long past the time when it should be necessary. He feels trapped by his striving for independence on one hand and his complete dependence on the other . . . he needs to feel that he is doing some things for himself.

"Will I ever be good enough for my parents?" said Jeff, aged thirteen.

"I hate getting tutored all the time. It makes me feel like a retard," said Tom, aged fourteen.

"I feel like a baby when I can never do anything by myself," said Jim, aged twelve.

"Every year they tell me that I'm doing better at school! What do I get for it . . . more remedial reading," said Caren, aged sixteen.

The use of tapes has become one significant way of providing an automatic support and tutor for the inadequate visual or auditory learner. Recording supplementary tapes for the reading-disabled is becoming an important community service project in many areas. Local women's groups and service organizations often provide volunteers to do this job for schools.

In Milton, Massachusetts, the Women's Club made a project of recording tapes of the twenty-eight hundred text volumes required in the courses at Curry College. The College Learning Lab and PAL Program, administered by Mrs. Gertrude Webb, utilizes these tapes for the fifty students in the college with diagnosed learning-disability problems who attend regular classes at the college. These students are tutored and given free access to all materials on tape. They are required to read while listening to the tapes to gain multi-sensory reinforcement.

Many ACLD groups and Help for Children with Learning Disabilities groups are working on the augmenting of school resource materials by use of volunteer recordings of tapes. SOLD, a parent group in Scarsdale, New York, has undertaken to build a library of tapes and make them available to Scarsdale high schoolers who cannot read the material required adequately. These are available on loan to other school districts.

Most of these efforts have come to fruition as a result of parent activism in communities. They cost time, energy, taping materials, and the expense of a few loanable tape recorders; little enough when one considers the value of such a service.

Books for the Blind, an organization originally set up to provide recordings for blind people, will also loan materials for youngsters with an identifiable visual perceptual handicap. Their resources are enormous. However, the teacher must know their resource listings before assignments are given out at a school. Unless the teacher preplans, there is some delay in getting the materials, depending upon their availability and proximity to your community. However, the use of this library might be explored by parents with their junior and senior high school administrators.

If some high schools have begun this practice, in time, with parents' active support, the others will follow. If a few colleges have begun to establish the alternative approach and supportive procedures of the PAL programs, others will develop programs, too. None of these things will happen unless parents and educators work together as activists on behalf of the learning-disabled child.

Parents must engage in rethinking their own "homework." They must, as well, rethink and restructure learning in the home to assist their children. Each child needs a specially modified structure to meet his particular learning needs at home as well as in school.

In general, the scattered, disorganized, distractible youngster may need a more programmed, scheduled life-style. He always needs to know exactly when things will happen, and where they will happen to keep his unpredictable self in more predictable control. He has to work in a quiet place, away from noise and distraction, with an adult within calling distance. The middle of the dining room is not the ideal place for him to do reading or homework.

The shy, fearful youngster may need opportunities to be free of organized activities. He may need more free time, free play, fewer lessons. He will benefit from moments to relax and talk with his parents alone whenever possible. He may simply be unable to get a word in edgewise in the company of his aggressive, talkative siblings. To make time just for him may be the first constructive step in assisting him to learn.

The auditorily impaired child may need ongoing opportunities to learn from visual clues while he listens. The visually impaired youngster may need to listen to tapes, records, or Mother while he sees visual images, symbols, etc.

ON CONCENTRATION

Children with perceptual disabilities often have difficulty in focusing their attention. When children tend to be restless, it is often helpful to reduce the amount of distraction by keeping the room fairly plain and undecorated. Toys or games within reach become a convenient distraction that intrudes upon maintaining attention. Sometimes it may be necessary to have your child sit facing the wall in order to separate him from potential distractions.

School textbooks are often filled with cluttered pages that are difficult to handle. There are simply too many pictures, charts, colors, words, or numbers on a page. He may be unable to pay attention to the specific tasks, words or examples on his homework pages.

If such problems have not been taken into consideration in the planning of texts or workbooks, you may have to devise techniques to make the pages appear less cluttered and keep the important material in the focus of his attention.

There are a number of methods to accomplish this. Always remember that your primary goal is drawing his attention to the specific problem to be solved.

ON DIRECTIONAL LEARNING

If the aim of the activity is getting your child to start work at the left side of the page or to begin writing at a certain point, accentuate that starting point with a heavy pencil line, an arrow, a pointer, or a stick figure to help him locate the spot in his workbook.

Bright colors can also stimulate attention and help an inattentive child focus. Use of a red or green marker may highlight a spelling pattern:

might

mat   mitt   met

knock   limb

Introduction of body movement helps a child to understand and follow instructions. By using your fingers as a pointer, tracing of words can be initiated.

Concept words such as *above, below, before, behind, in, out,* etc., can all be taught by games of charades involving body movement.

Later, the use of a finger as a pointer can help draw your child's visual attention from paragraph to paragraph down a page of reading. The finger as a place marker or a pointer is used frequently in reading programs for young adults to help lead the eye across a page more efficiently when reading.

The cluttered page can be made less cluttered by use of a window marker. To make a window marker, you simply decide upon a reasonable number of words that can be handled by your child. Take a piece of cardboard or scrap paper the size of the whole page and cut a window in it any size desired (see below).

bat	fan	jam	man	van

In the illustration a blank index card is used to cover the rest of the page and draw attention visually to the work that the child must focus on.

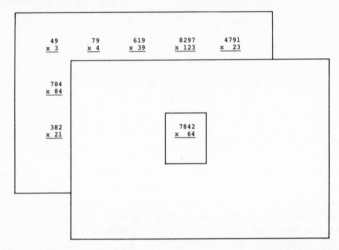

The window marker helps to block out the distracting stimuli from the rest of the page. The child can concentrate his attention on each example as he performs the computation.

PAY ATTENTION TO HIS LEARNING STYLE

If your youngster is a visual learner, try to give him visual clues to hold his attention. However, if he is basically an auditory learner, then he may need simple, repetitive verbal clues and explanations.

Try to avoid prolonged, complicated verbal explanations with any child, but most of all with your learning-disabled child. Too many words tend to get in the way. He may lose track of what you say and probably will lose interest immediately. Treat him as if English were a foreign language when you are giving instructions. He cannot absorb long, wordy, detailed explanations. Try to give short pointed directions!

E.g., "Look, watch me!"

(to make a **b**) Draw a line down and then a loop.

(to make a **d**) Say, "It starts like a **c** — which comes before **d.** First a loop, then a line. Make it like mine!"

The use of simple and repetitive language to give auditory cues can be extended to any phase of learning activity. One should not simply write an "a" on paper and say, "This is an 'a,'" for example. You might, rather, give a description of what you are doing as you write the letter. Rhyming is an additional help to recall. Children will learn rhymes faster than prose.

To illustrate any fact, try to use ideas or stories that will hold a child's attention. Especially good are those concerning cars, planes, or trains.

USING A MULTISENSORY APPROACH

(We hear more and more terminology in our educational circles with the advent of learning-disability research!)

By multisensory approaches, we simply mean the use of a number of physical and psychological functions at the same time in order to teach. This method has proven especially effective for children experiencing difficulties in learning.

The child who cannot seem to remember what he learns through just one experience or mode, i.e., reading, hearing, saying, may learn better through the use of two or more senses simultaneously.

For a parent who is trying to help his child at home, an understanding of this concept is extremely important. The use of any kind of supplementary modes of learning help the child absorb and recall.

Why is any multisensory approach to learning more successful? The physiological reasoning seems to be that all of our actions involve a number of physical and psychological functions rather than any one alone.

Perception, thought, speech, movement, and emotion may be involved in a single act. As each of these functions always occurs with others, it cannot be trained alone and without the others. When we speak about language training, for instance, we mean that language is given the primary emphasis but the thought processes, perceptual abilities, feelings are also included. The simple act of walking depends upon the interaction and coordination of muscle sense, vision, touch, sense of balance, and awareness of direction. Our emotions, too, commonly depend upon evidence collected by several sensory channels working together. This interrelationship of many physical and sensory activities can be utilized in training children with disabilities in a particular modality.

In research work, it has long been demonstrated that organisms trained to respond to the simultaneous stimuli of light and sound will then respond to either of the stimuli occurring alone. A perceptually handicapped child can be trained to understand visual shapes and forms accurately if he experiences them by touch as well as visually (by tracing with his finger). Later he can undertake the same task using only the visual clues and the previous experience will help him to recall what he sees.

ON TEACHING BY ASSOCIATION

One of the ways in which parents are best able to serve as teachers is by discovering techniques to associate information for the child. The teacher teaches a subject to a large group of youngsters. He has little or no contact with what is meaningful in the child's daily life.

The parent, however, has the unique opportunity to help a child make practical daily use of information, fitting it into the texture of his experience. Information is abstract and difficult to remember if it is apart from personal experience. We all learn and recall the things that have personal meaning for us.

The child who loves sports may be reached through his craving for information on that subject. He may balk at reading, but examine *Sports Illustrated* from cover to cover. He may refuse to complete homework assignments, but will do anything to be able to go to a football game with his dad. Parents are in a unique position to manage such preferences and interests to gain good study and work habits at home and in school.

In addition, math skills can be taught to him through the computing of ballplayers' averages in baseball. Eye-hand coordination, timing, and gross motor skills can be improved through pitching, batting, running, and other training.

Whatever his interest it can be associated with some kind of school learning, and managed so that it becomes an educational support and a behavior modifier.

Be it sports, carpentry, music, automobiles, bicycling, sewing, cooking, or just riding in the car, meaningful learning comes from all of these activities and such learning can be directly related to school performance.

If your child is too young for such activities, important information can still be cubbyholed in a way that will relate to his personal experience. If he visits the supermarket with you, the ride in the cart can be an education for him.

"Chickens really don't come from refrigerator compartments," I said to Richie. He needed to be told all of these little items of information that we often take for granted. I followed up with a whole discussion of the chicken-egg cycle. Though he was only six at the time, it had meaning for him and made sense. For months after he would announce to the whole family that:

"Eggs could have been baby chickens, if the man in the store had let them . . . he took them away from the hen too soon!"

ON REMEMBERING

Remembering important information was often a problem for Richie as it is with so many youngsters. He had great difficulty in recalling when holidays come, and what we celebrate on those holidays. To help him associate the holiday with a time of year we made pictures of the holiday and the season of the year in which it occurred.

Snow was associated with Christmas, flowers with Easter, a swimmer diving with July Fourth, and browning leaves with Thanksgiving. We made these associations when we spoke about the holidays as well so that they would be learned by seeing, hearing, and associating.

We made weekly schedules so that he could see what was going to happen each week. If we were going to do something special we put a picture of that activity on that day. Richie had calisthenics classes on Monday to help improve gross motor coordination, balance, and overall skills. We took his picture in one of the activities, tacked it up on the board with each week's Monday schedule. He associated a real experience with the day, and learned to expect that activity. He would plan to be home on time, rather than straggling in at any time, irritating me and rushing all of us. We tried to find pictures to represent any activities that we were going to have during the week, and later we added words to the schedule to help him associate the language as well. Such picture schedules help a child learn to plan time and assisted us in avoiding the lateness-forgetting syndrome so common with learning-disabled youngsters.

CONCERNING TELEVISION

We found that television could be used as a supplementary learning experience. Instead of damning it for violence, abusive programming, and "boob tube-itis," we found that it offered some important learning experiences as long as we monitored the watching hours and the schedule.

We used it to help our children learn to take turns, a task so difficult for learning-disabled youngsters. Each one selected one program and we rotated turns so that we all took a turn. We made up a schedule and associated certain programs with the weekdays in sequence. It helped Richard to remember the order of the days in the week, by associating each day with his particular program. We also used the TV schedule as a way of teaching the boys to tell time. We made a clock of cardboard. A large white paper plate represented the face of the clock with numbers marked in. A brass fastener and two colored arrows represented the minute and hour hands. When each boy chose a program he was required to show us the time at which it was scheduled by moving the hands of the clock. Constant reinforcement of the day, its name, the time, manipulating the clock hands, and seeing the program helped him learn all of this information more easily.

Richie's bicycle was used to help him gain a better awareness of right and left direction outside of his own body. We felt that this was especially important, since riding in the street on a two-wheeler bike was a stage just around the corner, and his awareness of right and left turns might be necessary in a life-or-death situation.

The handlebars were color coded, green for left, red for right. We placed tape letters on the handlebars as well for further reinforcement.

The pedals were color coded as well and his sneakers were given a colored dot on the front. We played right and left turn directional games on bicycle and off. He became quite adept at identifying turns vis-à-vis his own body.

The bicycle became a vehicle for teaching time—rate of speed and distance. As his radius of travel increased, so too did our expectations. He was helped to compute rate of speed and distance traveled using a speedometer we installed on the bike.

ON BEHAVIOR

One of the most difficult things to restructure at home was the tendency to act inappropriately. Youngsters who have learning problems often say and do things that make them appear bizarre or different to others. They do not see the social reaction of others to their behavior nor do they judge the responses of others. The impulsive threat of the teenager — "you want a punch in the face" — is not necessarily a real threat but rather an inappropriate over-reaction.

However, such a comment is often misinterpreted by the adult observer, the youngster is responded to with anger, and the situation gets out of control and worsens. Things are said that are not meant. If ignored, placed in perspective, and handled with quiet patience, they need not become a problem.

As the parents of a hyperactive, volatile youngster who could get out of bounds, overreact, and respond inappropriately, we are well aware of the parents' role as manager in such situations. We were well aware that an impulsive response or poorly chosen reply could cause Richie to explode. We know the tone of voice, the body language, the three or four chosen words that can "tick him off." All we need do is suggest by our response that he is inadequate, and he will blow. On the other hand, we are also aware of the few words that can give him sympathy, direction and self-control when he meets with frustration.

ON SUCCESS

Most important to learning-disabled youngsters in home management is the setting up of situations that foster success. Too often we give them tasks that are setups for failure. We are quite aware of their inability to do certain things and yet we allow them to take on jobs or face demands that are totally inappropriate to their abilities. Doing this with a child is damning him to failure.

True, John may need Regents Math in order to go to the college of his father's choice, but John won't pass that course, nor is he able to understand the subject.

Jimmy is trying to help his father repair the screens, but his poorly coordinated fingers are bound to cause some damage if he is given more to do than he is ready to handle. Better stand by and observe what he does and how he does it than let him hammer a hole through the new screening material.

Billy has difficulty recalling addition and subtraction facts. Let him use a number line or counting line when he does his homework. If you don't allow him such support, he will guess, or utilize his fingers. Then you may become angry with him, and he will become angry with his "stupid old self." Your help will turn him off.

You will be the one supportive follow-up that assists your child for twelve years or more. Your help is critical.

Somewhere, a mythological character in the form of a school administrator once told a parent that he should not help his child because:

a) he might confuse him;
b) he might make him feel nervous and pressured;
c) a parent should only act as a parent.

Thus there grew an aura of "hands-off" psychology, especially with youngsters who are experiencing difficulty. However, this same mythological educator never told parents who would be available to devise the alternative teaching techniques that their child needed during all his waking hours.

Many of the present-day special educators who are working with learning-disabled youngsters are in fact parents who started in the field by working at home with their own children. They felt pain, saw a need, and developed their own techniques because they cared so much.

Certainly pressure is bad for parents and children: confusion results from conflicting educational theory, and a parent is first and foremost a parent. However, common sense, a success-oriented approach, frequent school conferences, and some good guidelines can do away with many of these home-tutoring problems.

Parents are teachers, like it or not. They are teachers of good manners, practical living skills, behavior, and budgeting. They teach their children cooking, housework, responsibility . . . why not educational subjects as well?

TWO

UP THE LADDER
OF DEVELOPMENT

13

Gross Motor Development

ACTIVITIES TO DEVELOP GROSS MOTOR SKILLS

In May of his kindergarten year, our youngest son, Alan, appeared to be having some difficulty in school. We were called to school for one of the many conferences that we have experienced as the result of our children's personal needs.

It was suggested that Alan was not ready to move on into grade one due to apparent immaturity in a number of areas. Among these areas were the development of gross motor skills, such as those required in running, jumping, hopping, skipping, etc. He was also experiencing great difficulty in developing the skills of visual-to-motor integration, especially fine motor coordination and manual dexterity.

Once again, we embarked on a home program. We discussed the idea of retention and due to our previous experience with Richard and Ira decided against this solution. We have become increasingly convinced that only children who indicate complete social immaturity and inability to relate to their age group should be retained. Children with strong verbal and receptive skills, who can understand spoken language and can communicate verbally at high levels, can keep up with their peers as a general rule, if allowance is made for their learning needs and modes of expression.

Alan was just such a child. We recognized that it would mean much work at home on our part, but working at home with the boys in a learning situation had become an ongoing part of our daily lives and this was just a slight variation on a well-established theme.

Our previous experience had taught us that we could not wait for intensive remedial activities to be undertaken at school. Things were being done but those things were not enough to handle the problem. We returned to our home game activities to assist Alan as well as our older boys.

We set aside short daily time periods to help him develop the gross and fine motor skills that are essential to writing activities in school. We noticed that he seemed to have the greatest difficulty in handling written forms in which two-sidedness or bilateral symmetry was necessary. (This means that objects had to match on the right and left side to be accurate.) We had read in Dr. Kephart's books of the close relationship between gross motor coordination of the whole body (arms-legs, etc.), balance and coordination, and the higher level development of small muscle movement or fine motor coordination.[1]

In observing Alan more closely, we noticed that he had a great deal of trouble performing some of the body coordination activities that had come to his older brothers so easily. For Alan, skating was extremely frustrating, balancing on a balance beam was a chore, and learning to ride a two-wheeler bicycle was delayed by nearly two years.

We played daily balance activities together. All the boys participated but it was Alan we aimed our activities at most carefully.

Alan was not sure of how he could maneuver his body in all kinds of ways. With a variety of activities, he refined his actions, improving agility and coordination that benefited all motor coordination. For example:

GROSS MOTOR DEVELOPMENT

WALKING TO MUSIC

We played marching music with a strong beat and had the boys walk around a table to the rhythm of the music. We made a game of this by putting chairs in the center and having one chair less than the number of children playing the game. When the music stopped, the boys rushed for the available chair and the one who did not reach a chair in time was out. When you were counted out, however, you continued beating the tempo in place with your hands (clapping) or with your feet (stamping).

WALKING "HAPPY" AND "SAD"

At times we played walking games to the music. We had the boys follow a variety of directions and walk the way the music sounded to them. For example, we asked them to walk in tiny little steps or big giant steps. We might ask them to:
Walk around the room without touching anyone or anything.
Walk on the ice at the pond.
Walk on sand.
Walk as if you're happy, and walk as if you're sad.
Walk as if you're cold, and walk as if you're hot.
Walk as if you're in a hurry, and walk as if you don't want to walk at all.

ROBOT WALK: For Alan at age six to seven

Here the object was to teach him how to control the rigidity or relaxation of arms and legs. Alan put towel tubes on his hands and "became" a mechanical robot man. One of the other boys controlled the robot by telling him what to do and how to do it.

CLEMENTINE'S WALK: For Alan at age seven

We took this idea from the song "Clementine": "herring boxes without topses, sandals were for Clementine." We collected shoe boxes, taped the lids on, and cut out holes in the tops for feet and shoes to fit inside. We had him walk on a course with the boxes as sandals. Sometimes we held races with all the boys and their friends donning cardboard shoe boxes for the contest.

This was lots of fun and by causing all leg movements to be exaggerated, it helped him to be more flexible in leg motions.

RACES

Running races is a wonderful way for parents to help the less-coordinated child develop skill. But it is important to race only if the competitors do not outclass the child with a motor problem. Too much competition can be destructive and cause the child to avoid the activity. We had Alan race against the clock. His older brothers game him a time handicap of a realistic amount so that he could tie them or even win the race.

It was extremely difficult for Alan to lift both feet off the ground in jumping activities. We worked hard on this skill and tried to show him how to leave the ground and allow his arms to assist him in the lift-off. He seemed somewhat insecure about letting go and allowing space and gravity to take over. We held both his hands first, then gradually only held one hand. Finally, when he seemed more confident, we let go of both his hands and he took off by himself.

JUMPING ACTIVITIES: For Alan at ages six to eight

Jump in place, put down two footprints with tape on a tile floor.
Squat down and jump up high to reach the ceiling.
Jump backward from one set of footprints to another or jump forward from one set of footprints to another.
Jump over a piece of tape, a pillow or any other small object.
Jump down from a height, using small stool or wooden box.
Jump from the last step on a flight of steps, making sure that knees are bent to absorb the shock when landing.

HOPPING ACTIVITIES

Once Alan had learned how to handle jumping activities, we realized that weighting the body on one foot was an important exercise for him. We began including hopping activities when jumping had improved sufficiently so that he was not as afraid of letting go of his contact with the ground.

We held his hands initially, as with the jumping activities. After he became more secure, we only held one hand and finally no hands.

We would beat out a rhythm by clapping or drumbeat and have

him hop to that beat. When he could do this, we added hopping forward, hopping backward, hopping right, and hopping left.

MOTOR MATH

Using masking tape, we marked off spaces on a linoleum floor into squares, each measuring approximately one foot by one foot. This resembled a traditional hopscotch court (as shown below). We

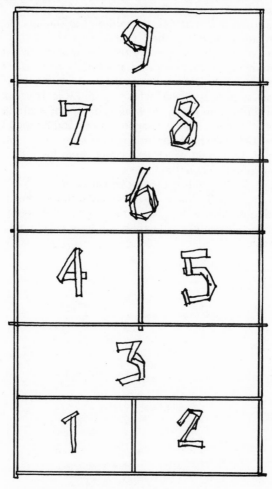

taped precut numbers (one through ten) into the center of each square, one number in each square.

We used this game to teach Alan and our other boys a number of different skills.

First Alan learned to hop from box to box without touching the lines as he hopped. He would throw a beanbag into one of the numbered boxes. Then he was asked to hop to the box in which he threw the beanbag (taking care not to hop on the lines), put both feet down, pick up the bag, turn, and hop back. As he became more proficient at this, we told him to stay on one foot, get the beanbag, turn, and hop back from box to box.

When he was able to identify number symbols, we turned this into a number recognition game and taught him how to identify numbers as he hopped from box to box.

The last step, at approximately age eight, was its use as an addition and subtraction game. He would add up the score he received every time he threw the beanbag into a box and hopped to retrieve it successfully. Whenever he stepped on a line, we subtracted the number of the box in which he faltered from his total score. This proved helpful to all our boys in learning math.

Not every child with learning difficulties experiences difficulties in gross motor skills. Many are extremely well coordinated and are good athletes. However, good gross motor development is not necessarily a guarantee that a child will have developed in the fine motor areas.

14

Sensory Motor Development

Sensory Motor Development: *Child begins to
integrate fine motor muscles and large muscles,
gains balance and rhythm; becomes aware of
direction out from the body and body in space.
Begins to develop right- and left-sidedness.*

PULLING IT ALL TOGETHER — LEARNING HOW TO WRITE

A young child learns to copy and write forms, letters, and numbers from observation and imitation.

We call this process the development of visual-motor integration skills. More than 75 percent of the work done in a classroom involves the copying of visual symbols onto paper. Some of these tasks require seeing forms and shapes near the eye. Others require seeing forms and shapes far from the eye. Academic achievement is determined to a large degree by the way a child sees and perceives shapes, understands them, and can write them on paper.

Children are ready for these observing and writing tasks at different ages. Readiness to perform complicated written tasks can vary from six months to four years at any given age. Since so many school tasks depend upon these skills, the child who is not ready is placed at a great disadvantage in a group setting unless modified demands are made upon him.

A parent can observe his child's written performance and give some assistance if it appears necessary. Many home-oriented activities contribute indirectly to the development of visual-motor integration skills. Two fine resource books of activities for home and school must be mentioned among others. They are the *Handbook of Psychoeducational Resource Programs*,[1] and *Motoric Aids to Learning*.[2]

A child can "experience" or "feel" the shape and direction of visual images before he has to draw these on paper.

Two of our sons, Richard and Alan, needed help in gaining better writing skills. For Richard, we found that recall of letters and numbers was improved by writing them on his back or arm. Thus, he could feel the shape before he had to copy it on paper.

After Richard had learned to handle single letters and numbers in this fashion, we used the same technique to help him remember two- and three-letter sight words.

Step two in the process was aimed at helping Richard translate what he understood about the shape and direction to written work. However, we tried to provide him with some structure to help him stay with the general shapes. We created dot-to-dot exercises with letters and numbers. He was then asked to connect the dots and identify the letter.

He was given a thick primary pencil and plastic gripper so that he would hold the pencil in the correct position.[3] Quite often, it is the narrowness of a conventional pen or pencil and the fine motor control necessary that also gets in the way of good symbol formation. A thick Magic Marker or grease pencil will work as well for firm grip and positioning.

As Richie moved on in school, he was required to use a regular pencil in class. He wrapped a rubber band around the pencil, approximately three-quarters of an inch above the point. He grasped the pencil over the rubber band and it helped him direct the movement of the pencil more accurately.

We tried to move him from concrete activities to more abstract ones. In order to help him remember shapes of letters and numbers, we played memory games without writing.

SENSORY MOTOR DEVELOPMENT

Mystery Bag: We placed ten plastic Playschool-like letters in a drawstring or brown paper bag. Richie would reach in and pick one, finger it and tell us what letter he chose. He then pulled it out of the bag, looked at it, and checked for himself.

Pipe-cleaner Projects: We gave him pipe cleaners cut in various lengths. We showed him a letter on a flash card. He would take his pipe cleaners and form that letter by bending and folding the various pieces.

We showed him the card a second time and he checked it with the shape he had made.

Rechecking and comparing for similarities and differences are an important task. We had Richie compare his work with the original form because we felt that learning to compare forms accurately is as important as learning to create the form initially.

There are so many letters in our alphabet that are of similar configuration. They often differ only by directional rotation. For example:

b – p – d – g – q
j – t – f
h – y
u – n – m – w

Many different kinds of practice techniques must be used to help children like Richie develop a consistent awareness of the shape and direction of these confusing letter forms.

Most important in working toward skills of form constancy is that forms that are *touchable* be used before pencil and paper activities are encouraged.

The skills of writing require that four stages of development have occurred:

At stage one a child must have adequate motor coordination and fine motor finger dexterity.

At stage two a child must be aware of the shape and direction of a form he learned. This is best absorbed through body movement.

When stage three is reached a child is trained to observe that some shapes are similar. The child must also be able to notice and point out the forms that are different and to explain and show to us the way they are different.

During the final stage of development, the ability to integrate the shape he sees with what he writes is formed. This comes after a period of trial and error, involving tracing activities, dot-to-dot drawing, and free-flowing art exercises. Getting the shape and feel of something is always easier if one uses the whole arm with large flowing strokes across the paper.

Confining a child to the small writing areas between the narrow printed notebook lines (approximately ⅜″) restricts movement and may prevent learning. It is after shapes have been mastered that we can then aid a child in reducing the size of the letter and number forms by gradually reducing the size of the area in which he must work. Teachers in the early primary grades are aware of this but upper grade teachers' expectations may be beyond the child's development level. E.g., use a large piece of drawing paper (16 × 24). We had Richie draw a large letter on the sheet with a paintbrush, finger paints, even chocolate syrup!

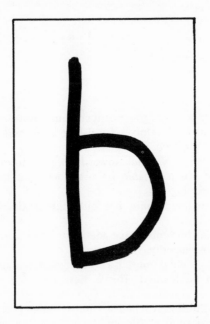

As he perfected the strokes, we introduced a smaller area. We folded the 16″ × 24″ sheet in half to approximately 8″ × 12″. Now we had him make a letter form half the size of the one above. He was beginning to scale down his performance.

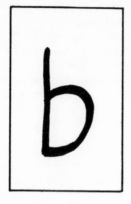

We worked on this size for a while with many letters and numbers. When he was proficient in motor control, we repeated the operation and gave him a sheet 4″ × 6″:

Now we had a letter form one-fourth the size of the original.

The smaller the sheet, the greater his need to exert fine motor control. He needed a longer period of practice on the smaller sheets. However, he mastered this one and we were able to reduce the paper size again.

When a child has mastered the fine finger dexterity required in legible writing, and an awareness of some similarities and differences in shapes, he is ready for writing. However, a multitude of factors interfere with the production of accurate written work. One of the most important of these factors is an automatic awareness of form constancy and direction.

The fact that a youngster may be able to copy a form or trace it correctly does not necessarily mean that he will recall that shape whenever he sees it again in a different context.

One of the most important tasks recognized by teachers in the early primary grades is the mastering of form constancy and direction.

15

Perceptual Motor Skills

"I think I know why I am always mixing up a **b** *a* **p** *and a* **d**, *my right eye is left-handed!" said Billie, aged nine. What Billie referred to rather comically is the third step in our developmental ladder, the development of perceptual motor skills.*

FORM CONSTANCY AND DIRECTION — LEARNING TO REMEMBER THINGS OF SIMILAR SHAPE

Certain objects make pictures that we can recall more easily. We can use, taste and touch them and allow our bodies to be in contact with these real sensations. For example, the taste of a toasted marshmallow, the takeoff of an airplane, the warmth of a hot bath, and the aroma of a skunk. These are easy to remember.

However, letters and numbers are symbols. They are not real things; they are abstract and have no direct physical experience that we can associate with their meaning. They must be learned in a specific direction. If we turn them, unlike real things, their meaning changes due to a rotation in space!

Such as:

In order to make use of letters, they must be grouped into meaningful words. Any switch in the grouping changes the meaning of the words. Not only must we learn to identify shapes and direction but we must also identify them by the way they are placed in groups. In order to do this, we must be able to recognize the same shapes and forms whenever we see them. This is called *form constancy,* the ability to identify a form embedded in any context.

We found that the most successful at-home activities were those that let Richie get involved in what he was doing physically. So we tried to avoid pencil and paper tasks whenever possible.

For example, we would show him words and sentences and ask that he clap his hands when he saw a **b,** stamp his feet when he saw a **d.**

We used this for teaching all kinds of forms and shapes. We gave special attention to the commonly reversed, rotated or inverted letters such as:

u-n; b-p-d; p-q; 6-9

Here are some games that we found helpful.

"MIND-DETECTOR"

We used old magazines or typed simple sentences on a sheet. We told Richie to cross out the specified letter each time it appeared. Such as:

> Find **b**
> The ̶b̶a̶b̶y went to touch the ̶b̶rown dog.

"SIMON SEZ" — ALPHABET:

Using a combination of body movement and touching was an effective way to teach Richie symbols and forms.

We call learning by touch *tactile learning* and the learning via body movement *kinesthetic learning*. Both were useful in establishing form constancy.

"SAND SCRIPT"

We tried many of the following games to learn letters. We used sand writing (sand in a shoebox) and he made letter forms. First, we would name the letter and he would respond by tracing that letter with his second and third fingers in the sandbox. As the forms and names were learned, we introduced sounds to the task. Then we varied the game. As he was learning phonetic sounds, we gave him a word . . . *"dog."* He identified the first sound he heard and drew that letter in the sandbox for us.

Finally, we asked him to draw the last sound he heard of a word, and then the middle vowel sound.

First Sound		Last Sound		Middle Sound	
big	jump	rip	pig	map	wet
girl	rip	hot	dip	tan	sun
hat	pin	bus	pad	hit	send
man	dog	box	rock	rob	hen
	fat			run	tap

What we were trying to help him do was to associate a sound that he heard — **b** — with a letter form that he would make: **b**. We then asked him to associate more than one sound with more than one letter . . . **b** . . . **i** . . . **g** . . . and to make words. We did a great deal of overteaching to help him overlearn.

The use of a tracing sand- or saltbox takes this game out of the regular classroom category. It is tactile, unusual, and this makes the experience different from a typical workbook task at school. That is one reason why children are so willing to use the sand- or saltbox for learning forms.

Other activities that help to reinforce form constancy are walk-on forms, made of tape, rope, or fabric. Once more body learning comes into play as the child actually walks on the shape of the letter form, barefoot. He has the fun of the tactile sensation, the learning that comes with a three-dimensional experience.

A variety of tracing experiences can be used so that no one task seems monotonous. Sandpaper letters or those made of string can be used to supplement pipe cleaners.

After the letter forms have been identified and formed repeatedly, the tracing, naming, sounding experience should become one simultaneous operation. This will use all the senses simultaneously, helping to make the learning an integral part of the child's memory bank.

The goal of this activity is to help the child learn the letter names, shapes, sounds, and a key word to associate with each consonant letter.

The same learning steps are undertaken to teach each letter form and to integrate all the operations into one multisensory task. These steps should be done in sequence. The letters learned should be practiced and then each of the letters learned should be reviewed daily if possible.[1]

Step I: The child is shown a card ten inches high with the letter form drawn in thick half-inch Magic Marker felt tip. The child is told the name of the letter and helped to associate the name with words that begin with that letter sound. For example: show him. Say. . . it is the word that starts **h–a–t, h–a–m, h–i–p, h–o–g, h–u–t,** etc.

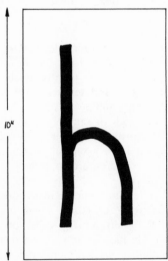

10"

Then with his whole arm held straight out from the shoulder, and pointer and middle finger outstretched, he traces the shape of the letter, saying the name as he traces the form. The two must be done simultaneously. "Name it and form it." . . .

Step II: After this has been done a number of times, the child is ready to hear the key word that he can associate with that form.

If possible, he can be given a picture of the object or a toy object itself to be associated with the letter.

For example: **"h."** He forms it . . . show him a hat. As the hat is shown he now makes the statement: **"h."** He forms it in air, whole arm extended, as he names it. Then he says, "It says **h** as in **h**at."

This procedure is repeated three or four times for each letter in the daily drill. As the child becomes better at the name-it form-it exercise, once or twice daily is enough.

Step III: After three token consonants have been introduced, the first vowel, short **a,** sound can be taught. Now the youngster is ready to decode words and blend sounds together.

Place one of the known consonants next to the vowel **a** and show how it is said: **"h . . . a."**

Stretch it out like taffy.

Repeat this with each of the known consonants and then have the youngster say each pattern after you for visual and auditory feedback.

Step IV: Make a set of three by five card letter patterns just like the eight by ten cards . . . always keep these in alphabetical order. Add letters as they are taught and put them in sequence.

Such multisensory approaches help to make the learning of letter shapes and forms a more consistent and predictable experience for the child with learning difficulties.

Often they will overcome the most common problem associated with the teaching of letter shapes and forms, that of directional learning and reversals.

16

Overcoming Reversals

"How come teachers can't mark the ones that are right — ?
— (cause I have so few!!)"

— Kurt: age nine

Reversals are prevalent in young children age four, five, and six when they are beginning to read and write. Because of a poorly developed sense of the direction of things outside of their own bodies they confuse similar forms. Symbols are not as easy to identify as concrete things which can be recognized no matter how they are rotated in space. A pipe is a pipe whether it is upside down, right side up or turned on its side. The same is true of a table, a chair, etc.

After our son Richie was able to remember shapes and forms in spite of variations of size, directions, or color, he had to learn to recall the sequences or order in which he saw them. Recalling a sequence of letters was particularly difficult for him.

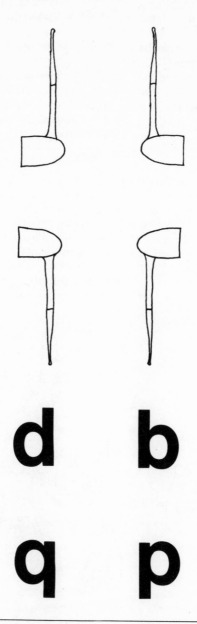

The words **tap** and **pat** are different although he often interchanged the two.

Spot, pots, and **tops** have different meanings, but they caused him great confusion.

We became aware of the kind of errors he made by collecting the papers coming home from school. We realized that reversals of words, parts of words, and the order of words in sentences usually indicated that he needed specific training to develop a consistent left-to-right sequence in reading and writing.

1. LEFT-RIGHT DIRECTIONALITY

We designed a left-right walking pattern. Arranged a series of plastic bottles as *"bowling pins,"* allowing enough room for him to pass between them. We often used chairs, pillows, blocks or *color-coded bowling pins* and had him walk to the *right of those marked with red* and to the *left of the green* pins.

(Throwaway plastic bottles or any cardboard tubes such as on paper towels could be numbered and used as "bowling pins.")

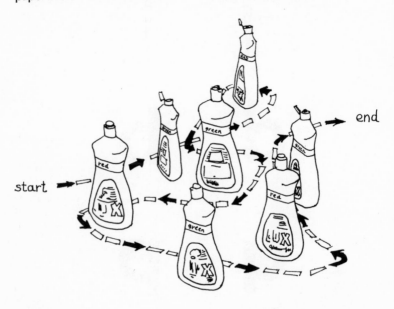

As your child grows older, the game can be made a bit more difficult. You can draw a pirate's *treasure map* or *map of the moon*, indicating the way the child must go to reach the buried treasure (prize).

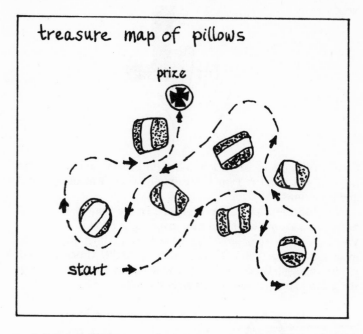

treasure map of pillows

prize

start →

By following the map and moving around the objects he may begin to *abstract direction*. He is forced to think about his movement through space in relation to things. He is obliged to follow a drawing rather than a feeling that comes from his own body. He has to think — the map tells me to go right around that bowling pin, which way is right? Now the map tells me to go in this direction: ——→ is this right or left? With each decision he makes, he is reinforcing his understanding of himself in space, his sense of direction and his body movement.

We would make a room *obstacle course* using square pillows or 8″ × 10″ sheets of colored paper. We told Richie to move to the right of the red sheets and to the left of the green. *Right* and *left* identification continued to give him difficulty.

We showed him that the left hand makes a letter "L" when you hold it up. We put a letter up against his hand to show the shape. We said to him: "Listen to the word Left . . . the first sound you hear is *L* for *Left*. This is your *left* hand. When you hear the direction *Left* or see an arrow pointing toward this hand you go *left!*"

Gradually, the sense of left and right became automatic, though he must still preplan a car trip carefully when it involves many left and right turns.

We observed Richie's work papers. He had difficulty in remembering to start his writing on the paper in a *left to right* direction. We decided to *color code* his papers with something that had a meaningful association for him. **Red** for **right, Green** for **left** for writing papers. **Green** means **go**. **Red** means **stop**. You can **go** at the **green** light. But you must **stop** at the **red** one.

By doing this with your child, you are giving him real ways of associating concrete things, i.e., "traffic lights" with abstract work in writing.

You are using real clues to help him remember which way to go. Drawing arrows on work papers may also be helpful.

We tried to give him cues to signal right and left. We called them *traffic lights*. We often began the first letter of an easily confused word in *green* and ended the last letter in *red*, e.g., was-saw, or we put a *green* dot or arrow on the left-hand side of the page to indicate where to start and a *red* dot on the right-hand side of the page to indicate where to stop.

When he began to learn longer words, we taught him to use a window marker to block out parts of words so that he could read syllables in the correct sequence.

Like this:

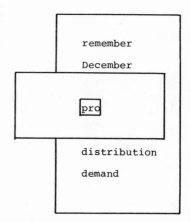

(Slide marker slowly left to right so that he reads syllables properly.)

For Richie, the most persistent ongoing directional difficulties occurred when he tried to write **b**'s, **p**'s, and **d**'s in words. We found that he had great difficulty in learning to discriminate **b** from **d**. We had to reteach the two symbols. We showed him that *to make the b,* he must begin his letter at the top of the space; move his pencil line down until the pencil touches the bottom line; move back up halfway along that line and then move around to the right forming the circle part of the letter.

We always described it verbally. DOWN — UP — AROUND to give him auditory clues. We had him draw it in the air and give the name of the letter simultaneously.

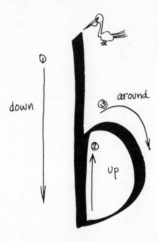

We also showed him that he could *see the small b in the Big B.* It helped him to become aware that by knowing how to make the capital **B,** he will also know how to make the lower case letter. (He will know in which direction to go to form the letter correctly.) We practiced on a page which begins with forming both versions of the letter **b.** We tried several words beginning with capital **B.** Then we had him use a colored pencil and outline the little **b** in the Big **B.**

We made a poster chart of the word **bed** and told him to remember the word **bed,** and associate it with the picture.

He found this illustration useful.

After the letter **b** had been well learned and his identification of it was almost an automatic response, we retaught him the look-alike form **d.**

As he formed the **d,** we gave verbal instructions in order to help him hear and do at the same time. When a child like Richie has difficulties with letter form rotation and his listening skills are stronger, it is helpful to give him talking clues when he makes forms from visual clues.

We said: You start to make the letter **d** by putting your pencil in the middle between the upper and lower lines. Find the middle! Then go *around-up* in a straight line and *down*.

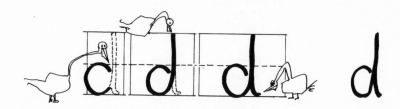

We focused his attention on the fact that you start at a different point when you make **b** and **d** to help him differentiate between them.

We showed him that there was a letter **a** within the **d.**

We made the small **a** within the **d** in color to help him see it superimposed upon the letter.

Again we reviewed the **bed** visual clue card to help him retain a picture-word mental image that he might call upon when he was confused.

Other kinds of touching activities that we used to help Richie learn to associate shapes with sounds were:

sandpaper letters (cut from sheets) purchased in a hardware store

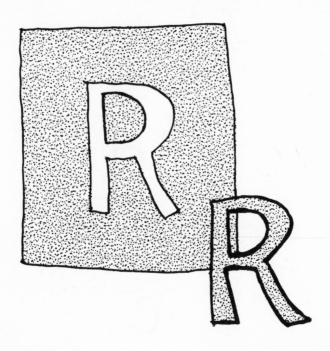

finger paint

(or large paint brush and water) on blackboard.

We had him use an ice cream pop stick and write in slightly moistened clay. Then we told him to close his eyes and feel the shape, and tell us the name of the letter;

the sound it made;

and give us a word that started with that letter sound.

When all other games were a bore, we found that the one he enjoyed the most was to have us trace letters on his palm or back. We tried to verbalize the sequence of actions as you make the letter. He identified the letter and then wrote it for us or traced it on our backs.

As Richie grew better able to handle letters and sounds, we found that remembering the sequence of a group of letters gave him increasing difficulty. This was especially true of words that are not sounded the way they look, such as "night" or "enough."

We would write words on his back and have him tell us the word we had written. Then he tested his recall by writing on our backs and we would respond with the letters he had written. He would say the word.

As he became better able to handle the writing and more confident, we tried to do more pencil-to-paper activities. For spelling we found that the regular weekly list of ten to twenty words was impossible for him to handle. Initially we had him copy the words from a model. We asked him to say the letters as he wrote it and eventually he was able to write the shorter word correctly without a visual cue. Where confusion occurred, we had to devise our own study technique that kept him writing the word a number of times without its becoming monotonous or frustrating.

We designed exercises in which he first saw the complete word, and then letters were omitted and he filled them in. For example:

and	saw	w_s
a_d	s_w	was
an_	sa_	wa–
_d	s__	w__
a__	_aw	_as
_n_	__w	_a_
___	___	___

As he became more adept at this, we had him cover the word above and try to write the missing letters in the second, third, and fourth words from memory. When he could handle three-letter words, we tried four letters and five letters. He needed a good

deal of reviewing but this became his practice technique of learning to spell.

```
and
a_d      a_d
an_      an_      an_
_d       _d       _d       _d
a_       a_       a_       a_       a_
_n_      _n_      _n_      _n_      _n_      _n_
___      ___      ___      ___      ___      ___      ___
```

One of the primary difficulties experienced by youngsters with
learning difficulties is their poor memory for things seen or things
heard. The child with a poor visual memory may appear to make
careless errors, mispronounce words, guess at words, etc. The child
with a poor auditory memory will appear to be inattentive to what
is being said. He will often answer "What did you say?," frustrating
his parents and teachers. He will often have difficulty spelling
words, recalling information, selecting correct vocabulary to use,
and will probably not do well when studying a foreign language.

Memory is critical to learning and visual memory is the ability to
recall what one has seen and revisualize; that is, to see a mental
picture once more from recall.

17

Learning to Revisualize (Remembering)

*"But if I take a picture with my eyes,
how do I know it will come out?"*

— Mark: age ten

We asked Richie for a definition of the word "memory." His reply . . . "Oh, memory . . . that's the thing I always forget!"

Revisualization is the ability to retain a mental picture in the mind's eye.

When a child hears the name of a letter, he must have a mental picture of that letter. If he cannot recall the shape of that letter, or its direction, he may write the letter incorrectly. Consequently, developing this skill is essential to the learning of letters, numbers, and words.

As the child grows older, more demands are made upon him. He must revisualize specific objects when he hears their *names*.

As Gertrude Stein said:

"A rose is a rose is a rose."

For children . . .

A rose may be a . . . "hose."

If he reads **h** for **r** . . . or it may be a . . .

    "nose" if **r** is read as **n.**

Developing the ability to associate information such as letter forms with specific sounds is a complex task. Often a child is asked to learn the name of a letter and then its sound.

For our second son, Ira, the problem of revisualizing letter forms and associating the forms with sounds was especially difficult. The fact that **c** said **k** as in cake or **q** said **kw** as in queen was difficult.

We found that Ira learned best by becoming physically involved in the process and using all his senses simultaneously. He would name letters, form them by tracing them in the air, and say a word beginning with that sound to help him recall it. The final step was to say the sound that the letter made when analyzed from the word.

For example, he might say the sound "eff as in fish" when forming it in the air.

Through this process, he was able to revisualize letter forms. His memory for sight and sound improved by doing things. This multi-sensory approach is from the Slingerland Program and the Orton-Gillingham Approach. (See pages 155–159.)

He could remember better when he became physically involved in the learning and he used seeing, hearing, and tracing to help him remember.

As he moved on through the grades, he learned words in this fashion. He needed the constant reinforcement of tracing and spelling out loud to reinforce visual recall.

Some of the things that we did to assist him in developing visual recall were dependent upon his age and attention span.

Our earliest method was the Slingerland technique mentioned before. However, as he grew older we had to look for alternative techniques for word learning.

We tried limited exposure of words, letter by letter, or part by part until the whole word could be remembered.

We used a cardboard marker strip about one inch by four inches. We slid the marker across the word in a left to right direction. As we did this, he would sound out the word part by part. After grade four level, he was able to understand what a syllable was. We then broke the words down syllable by syllable, exposing one syllable at a time.

We aimed at two skills. The first was the smooth reading process of word attack in a left-to-right direction.

We did many preparatory activities to help him develop recall (revisualization). After a while, Ira could hold a word image for purposes of recognition of word in reading. However, he could not recall spelling and writing. We worked from recognition of words to recall skills needed in spelling and writing. We tried to simplify the demands by expecting him to recall only parts of the word before we asked him to recall the whole word.

We would expose a picture for four to five seconds. Then we removed it and showed him another one. We asked Ira if it was the same.

Sometimes we used similar pictures and sometimes we used pictures that were slightly different. We called the activity a "detective game." Ira was the detective looking for the clues that made the pictures different. He enjoyed this and became good at it. Gradually, as his expertise grew, we decreased the time of exposure.

After pictures had been mastered, we moved to more abstract activities. We exposed a picture, letter or word as above. We gave Ira a paper containing three-by-five-inch figures similar to that he had seen and asked him to circle the one he saw. It helped him to say the letters or numbers subvocally when he saw them. Then he would turn to the page and find them. We were helping him to pay close attention to the details of what he had seen, but we also allowed him to compensate for his poorer visual recall by *saying* words to help him remember. Ira was not a visual learner by nature; however, he needed to develop some basic skills to retain visual images, symbols and words. We could help him make better use of his visual skills and let him learn to compensate using other skills.

He has moved through middle school and high school using these same basic compensatory skills. He has learned to use these skills and has modified them to meet his own needs as he has moved along in school.

He may *verbalize* in order to remember saying what he wanted to remember, so that he could hear it, or . . .

He may *group* information in some logical way to help him recall a series of numbers or random facts. Also he may actually try to rehearse the material, see it, say it, close his eyes and try to recall it, then open his eyes and recheck himself. By rehearsing the material, he can actually design a mental picture that is simpler to recall than abstract words. By practicing this technique, *word* pictures can become *real* pictures that can be more easily remembered. Whenever we can, we try to supply a real picture that explains an idea.

For example, it isn't enough to talk about kinds of rocks in geology. If we could not find samples of rock, we tried to find pictures of these rock types. We would then describe the type in a way that made it relevant to his personal experience.

Sedimentary rock could be described as looking like a chocolate layer cake with each layer representing a layer of particles set down during a period of geologic time. Layers were deposited in lakes over long periods of time. The layers dried out as the body of water dried up and the weight and pressure of the top layers forced the layers to be packed together. What he retained was the picture of layer cake and that was revisualized whenever the word *sedimentary* was mentioned.

One of the complicating factors in working with youngsters with learning disabilities is the complexity of tasks. No one learning mode or skill can be singled out and taught with assurance that it is "the answer" to the problem. All learning modes are dependent upon each other and no one can work well without being integrated with the workings of the other.

For example, the seeing of sedimentary rock formation in a picture is fine; however, the word *sedimentary* must be recalled simultaneously in order that a real thing is associated with its name or symbol. If we can't learn language on schedule, we will lag behind in the learning of the information directly dependent upon that language.

The learning of language or symbolism, then, is critical to our retaining of information, and to our ability to sort information and categorize it as we mature.

18

Language Development

Language is the way we communicate. It is the means by which we express ourselves and how we understand the communication of others. Not all language is expressed in the spoken word. Our inner thoughts are translated into words as well. Without thinking in words our thoughts would be little but random images with no meaning for us.

Thus, there are three kinds of language: that which we speak, called expressive language; that which we hear and understand, called receptive language; and that which translates our thoughts, called inner language.

Our skills may vary in these three types of language. If we are gifted in our use of verbal expressive language we will be able to communicate well conversationally, perform well in classes where public speaking is important, and do well on tests of verbal vocabulary.

However, we may be poor in the skill of receptive language. If so, we will probably miss the subtle differences in meaning among words heard. We may misunderstand much of what we hear and thus do poorly on tests in which we must decide on meanings of words heard.

Someone else may excel in receptive vocabulary and have a fine ability to understand what he hears, yet be less well able to express himself orally.

In addition to these three modes of language, other qualities enter into our understanding of language. We also express ourselves via body language, voice, tone, and manner. We may give off consistent messages or conflicting ones. Life would be so simple if we always meant "no" when we said "no." Unfortunately that just isn't true.

In the classroom, and at home, such obvious inconsistencies confuse parents and teachers. The child who experiences difficulty in expressive language may know much more than he is able to communicate through the spoken word. He may find it difficult to choose appropriate words, use them properly, and may lack the confidence to speak without anxiety and fear. Any one of these, or in any combination, may block verbal expression on the part of a knowledgeable, intelligent child.

On the other hand, a youngster may be able to speak well, and have a lower level of receptive language. He is the youngster who may bluff his way through a course by answering any question, offering misinformation or partial responses, even when he is unsure of what he is saying.

Not only can we have different ways of showing our language aptitude, we also can experience confusion when we receive conflicting messages through the various modes of communication.

When Richie said to me, "I won't do it and you can't make me," I received his statement as "You are testing my authority and I can make you do what I want, though I might have to resort to force."

My inner language told me, "He is a child with a problem and I don't want to resort to force to control his behavior. I would rather reason with him."

He may sense my ambivalence and respond to my voice and body language as meaning: "She won't force me to do it. I'll keep fighting and maybe I'll be lucky and get away with it this time."

When one lives with a learning-disabled child, it becomes increasingly apparent that our expressed language and the meaning the child receives from it do not always coincide.

Often we felt as if we were speaking a foreign language from their response. They seemed to totally misunderstand what we were saying and needed ongoing translation. This puzzled us at first and caused us to be extremely careful about our choice of words. We observed that their attention was sustained in short intervals. Following these spurts of attention, their interest seemed to wander and then refocus seconds later. We observed that they really did not appear to hear everything we said.

Another factor that entered into their understanding of language was their expectations. They expected a particular response from us and no matter what we would reply they would interpret the response according to a preconceived idea.

For example, one day we were trying to explain something to Richard concerning his lack of follow-through on jobs and chores at home. We were careful to make the suggestions constructive, and were controlled and patient in our explanation.

He responded: "Well, you don't have to yell about it!"

His response took us by surprise.

"We weren't yelling!"

Afterwards we realized that most of his previous experiences had convinced him that adults always yell when they give advice. No matter how our statement had been worded or expressed he probably would have felt that someone was yelling.

We realized that such youngsters (perhaps all youngsters) hear what they expect to hear!

Much of what we hear is determined by our attention and what is called auditory perception. It is also determined by how well we remember auditory sounds and symbols.

Hearing others speak is the first introduction the young infant has into the world of communication. Assuming he has normal hearing acuity, and normal speech equipment, he begins to learn to understand that different sounds mean different things. He becomes aware of his own ability to control the reproduction of sounds, and by listening and imitating he is introduced to the spoken word.

Our developmental timetable tells us that most children begin to imitate sounds and words, respond to their name and the words yes or no, at about twelve months. By the age of two, they can usually recognize the names of familiar objects, and recognize some parts of the body. Their expressive vocabulary should have grown to approximately twenty-five words from the one or two words spoken at twelve months.

By the age of three, a speaking vocabulary of some fifty words or more, including some phrases and sentences, and recognition of common objects in pictures should be developed.

We can then develop a chart of expectations as to what they "should" be able to say and do at each stage and age. However, there is no assurance that all children will reach these stages at the same time. There can be a great variance in the readiness level for speech. This readiness for the spoken language may affect the child's total timetable for language acquisition, learning symbols, and reading and writing skills. Each stage is affected by the one that precedes it. Thus, the delay in development of the skill of spoken language can delay the whole "language continuum."

Certain dysfunctions can also affect the smooth process of expressive language. Two of these are discussed in the following section.

CLUTTERING AND STUTTERING

Two of the most common early speech disorders are those of cluttering and stuttering. Although stuttering is a well-known problem, little is known by many concerning the cluttering pattern.

The stutterer is generally a child (or adult) who starts speaking at a normal age. His speech may develop quite rapidly and articulation may be good to excellent in quality. The onset of his stuttering disorder is generally at a specific period of time and may have psychosocial implications. It may begin as a result of some traumatic event in life that affects his interpersonal relationships or threatens his sense of security. Stutterers are usually quite sensitive and aware of their difficulties, and reminding them of their problem by calling attention to any errors will often make matters worse. The less attention paid to the stutter, the better off the stutterer may be. Stutterers often cover up their anger and repress it, or become aggressive in their relationships with peers to compensate for their feelings.

On the other hand, a clutterer is a far different kind of individual generally. He is often an individual who has relatives with speech and language disability problems. His whole pattern of speech development is usually slow, and the onset of speech is often delayed. He often has such difficulties in combination with other language problems, such as difficulties in articulation, problems in finding the right word when speaking, difficulties in building syntactical sentences, telling stories, spelling, and even reading.

The child who exhibits cluttered speech tends to be a scattered, disorganized, untidy, impulsive youngster. He is often short on attention span and seems confused in his retelling of stories and expressing himself. Gradually his speech patterns and garbled language will often improve if he is handled with slow, patient attention. He will benefit from specific directed work in sound patterns, syllabification, and oral expression to help him gain better organization. He will accept help, does not appear oversensitive to correction, and is even amused by his own funny comments. He may stop and correct himself, smile, and continue to talk.

These two kinds of problems need careful differentiation because planned therapy is different. Corrective drill for the clutterer may increase the frustration of the stutterer.

Parents need to know the kind of problem their child is experiencing to know how to handle the home therapy aspects.

The clutterer may say "revy, revy, revelant" instead of "very, very relevant," while the stutterer is still trying to get the first "veh-vuh-vuh-vuhr-vuhry" off the ground. Mike, a nine-year-old stutterer with whom we worked, became so frustrated when he had to say a word beginning with a **b** or **d** or **p,** that he would punch the desk hard with his fist in anger.

Peter, a youngster of the same age with cluttered speech who had severe auditory processing problems, decided to have us collect all of his "bloopers" and funny lines to write a book and publish it.

The problem and accompanying self-image on the part of the stutterer and clutterer may be quite different. The delayed talker may be a potential clutterer; however, stuttering can occur in any youngster given the appropriate personality type and the right set of circumstances.

The child with delayed language skills is often a youngster who will experience learning disability problems of varying degree. Delayed language acquisition is considered by many to be a prime warning signal. This kind of youngster often exhibits a massive unreadiness in many areas of perceptual development.

Terry was such a child. When early language stimulation opportunities presented themselves Terry was just not ready to respond. Later, when he was ready for such an experience, the same kind of opportunities were no longer available. His mother and father both worked and he was left in the care of a grandmother. She had little patience and was disappointed at the child's slow rate of response. She expected little from Terry and met his needs expressed through pointing or making a sort of sign language. He was accepted and tolerated as an uncommunicative child and allowed to remain that way.

We explained that Terry, who was communicating in single incoherent words at age four, needed more stimulation than other children. He needed this help over a long period of time. He needed to be spoken to in simple descriptive sentences. His imitative skills were developing and someone needed to help him by supplying the words so that he could practice saying them. He needed the ongoing feedback of success.

His poor progress frustrated his parents. They responded to his gestures and gave him what he wanted. We pointed out that this kind of action would give him no reason to try to talk. Uncommunicative children can try your patience and test your will.

Our oldest son, Richard, was such a late-talking child. If we gave him what he wanted when he pointed, he would not attempt to speak. We often found that we had to force him to talk, not gesture.

"Don't show me . . . tell me!"

"What do you want? You must say the word!"

Initially our insistence often caused a temper tantrum, but gradually he began to respond. If he did not know the right word we would supply it. However, he had to say it and imitate us a number of times before we would respond to his request.

At the beginning we accepted just the first sounds in the word as his best attempt at saying that word. We understood him and "aap" meant apple; "sod" meant soda; "gaga" meant dog. As time went on we helped him learn to complete the words. We found that using a small metal mirror was helpful. Richie could watch himself form the sounds with his lips, and correct himself by observing one of us say the word simultaneously. If he had some difficulty hearing the sounds correctly, he could observe the mouth formation to help himself.

We worked constantly day after day to help him acquire the ability to associate things he saw with words that he heard, and to associate things in pictures with their names as well. We played many listening games with him as well. We kept our game time short in response to his shorter attention span. We tried to include games involving movement to help him get involved in the task. We worked for ten to fifteen minutes twice a day rather than trying to keep his attention for thirty minutes at any one time. We did not work when he was sick. We found through harsh experience that hyperactive, learning-disabled youngsters overreact to frustration and are far more impulsive when they are not feeling well.

This kind of early speech and language enrichment must go on during all a child's waking hours if it is to be successful. It is not an activity to be turned on and off for one hour of speech training per week. Learning language is an ongoing activity and correct articulation requires daily work.

Improving a child's vocabulary and word usage is often a direct result of constant teaching by adults at home. Whenever unusual ideas or difficult concepts are discussed, special attention must be paid to the child with slower-developing language. Explanations must be offered constantly. The child must be encouraged to re-state these in his own words. Talking to children is a primary art that seems to be almost lost in our fragmented, hurried daily life. Much learning occurs through talking. Talking goes on in the province of the home. Talking is a three-hundred-and-sixty-five-day-a-year educational operation.

Sometimes opportunities just for talking must be made. If we wait for the average family to have time to talk we may be waiting forever. Opportunities exist during car trips, mealtime, bath time, bedtime, supermarket trips, vacations. Communication in some families is limited to talking "at" the kids rather than talking "to" the kids.

Attention must be paid to listening "to" the kids as well. Their speeches may be long-winded and tangential. Their material may bore us, but we bore them as well and we expect them to be polite to us. If no one is willing to listen to the child with slower speech development, why should he bother trying to talk? What value judgment will he place upon himself?

We played many vocabulary-building games with our children. We found them helpful to all the boys in making them more selective concerning words and definitions.

Your goal in games such as these is getting your child to listen carefully and follow directions that are only given through language. In order to challenge him, each set of directions is a little longer and each one becomes a little more demanding of increased attention span. Teachers give many auditory instructions in school activities, and your child must be able to attend to them. Distractible youngsters need practice in developing such skills. The best practice comes through game activities and the desire to succeed and win.

The aim of all the activities to enhance development of spoken language is to get your child to be more relaxed and fluent in his expressive communication. Any pressure or tension applied during these games will turn him off. It will negate the successes he has felt. He needs warmth and patience, time and attention, to feel success.

Children develop language skills through imitation of sounds they hear. They must be corrected kindly when they mispronounce words. Any laughter at their expense is interpreted as an insult. If they are to be free to make mistakes, we must not laugh at their baby talk or ridicule their errors.

Children develop a better awareness of word meanings and language usage by practice. When dealing with new words, it is always best to illustrate the new concept by showing a concrete object, picture, or real representation of the concept. If this is not possible, try to explain what you mean in terms of something they have seen or experienced.

For example, in explaining the appearance of sedimentary rock, the only illustration that came to mind was the chocolate layer cake mentioned before. It looked like sedimentary rock, it helped explain the way successive layers are set down. Cutting through it was especially helpful. This proved to be so much fun that we used a marble cake to show what glowing volcanic granite would appear to be like as well. There are so many real things that help to explain abstract concepts for the unsophisticated child. For example:

1) Balloons filled with air explain jet propulsion.

2) Drinking straws help explain suction, a vacuum, pressure.

3) A bathtub filled with water helps explain immersion and displacement (when the water rises in the tub after you have gotten in).

4) A bat hitting a ball explains that every action has a reaction.

5) Brushing your hair explains static electricity.

6) Striking a match explains friction, leading to combustion.

7) A cake mixer explains centrifugal force.

8) Observation of the difference in temperature in the shade and in the sun will illustrate solar heating energy.

9) Dropping different objects of varying weights helps to explain gravity.

10) The variation in the amount of daylight time helps explain the change of seasons.

There are so many real experiences that can be used to explain abstract concepts if we look around. The key to making it real and meaningful is attempting to relate it to personal experience.

MYSTERY GAMES (Ages Five to Ten)

Aim: To improve observation and recall of language.

Have your child look around the room very carefully. Tell him to notice as many objects as he can and to say them to himself as he looks around. Then tell him to tell you as many objects as he can identify. Ask him to put each in a category (age seven and over):

Categories: (1) Is it a vegetable (something that grows)?
                  (2) Can it be eaten by him?
                  (3) Is it a mineral, made of a resource of natural origin found in the ground?
                  (4) Is it a garment of clothing, something to wear?
                  (5) Is it a piece of furniture?

NAME THE JOB (Ages Six to Nine)

Aim: To improve vocabulary and acquire information.

Goal: To help the child learn to identify the kinds of jobs and professions in our community. To learn to associate these people with the kinds of services that they do for us. Below are types of questions. The answer to each question is a job or profession:

(1) Whom do we go to see when we are sick?_____(doctor)

(2) Who fixes things in our house when they break?_____ (Daddy or handyman)

(3) Who fixes your teeth when you have a cavity or toothache? _____(dentist)

(4) Who teaches you how to read and write at school?_____ (teacher)

(5) Who flies a big airplane?_____(pilot)

(6) What do we call the men who went to the moon in space ships?_____(astronauts)

RIDDLES (Ages Six to Nine)

Aim: To improve vocabulary and give general information.

Who am I?

(1) I can fly . . . who am I? (bird)
I can swim . . . who am I? (fish)
I can hop . . . who am I? (rabbit)
I can chew food . . . who am I? (teeth)
I can take you flying . . . who am I? (a plane)
I help you kick a ball . . . what am I? (a foot)

Any variation on this game is fun to play . . . children love it especially at bedtime.

(2) For older children try these (ages seven and eight):
I make milk for you to drink . . . who am I? (cow)
I make honey in my hive . . . who am I? (bee)
I can bark very loud . . . who am I? (dog)
I lay eggs for your mother to fry . . . who am I? (chicken)

(3) Older children will like these (ages nine to eleven):
I explore under the surface of the ocean . . . who am I? (aquanaut)
I sell tickets on the train and take care of the passengers . . . who am I? (conductor)
I work in a laboratory making medicines to help people who are sick . . . who am I? (chemist or scientist)
I have traveled to faraway places to discover new things . . . who am I? (explorer)

GAMES OF CHARADES

Here the child acts out the words you say (if he can read, he reads it from a piece of paper and then acts it out).

Sequence and remember . . . do these things in the order in which I tell you:

(1) Clap your hands . . . jump up and down (two instructions).

---

(2) Stand up, hold up your right hand, and touch your nose (three instructions).

(3) Hop three times on your left foot . . . sit down . . . clap your hands three times . . . and close your eyes (four instructions).

RECEPTIVE OR LISTENING LANGUAGE

There are many factors that affect the growth of receptive or listening language. Among these factors are our attention span, auditory memory, perception of sounds, understanding of vocabulary, and previous language experience.

With regard to the development of auditory attention span, most listening is done in spurts at intervals of approximately thirty seconds' duration. Between these thirty second intervals interest wanders and then returns to the attentive listening stage. We do not hear everything said by anyone.

We have also observed that children listen best when they are actively involved in the listening process. When we are doing something else at the same time it distracts us from what is being said.

The distractible youngster who is fidgeting with toys, paper clips, coins, bottle caps, and buried treasures from his pocket or desk cannot listen as well. The objects he holds distract him.

You may have to frisk him and empty his pockets into a "treasure box," empty his desk, and put knickknacks out of reach to get his full attention.

Other youngsters seem to have difficulty when faced with listening to a voice combined with some background noise. They appear unable to separate the central voice from the background. It is almost like a telephone switchboard with all circuits left open for incoming calls. They simply can't decide which call to answer.

Unfortunately we cannot provide them with a totally noiseless environment in which to work. We may have to look for other ways to help them focus their attention.

In addition to that, the child needs some direction to help him hold his attention to what he hears. If what he audits is without some specific purpose or goal, he will remember less of it than if you give him a specific question to answer before or after listening. Active involvement is often the direct result of definite direction and the need to answer questions to get specific information.

Often as teachers we have found that the "follow-up" questions concerning a report or tape should be given in advance. The traditional practice is to give the questions at the end of any reading or listening assignment. However, one of the primary directive techiques for listening and reading remediation is to give questions to be answered in advance. This highlights what is important, and what should be recalled. It places the child in the role of detective; finding clues to a mystery.

We expect too much from children in the handling of auditory recall. Actually, a normal adult may forget as much as 90 percent of what he has heard during any two-week period. Thus, they recall only 10 percent of what they have heard. Interestingly enough, what they recall is determined by their ability to associate it with something they have experienced or learned previously, their retention of a visual picture of the information, the importance they place on the material, and the way in which they develop recall techniques or devices.

These clues tell us much about the way both adults and children recall information that they hear. If it can be:

1) linked to something they knew previously;
2) drawn or associated with a meaningful picture;
3) made important or personally significant to them; or
4) adapted to become a rhyme, or acronym.

It is much easier to recall the acronym CREEP than to remember Committee to Reelect the President. Rhyming assists memory as with. . . "30 days has September, April, June, and November; all the rest have 31; except February which has 28 and leap year gives it 29."

The deduction from my own paycheck has more meaning and significance than a general discussion of federal income taxes and Social Security systems. It is my money being deducted, personal and important to me.

I can readily remember fractions as real things, rather than segments of an abstract whole. Cutting up pie plates, felt circles, etc., can make this a real experience and far easier to remember.

The most significant symptoms suggesting a possible difficulty in auditory skill development are often those that can be first noticed by the aware parent. Characteristically, youngsters exhibiting late development of verbal expressive language skills are those who seem most prone to experience auditory processing problems.

When we examine case studies of older youngsters who are experiencing difficulties in spelling, reading, verbal expressive skills, and foreign language, among the most significant symptoms in their records are:

1) late development of understandable speech (after age two);
2) garbled speech or baby talk (after age three);
3) omission of beginnings and endings on words (after age three);
4) the inability to speak in sentences (after age three);
5) a decrease in verbal expression rather than a gradual increase (from age three on);
6) nonfluent speech or stuttering (after age four);
7) distortions, reversals, omission of sounds or telescoping, or unusual confusion (cluttering) (after age seven).

For example: the kind of humorous comments youngsters make may be indicative of far more than comedy:

"I get help at school. I go to trituteral (tutorial) every day."
— Jerry: age eleven

"I saw this movie called *Increbidible Journey*. There were two dogs in the story, a Gordon Retrieval and an Irish Settler."
— Peter: age eleven

"We were studying about that city in Italy that was buried under the ashes of a volcano . . . you know, *The Last Days of Bombay*."
— Richie: age ten

"Someone who has a way of telling what is gonna happen in the future is someone with STP."
— Mark: age ten

Such errors are humorous, but confusing for the child who is experiencing such difficulty. It is important to note that the words learned can be associated with nonmeaningful clues and become a welter of confusion for such a child. Richie searched the map of Asia for Bombay to associate the story he was reading with the historical information. He was on the wrong map, the wrong continent, and certainly confusing a period of European history with that of Asia.

What we say is based upon what we hear said by others. Thus, our speech is largely dependent upon the way we are able to receive and understand what others say to us.

Auditory perception is the ability to differentiate the similarities and differences in the sounds we hear. If our auditory acuity is normal (hearing) and our auditory perception is accurate, then we can discriminate sounds normally.

Decoding words from what we hear is the ability to understand that groups of sounds make words. We must be able to put together meaningful groupings of sounds to make understandable words or we will not be able to comprehend what is being said to us!

A child may have learned to recognize the word *dog* or *cat*. He says it but he does not hear the sounds in isolation. In order to help him with such a problem, we must stretch out the sounds for him the way we would stretch out **t- -a- -f- -f- -y.** Then he will learn to isolate the single sounds better.

In this process we start with simple three letter words and move to words with increasingly difficult sound patterns.[1]

d-o-g **d-o-ll** **c-a-t** **c-a-p** **c-a-n** **c-a-b**

Such a youngster needs early training to improve his awareness of auditory stimuli. It is fun to perform a game called:

BLINDMAN'S BUFF

Have your child turn his back and tell him not to peek.

You make common sounds and he must identify them without seeing what you are doing. Some common sounds are:

clapping	kicking	tapping a pencil
crinkling paper	whistling	ringing a bell
glass tapping	finger snapping	ticking of a clock

Gradually, auditory sequencing can be added to the game. Make two sounds in series, then three, then four. The child must tell them in order.

As we introduce more complicated tasks of auditory sequencing, we must talk about auditory memory as well. This is our ability to hear and retain what we have heard. We must remember things we have heard in the far-distant past in order to make sense of what we hear in the present (long-term auditory memory). We must also be able to remember the sounds in a word that someone has just said if we are to understand the word and spell it (short-term auditory memory).

These skills — auditory perception, decoding, comprehension, sequencing, and memory — are all interdependent. They are all called into play every time someone speaks to us. If we receive proper information through our ears and have normal auditory acuity, then it should be received and understood. If, however, this information is improperly transmitted from ears to brain, or becomes scrambled in transmission, we will not be able to utilize it properly. If it is received correctly and associated with something we recall, then we can use this information. On the other hand, if we have no prior experience with it or can't recall it, it is useless to us. We might as well be listening to Chinese or Spanish without understanding the language.

Auditory acuity testing is not enough for school-aged youngsters. This does not tell us the use a child is making of the information that is coming in.

In addition to these skills, much of academic learning is based upon the ability to recall information in a correct sequence. If we cannot remember things in order after hearing them, we will have difficulty in spelling, mathematics, following instructions, etc.

The fifth grade class is waiting for Mrs. Smith to give out the homework assignment. Jerry waits with his pencil poised to get the information down on paper. Mrs. Smith doesn't write the assignment on the board.

She says: "Read in your history books to page 31. Answer the questions on page 32. List all of the products of the Southwest on a piece of paper and bring it in. Don't forget to put your name and the date on the paper you hand in tomorrow. Oh . . . by the way, review for a spelling test on the last three lessons."

One glance at Jerry's paper tells the story. He has written:

History page 13 . . . questshuns.
Name and day . . . spelling

When he gets home he may not understand what he has written.

He will not do the assignment nor will he remember the spelling lessons to study. He will put his name and the date on a piece of paper, however, and probably hand that in.

Jerry has problems in auditory processing to written work, sequencing sounds in words for spelling, and sequencing numbers from auditory stimuli. If Mrs. Smith had just written the homework on the board Jerry might have been able to complete at least part of the work expected. However, now he is due for a lecture, a failing mark, and another disgrace in front of his friends.

Difficulties in auditory skills appear in many disguises. They appear in a different pose when we deal with youngsters of ages eleven to eighteen. For such youngsters, the frustrations experienced have become an integral part of their daily lives at home and at school. Life is a constant series of the following:

"You didn't follow my directions so you get a zero on that paper!"

"Why can't you ever do what you are told?"

"Sometimes I think you must be deaf the way you don't hear me."

"You were told to bring your history books today. Why do you always have excuses?"

The auditory-impaired adolescent appears to be disinterested, apathetic, and out of touch with what is going on both at school and at home. He may be disorganized, forgetful, out of "sync" with his environment. He rarely completes all assignments, and does very poorly in classes that involve a good deal of lecturing. He may learn to read but not to spell. He may be a nonverbal, uncommunicative youngster, who never volunteers in class. When called upon he seems not to have heard the question — daydreaming. He may have difficulty abstracting information because he doesn't understand the language of the course. He will probably experience difficulty writing interesting descriptive paragraphs. His writing appears rather primitive with simple "baby" words.

His parents become impatient with him.

His teachers are frustrated trying to reach him.

They try alternate doses of patience, friendship, anger, and punishment. But nothing seems to make him "listen any better." On the other hand, he may perform adequately or excel in tasks that require building, drawing, painting, and constructing. Here we have hands-on activities that allow him to become physically involved in the learning process. He will probably do well in science laboratory work, although he doesn't pick up information as well through the lecture classes.

Often the inability to discriminate sounds heard, and confusion of words heard, goes hand in hand with overall language difficulty, in speaking, understanding, and inner-language development.

Our son Richard needed visual assistance to handle information heard. If the class was discussing abstract concepts in mathematics or science, he needed concrete illustrations of the concept using real objects, sketches or pictures. When this was done simultaneously, he received input via two modes, auditory and visual.

When given homonyms (words that sound alike but have different spellings and meanings, such as *their, there, here, hear*), he will need a good deal of explanation concerning their different usage. Help in associating specific meanings and spelling via some device or technique such as rhymes makes recall easier.

For hear and ear: "I hear with my ear . . . ear is found in hear."

Or for here and there . . . "Here and there are places. Here is found in there."

The children need many kinds of learning by seeing and doing. Subtle differences among words will elude them, and selecting the main idea from what is read or heard may be difficult. Words are the problem: understanding, spelling, defining, and writing them. Thus, acquiring a technical vocabulary in any subject may be their nemesis. Such youngsters are a setup for failure in foreign language classes, unless the course is specifically designed to meet their needs, or includes the study of Latin.

Generally, the auditory-impaired youngster learns best by a combination of seeing, doing, role-playing and experiencing. We would all probably learn better that way.

For example: to develop his ability to use descriptive words, use picture studies. He studies a picture, then names or describes everything he sees using as many adjectives as possible.

You can ask him to draw a picture from a word description, helping him to listen and visualize from spoken language. Without the learning of a more descriptive usage of vocabulary, such youngsters tend to stay with extremely simple, primitive language when writing. Often they will use more descriptive words if they are given a list of adjectives or adverbs when doing a writing assignment. However, they seem unable to select the correct words themselves.

Such youngsters should be facing the person speaking to them. They do not audit when they are not facing the speaker. Their attention wanders or they lose track of what the speaker is saying.

When assisting your child in spelling, try to find some structure in any group of words that he must study. By structure we mean similarities or word family groupings. If the words are completely unrelated and this is impossible, have the youngster spell subvocally (whisper) as he writes the words. Explain to him that he is better able to remember a sequence of letters if he says them to himself as well as writing them. Use the partial word recall techniques listed on pages 170 and 171. They will be helpful for better recall. It is also important to speak to your child's teacher and suggest that he might benefit from a slightly more structured spelling approach, varying only one letter or pattern at a time.

Auditory recall can be improved through learning to pay closer attention to what is being said. One game that children of any age enjoy is called "I took a trip and in my grandmother's trunk I carried" . . . then each person playing adds an item carried in the trunk. Start with **a** (apples) . . . second player must add something with **b** (bananas) and he must say "I took apples and bananas." Third player says something with a **c** . . . "I took apples, bananas, and a coat," and so on. This can be played with countries, cities, things to eat, clothing, furniture or any category that is being learned.

Another training game to improve listening skills is called "Messenger around the house." Mother sends a simple message to Father at the other end of the room. Six-year-old Jimmy is "the messenger." Each message gets more complex and longer. If Jimmy gets the message correct, then Mother must be the messenger.

Other sequential memory games to improve recall are:

1) Having your child copy clapped patterns.

2) Playing detective and having your child find a hidden object in the room, then two objects, then three, and so on.

3) Copycat game. Taking turns, each one must copy the leader and say what he says or do what he does.

Starting with simple sentences your child must repeat what you say . . . then move to more complicated sentences, and finally to short tongue-twisters.

4) Have your child close his eyes and tell you exactly what someone in the room has just said. He listens and repeats.

5) On long car trips the game of sightseeing is great fun and certainly cured the restlessness of five little boys for us. We gave each one a list of things to look for on our trip. They would check each word off as they saw that sight. We went over all of the words.

All games that are played to enhance the development of listening skills and auditory perception should aim at helping the child learn to listen more intently to different sounds, tempos, pitches, levels of noise. Any activity, therefore, that involves changes in sound pattern, etc., can be a remedial drill in auditory perception.

Moreover, games that require attention to specific word meaning and usage as in riddles, question and answer games, and sorting words into categories are vocabulary builders. Many commercial games are on the market that will help develop such skills.

Activities involving taping and listening, mimicking sounds and physical activities involved in articulation, help a child develop better expressive speech. Language Masters are used by schools for such activities.

Generally, memory improvement can be developed by recall of any sequential material in a preplanned order. Repeating numbers, letters, directions, objects, cooking recipes, etc., are all helpful activities.

Sound symbol association games are helpful in improving a child's overall skills in phonics, reading and spelling. See the section on phonics, pages 218–238, for specific activities. Generally, however, rhyming activities and picture cards to help remember sounds letters make are most helpful in this area.

Developing good listening and language skills is basic to nearly all school-related activities. Parents need to be aware of ways in which they can make all conversation at home a helpful support in this area.

One cannot learn without listening.

One cannot communicate without speaking.

19

Concept Skills (Math Activities)

*"There's nothing that spoils arithmetic more than
a lot of numbers."*
> — Lucy from
> *Peanuts Characters*
> © United Features Syndicate, Inc.

*"I guess I was in the bathroom when they taught
fractions."* (For six months?)
> — Skip: age twelve

*"I was flirting with Patrick Herlihy when they taught
decimals."*
> — Lois: age thirteen

The next group of activities that are essential to the learning process are those connected with the learning of math skills; to learn to identify numbers, to perceive their forms, and to differentiate the numbers one from another. The child who has perceptual and directional problems may have great difficulty in handling numbers, their shape and their values.

Many of the suggestions that we have made previously concerning directionality, rotation and form also apply to number-form and shape. For example: many children read a **6** for a **9** and vice versa. First and second grade teachers see many threes and sevens written backward. The problem is when the student continues to write the numbers in that manner in third and fourth grade.

The use of stencils, tracing paper, plastic overlays, and templates usually is of great help. Wooden numbers (and letters) can be made for the younger children as part of an industrial arts project. In the same manner, beanbag numbers can be made or purchased.[1] These give the number form and have substance.

VALUE AND CONCEPTS

In order for a child, any child, to be able to understand the value of an **8** he must be able:

1) to count on a one-to-one relationship; that is, if shown eight objects (chips, bottle caps, or blocks, etc.), can he, with his fingers or his entire hand, move them one-by-one as he counts and is saying "one, two, three . . . ?"

2) Then he must be able to identify the form of an eight (**8**).

3) Then he must be able to write an eight (**8**).

There are many different methods of helping a child to learn the above. The method that we used with all of our children is as follows:

We utilized three sets of homemade cards, approximately the size of playing cards. The first set has a different number of *dots* on each card.

The second set had the set of *dots* and the *numeral* represented by those dots.

The third set completed the concept, that is, the *value,* the *numeral,* and the *word* representing the value.

The three sets of cards are used separately; first to be able to "count," then to relate the above to a numeral, and finally the third set above, using the word of value.

When teaching addition, have these cards available. The child can then add the number of dots required to get the sum of any two numbers. For example: *Two* plus *five* is the sum of *two dots* plus the sum of *five dots* on the five card. He gets the sum of *seven dots.*

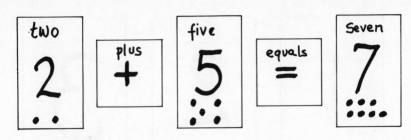

After the value of the numbers has been learned, equations can be introduced. One way to do this is to make up cards showing plus, minus, equals, etc. Cards with forms and signs in math need to have words on them as well to introduce the language of math visually. This is shown in the illustration above.

One method for form and shape learning is to have your child close his eyes and *finger* sandpaper numbers. You can then have him practice drawing these numerals with his paintbrush and water on the blackboard or with his crayon or a pencil on a piece of paper.

Another game for use in both letter form and number form is "Go Fishing" (for letters, sounds and words). As the child learns letters, numbers, and words, the fishing game may be used in a different way. A small index card with a name or number of the various things to be learned by memory will have a small paper clip attached to it. The child then fishes with his magnet, picks up the number, letter, or word with the magnet, and gets the number of points indicated on the card. He gets one point if he can say the word. This will be another memory reinforcer.

In order to teach ordinal number concepts, always emphasize the use of the words "first, second, third," etc., when playing a game. The use of these words is often confusing to a child who does not often associate the meaning of *1* with *first* and *2* with *second*. Make sure your game instructions are in simple, clear language that you should probably repeat and repeat.

The materials that you will need for this group of activities are found around most homes. For example:

(1) five or six spring-type clothespins. If you do not have the spring type, any clothespins will do.

(2) jacks and a ball

(3) a small paintbrush

(4) a paper cup

(5) plastic game chips or pennies

(6) a beanbag

(7) the lower part of two plastic egg cartons of the one dozen size. Cut off the tops and write the numbers one to twelve with a Magic Marker in the bottom of the little egg compartments, thirteen to twenty-four in the second carton.

(8) a Magic Marker

(9) a bag of balloons

(10) a candle at least twelve inches tall and a holder. Be sure that the candle is firmly placed in the candleholder.

(11) plastic container tops from the various foods that are available in the supermarkets, such as margarine containers or ice cream containers. Cut the centers out of these tops to make rings for a ring toss game.

(12) a hammer, nails with various size heads, and a piece of wood into which they can be hammered safely

(13) a magnet

(14) a piece of string

(15) paper clips that can be picked up with a magnet

(16) nuts, bolts, and tools that can be picked up with a magnet

(17) large inflatable ball or ordinary large ball (plastic or rubber)

ENCOURAGEMENT OF EYE-HAND COORDINATION — GAMES

There are many activities that can encourage a child's ability to use his eyes and his hands together. The combination of his eyes and hands working together is extremely important and basic to achievement in school and among peers on the game field. If a child lacks the ability to be able to reach his hands through space and grasp successfully for an object, he will have great difficulty in many areas. Try some of these games.

Beanbag Toss: The beanbags may be used in a number of ways. Beanbags can be tossed into any container available and a number of points can be gained for a successful toss. Beanbags can be tossed over the child's head and caught by the child himself. He can play toss with you or with one of his brothers or sisters. Note that he uses his dominant hand to throw the bag to you.

Egg Cartons can be used in a variety of ways:

As a counting frame: When scoring a game, place one chip in each numbered compartment to keep a cumulative check on the score. Different chips (blue or red) will differentiate the players' individual scores or can be used to teach odd and even.

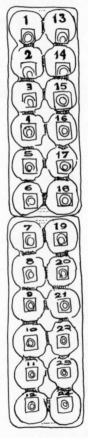

As a visual multiplier: Multiply by 2's, place a chip in each compartment representing a multiplier of 2 (2) (4) (6) (8) (10). Multiply by 3's (3) (6) (9) (12) (15), etc.

Sorting and categories: Have a preschooler sort objects into the compartments — screws, nuts, bolts, chips, clips, etc.

Go fishing (for younger children): Take your horseshoe-shaped magnet and tie it to a string. Place the many screws, nuts and bolts on the floor. Let the child go fishing with his magnet on a string. He may try to pick up as many of the small metal objects as possible.

PICK UP JACKS

For one-to-one correlation, *jacks* make a great game. *Pick Up Jacks:* If you have been able to obtain spring-type clothespins, spread the jack set out on the floor and let the child take the clothespin and try to pick up the jacks one by one. This is both a fine motor coordination and an eye-hand coordination reinforcer. Later on, of course, the child can use the whole set of jacks and the ball together and try to coordinate eye-hand and motor motions.

jacks

spring clothes pin

All of these games involve keeping score. It is through keeping score that counting can be reinforced in a very positive and natural manner.

Another method of teaching the additive function is to have each number represented by a block. To teach a young child the function of addition, add blocks in a cumulative vertical manner. The taller the tower, the higher the number. Avoid teaching addition in a horizontal direction. When taught in a vertical direction it can be seen and felt, and a visual picture can be associated with a fact to remember.

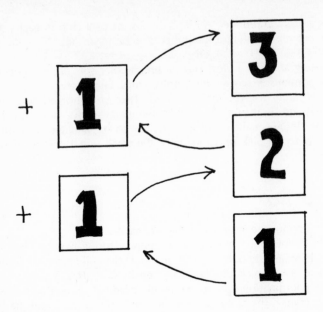

A COUNTING LINE

This is to be used by illustrating steps forward to represent the process of addition (adding to). Steps in the opposite direction represent taking away from a number.

The direction of the arrow represents the directional concept of positive and negative numbers. Movement to the right is positive; movement to the left is negative.

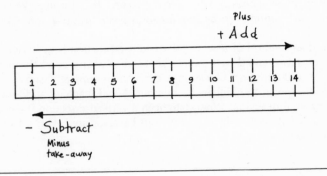

CONCEPT SKILLS (MATH ACTIVITIES)

DIRECTIONALITY

Why is a directional sense so important to your child? Directional sense is defined as an undertaking of his own body in relation to right and left, forward and backward, up and down, i.e., all the various directions a body will face. How does this relate to dominance problems? If your child indicates symptoms of mixed dominance, it is quite possible that he may have difficulty in orienting himself in space and in understanding direction. The right and left directional clues may be quite difficult for him and may require extra reinforcement. If this seems obvious in your child's case, try some of the following exercises.

Practice of left and right discrimination can be done in the home. When a child sets the table, he must observe that the fork goes on the left and the knife and spoon on the right. As he goes around the table, he must reverse his image in space and still put the fork on the left and the knife and spoon on the right.

In order to determine right and left consistently, it sometimes is necessary to use a Magic Marker to write R and L (right and left) on a child's hands or sneakers for a period of time. Then a daily exercise in playing Simon Says might be appropriate. For example:

"Simon Says"

Simon Says raise your right hand.

Simon Says raise your left hand.

Put your hands down.

When "Simon Says" does not precede your directions, the child should not follow the command.

A plastic sheeting can be taken and placed on a table. The child's hands can then be put palms down on the plastic sheeting and an outline drawn with a Magic Marker. The tracing of the right hand and the left hand can be pasted to your child's desk or wall until he has learned to match up his right and left hand and can clearly discriminate between them.

REVERSALS IN MATH

Just as directional learning is significant in learning to read words and spell them, so too directional learning plays a significant role in learning math. The child who has experienced difficulties in learning body direction and the relation of his body to things outside of his body in space will invariably have spatial difficulties. He may also perform the same kind of reversal and rotation errors in math that he does in other academic areas.

Moreover, in learning mathematical computational skill he must move from right to left for addition and subtraction:

$$\begin{array}{r} 72 \\ +51 \\ \hline \end{array} \qquad \begin{array}{r} 693 \\ -428 \\ \hline \end{array}$$

and multiplication:

$$\begin{array}{r} 32 \\ \times 12 \\ \hline \end{array}$$

and from left to right for division:

$$23\overline{)6431}$$

He must be able to process what he hears (auditory language) and understand the sequence of numbers as the teacher dictates them:

Three thousand four hundred and sixty-four

Is it 30464   or 3464   or 3644   or 3000600064?

This is much like the task of translating a foreign language for a child with auditory processing problems.

He may confuse the meaning of the words or transpose the numbers in the wrong sequence.

KEEPING NUMBERS IN COLUMNS
(SPATIAL DISORIENTATION)

Children need to use quadrant or graph paper on which to do their math whenever possible. The structure of boxes and lines enforces placing the numbers in columns. Thus correct addition, subtraction and multiplication is made easier. If such paper is not available, regular ruled paper held *sideways* so that the lines are vertical rather than horizontal is useful. Add the other lines if necessary. Encourage the use of such paper for all math computation.

							6	5	3	
							3	6	2	
						+	2	4	2	
						1	2	5	7	
	2	4	7							
−	1	3	5							
	1	1	2							
									3	
								+	2	
									5	

Often youngsters who have difficulty keeping numbers in columns to perform math computation also have some difficulty in deciding which direction math computation must go. They may add from left to right rather than right to left.

Our little pointer bird can be placed on the right side of the paper to indicate the place to begin:

845
+769

7456
670
+85364

85
×67

5 | 75689

An arrow can be drawn on each math paper until the direction of computation is overlearned.

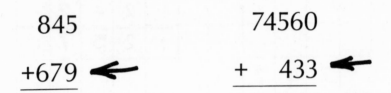

A window marker can be used to unclutter pages (as was mentioned in the section on reversals). These devices will make the child more secure in his sense of direction and he will be glad to dispense with them when they are no longer needed.

LEARNING THE CONCEPT WORDS:
MATH — THE "SECOND LANGUAGE"

Sometimes more than one expression can be used to say the same thing. To a child you can be teaching more than one problem. You must show that they mean the same thing.

(a) If you have 10 M&M's and I take away 5, how many will you have left to eat?

(b) If I have 10 M&M's and I subtract 5, how many will remain for you to eat?

The answer, of course, is five M&M's. When the child can understand that many problems using different vocabularies mean the same thing and can come up with the right answer, he may eat the five M&M's. This is an immediate, concrete reward for success.

When handing any object to your child always speak as follows:

(a) "Place these four spoons on the table, please."

(b) "Bring those two books over here, please."

This will help introduce the concept and the language meaning as early as possible. It will also help your child identify the names of the numerals. Always use concrete words when questioning your child.

(a) "Is John larger than Mary?"

(b) "Is John taller than Mary?"

(c) "Then Mary must be smaller than John."

(d) "Is Mary shorter than John?"

These questions will help the child understand the concept of relative size.

(a) "I have more in my glass of milk than you do."

(b) "You have had more of your milk; therefore you have less remaining in your glass."

(c) "How much money do you have for lunch?"

(d) "You have very little money remaining for lunch."

(e) "I have to put your team up at bat first, because they were up last yesterday."

(f) "See if the ball is inside the glove."

Use simple ideas such as:

(a) "How many bounces have I made with this ball?"

(b) "How many throws or how many catches?"

(c) "Is it more than Tommy did?"

(d) "How many cars, houses, etc.?"

(e) "How many classrooms in our school?"

(f) "Which floor has more classrooms; less classrooms?"

In order to help our children (and our students) learn and remember this special language, we utilized the answer sheet from the Boehm Test of Concepts[1] as a starting point. We would ask them to physically demonstrate the meaning of a word — not just to tell us with words. We are including that list for your use.

top	some, not	over	nearest
through	many	widest	second
away from	middle	most	corner
next to	few	between	several
inside	farthest	whole	behind
after	around	alike	almost
half	row	never	center
as many	different	beginning	other
below	not first or	always	right
forward	last	zero	every
	matches		
	medium-sized		

ABOUT MULTIPLICATION TABLES

The following table should be utilized after a child understands the concept of multiplication as a repeated process of addition. Do not hold a child back from handling multiplication or even division if he cannot recall the facts, but can understand the operation. One is a function of memory, the other of concepts and understanding. You can understand what $9 \times 7 = ?$ means but you may not be able to retrieve the answer out of your memory bank. Give him this table as a tool. Just as engineers have slide rules, statisticians have calculators, and researchers have computers or encyclopedias to remember for them, allow your child to use the table. Every time he traces down to seven and across to nine, he receives a visual reinforcement of the answer.

1	2	3	4	5	6	7	8	9	10	11	12
2	4	6	8	10	12	14	16	18	20	22	24
3	6	9	12	15	18	21	24	27	30	33	36
4	8	12	16	20	24	28	32	36	40	44	48
5	10	15	20	25	30	35	40	45	50	55	60
6	12	18	24	30	36	42	48	54	60	66	72
7	14	21	28	35	42	49	56	63	70	77	84
8	16	24	32	40	48	56	64	72	80	88	96
9	18	27	36	45	54	63	72	81	90	99	108
10	20	30	40	50	60	70	80	90	100	110	120
11	22	33	44	55	66	77	88	99	110	121	132
12	24	36	48	60	72	84	96	108	120	132	144

CONCEPT SKILLS (MATH ACTIVITIES)

Sometimes a deficit in arithmetic is obviously not a function of low intelligence, but rather a suggestion of some interference in dealing with recall of number facts, the relationship of numbers and language as symbols, and his ability to understand what is expected of him in dealing with the mathematical processes. Perhaps the instructional materials given to the student have been far too abstract and, therefore, somewhat meaningless for him to comprehend and incorporate. He may need a much more experiential approach; that is, he may need to touch, feel and actually experience relationships between numbers and number processes.

For example: Bill was still having considerable difficulty in retaining his multiplication and division facts. Bill had not developed the skill of learning isolated facts by rote memory. We took him back to the original concept of multiplication; that is, we had him develop a series of number strips on a small adding machine in which the printout would show that three plus three was equal to six, or two times three, that three plus three plus three was equal to nine, or the equivalent of three times three; and three plus three plus three plus three was equal to twelve, or the equivalent of four times three. Gradually as these sequential number strip tables were developed, Bill began to associate one number fact with the next number fact in a sequence.

The actual process of constructing his own math tables and the sequencing of the facts made it easier for him to develop memory through association and recall. Let's stay with Bill's problem for a moment. In eighth grade, to help him understand equations for his algebra homework, we used a small plastic children's scale. We developed a series of numbers and unknowns that would be placed on either side of the scale to help him to see that both sides of the scale must balance in order to develop an equation in which either knowns or unknowns were present. Bill began to understand why both sides of the equation had to have equivalent values when he could see them and work with them in a real concrete manner.

To teach the squaring of numbers, we gave Bill the following sheet upon which numerous circles were drawn. When asked to square the number three (that is, to multiply three by itself) he would physically draw a box around the number of zeroes that represented the squared number. He in turn could find the square root of the number.

We thank Alice Ansara for this suggestion.

$$4^2 = 16 \;,\quad 4 \times 4 = 16 \;,\quad \sqrt{16} = 4 \;.$$

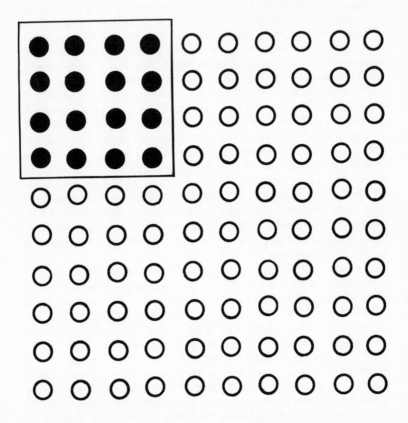

These are but a few of the types of techniques that helped Bill to understand arithmetic processes in a more concrete but mature fashion.

Now back to some basics. Here are some games having to do with directionality, organization, eye-hand coordination, and measurement meant to give you a small idea of what can be done at home.

There are many other aids in a home that can be utilized to encourage your child. The reading of labels can be a helpful reading practice. He can learn to repeatedly identify words by having to search out certain boxes or pans from the pantry shelf. The dusting of a room requires coordination when little objects are removed from the table. The tidying of a room requires visual perception to spot things that are out of order and which need to be correctly replaced. In order to do this, he must recall where they were in the first place.

Many tasks can also improve motor skills. Clipping laundry onto a clothesline with clothespins, mopping and sweeping the floor, helping to move furniture, helping to push a lawn mower, and raking leaves are all jobs which require motor coordination.

For eye-hand coordination and counting:

Ring Toss: Using the rings from the food container tops, make a game out of tossing them on the candles as a ring toss. Make sure the candle is firmly placed in the candleholder some distance away from the child. The child then tosses the plastic rings over the candleholder.

The legs of a chair turned upside down also make a great holder.

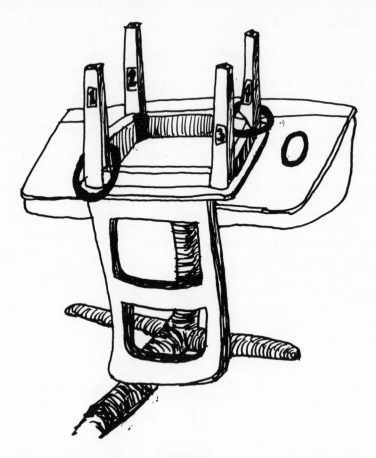

Write a different value for each leg, then add for individual scores.

Sorting and separating pairs of things gives your child experience both in examining the quality of things he is sorting and in learning how to multiply by two. If he sorts shoes or boots or a row of socks in pairs, he can then use those as multipliers of two:

"We have 6 pairs of shoes on the closet floor. How many do we have altogether?"

"6 sets of 2 equal 12." (For a third or fourth grader, show the example 6 × 2 = 12.)

"How many left shoes do we have?" Line up to his foot.

"How many right shoes do we have?" Line up to his foot.

AVOIDING THE "MAGIC CARPET" SYNDROME

Never assume that seeing a new place while traveling or seeing an exciting TV program means that your child truly understands what he is seeing or hearing. A place must be located on a map. Lines must be drawn from home to that place. Your child can draw those lines on a map, and maps are free at gas stations. He can then be the family navigator when you go on a trip. Ask your child questions about what he sees and hears along the way to a new place. This will increase his language and experience.

TABLE OF USEFUL INFORMATION

Remember the old black and white copybooks that we all carried? They contained a table similar to the one on page 214 for our use. Now, students are expected to recall all of this information without benefit of these tables in certain classes. Perhaps the old-fashioned technique was more realistic in its approach to memory and recall.

CATEGORIES — SORTING

Games can be utilized when going for a walk or taking a bicycle ride. Leaves can be picked up and categorized in a scrapbook. Sorting nuts, screws, and bolts into jars can be utilized as a visual perception and categorizing exercise too.

GAMES OF PLACES

Never take for granted that because a child travels with you he is gaining all the experience he needs. He must have things explained to him. When going to the grocery store, explain what happens in grocery stores. At the post office, explain where the letters go. At the bank, explain where his money is going. Teach him important addresses and phone numbers.

GAMES OF HOLIDAYS AND CALENDAR

Teach him the days of the week, the names of the months, and the seasons in a year. If you have difficulty, relate them to holidays

---

CONCEPT SKILLS (MATH ACTIVITIES)   213

USEFUL INFORMATION

MULTIPLICATION TABLE

1	2	3	4	5	6	7	8	9	10	11	12
2	4	6	8	10	12	14	16	18	20	22	24
3	6	9	12	15	18	21	24	27	30	33	36
4	8	12	16	20	24	28	32	36	40	44	48
5	10	15	20	25	30	35	40	45	50	55	60
6	12	18	24	30	36	42	48	54	60	66	72
7	14	21	28	35	42	49	56	63	70	77	84
8	16	24	32	40	48	56	64	72	80	88	96
9	18	27	36	45	54	63	72	81	90	99	108
10	20	30	40	50	60	70	80	90	100	110	120
11	22	33	44	55	66	77	88	99	110	121	132
12	24	36	48	60	72	84	96	108	120	132	144

Cubic Measure.

1728 cu. in._____1 cu. ft.
27 cu. ft._____1 cu. yd.
128 cu. ft. _____1 cord
1 cu. yd.____1 load (of earth, etc.)
24¾ cu. ft._____1 perch

Note: A cord of wood is a pile 8 ft. long, 4 ft. wide and 4 ft. high

A perch of stone varies in different parts of the country, but is usually considered as 1 rd. long, 1 ft. high and 1½ ft. thick.

Avoirdupois Weight

16 ounces make__1 pound
100 lbs. make _____1 cwt.
2000 pounds make__1 ton
24 grains__1 pennyweight

Troy Weight

20 pennyweight__1 ounce
12 ounces_____1 pound

Apothecaries' Weight _

20 grains make__1 scruple
3 scruples make__1 dram
8 drams make___1 ounce
12 ounces make__1 pound

Miscellaneous Weights

1 keg of nails_____100 lbs.
1 bbl. of salt_____280 lbs.
1 bbl. of Flour__196 lbs.
1 bbl. of Pork or Beef weighs____200 lbs.
1 firkin of Butter__56 lbs.

Square Measure.

144 sq. in. make__1 sq. ft.
9 sq. ft. make_____1 sq. yd.
30¼ sq. yds.____1 sq. rod
160 sq. rods_____1 acre
640 acres____1 sq. mile, or 1 section
36 sq. miles___1 township

Miscellaneous Cubic Measure.

231 cu. in. make__1 gallon
2150 cu. in._____1 bushel
40 cu. ft.____1 ton shipping

Dry Measure.

2 pints make_____1 quart
8 quarts make_____1 peck
4 pecks make____1 bushel

Liquid Measure.

4 gills make_____1 pint
2 pints make_____1 quart
4 quarts make___1 gallon
31½ gallons_____1 barrel
2 barrels, or 63 gallons, make _____1 hogshead

Miscellaneous Measures.

12 units make____1 dozen
12 dozen make____1 gross
12 gross_____1 great gross
20 units make_____1 score

Miscellaneous Long Meas.

4 inches make_____1 hand
6 feet make_____1 fathom
120 faths.__1 cable length
1.15 miles, nearly__1 knot

Surveyor's Long Measure

7.92 inches make___1 link
25 links make_____1 rod
4 rods or 100 links_1 chain
80 chains__ _____1 mile

Long Measure.

12 inches make_____1 foot
3 feet make_____1 yard
5½ yds or 16½ ft. make 1 rod, pole or perch
320 rods, or 5280 feet make_____1 mile
8 furlongs make___1 mile
40 rods make___1 furlong
69 1-6 miles. ___1 degree

Paper Measure.

24 sheets make_____1 quire
20 quires make_____1 ream
2 reams make___1 bundle
5 bundles make_____1 bale
1 bale contains 200 quires, or 4800 sheets.
480 sheets_____1 ream

For convenience in counting, 500 sheets are more often called a ream, and the word quire is used only for the folded note-paper.

Measure of Time.

60 seconds make__1 minute
60 minutes_____1 hour
24 hours_____1 day
7 days_____1 week
30 days_____1 commercial month
12 months_____1 year
360 days_1 commercial yr.
365 days__1 common year
366 days_____1 leap year
100 years_____1 century

United States Money.

10 mills make_____1 cent
10 cents_____1 dime
10 dimes_____1 dollar
10 dollars_____1 eagle

English Money.

4 farthings_____1 penny
12 pence_____1 shilling
20 shillings__1 pound, Sterling

or specific times that he can recall, such as Christmas in the winter when there is snow, and Easter in the spring when there are flowers. A special TV program that is on Friday night may relate to Friday. Put a calendar on the wall large enough for him to reach, and circle and color in important days as a reminder. He will learn sequencing of numbers, the days of the week, and the dates, from the calendar.

KINDS OF MEASURING

Teach him to observe speed on a speedometer; time on a clock; distance on a yardstick, ruler, or mileage guage; temperature on a thermometer; weight on a bathroom scale. All of these things cannot be taken for granted with a learning-disabled child. Let him measure the furniture in his room, compare his weight to an adult's, differentiate the level in the thermometer on a warm day as opposed to a cool day. Let him help to bake a cake, measure out the portions *slowly* and *carefully,* saying the amounts as he does it.

LEARNING IN THE KITCHEN

The kitchen is a fine place for learning to take place. Simple jobs help promote fine motor coordination. For example: rolling out cookie dough or cracker crumbs with a rolling pin is fun and promotes coordination of the two hands; using a cookie cutter to cut out shapes is a lesson in simple form perception and form constancy; learning to peel potatoes and using an eggbeater or hand mixer is helpful and requires coordination. Following a recipe is a way of learning to sequence activities in a logical step-by-step progression:

1) Assemble all ingredients.
2) Gather all the tools you need.
3) Open all cans and boxes you need.
4) Grease your pot or pan.
5) Heat the oven.
6) Measure (a mathematical exercise).
7) Mix the ingredients (if left-handed, stir clockwise; if right-handed, stir in a counterclockwise direction).
8) Pour into the pan.

9) Time the cooking . . . watching the clock.
10) When cooked and cooled, cut into pieces (fractions).

So-called clumsy, disorganized children often don't get the chance to measure, pour, stir, or slice when their mothers cook because they make such a mess. They need to handle such tasks more than other so-called normally coordinated children.

SCIENCE IN THE KITCHEN

Condensation of moisture, when cooking is taking place, can be explained. Facts about soluble substances that dissolve are apparent. Mixtures, compounds, and all kinds of chemical combinations are all important in cooking, and a child can observe them and work with them. Even without the vocabulary of chemistry, the experience of seeing and observing these things lays the groundwork to understanding them.

For a learning experience, use things that you have around your house or in your car. We have mentioned the use of egg cartons or empty food cans for games involving eye-hand coordination. You may also use wastepaper baskets, plastic containers, pegs or pennies for coordination and counting; small wooden sticks with the ends broken off make good counting sticks. All these things that can be found in your home can teach your child concepts with a game.

When your child is ready for fractions, have him cut out paper plates that you have helped him mark into halves, thirds, quarters, fifths, etc. Make sure that he sees the paper plate in terms of a whole plate and have him put it back together again. Mark the sections with the appropriate fractions, $\frac{1}{2}$, $\frac{1}{4}$, and so on. By having him compare the size of the sections, help him to understand the difference in relationship between one-half and one-quarter. Two-thirds makes a larger piece than one-half of the plate. Now he will be ready for fraction concepts when they are taken up in school. He will have less difficulty with abstract ideas if he can visualize concrete objects when he computes.

Mathematics can be learned through many things we do: traveling, measuring, shopping, budgeting, pairing socks, setting the dinner table, scoring games, and so many more. Often golden opportunities are overlooked by parents because of the annoyance of

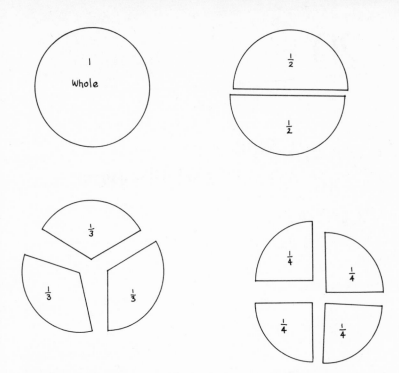

answering the multitude of questions. We emphasize that real experience is the best teacher and daily learning opportunities are there to be exploited.

20

Concept Skills
(Word Attack and Phonics
Activities)

Learning to read is one of the most important tasks any child will try to accomplish during his years in school. If he gets off to a good start, learning to read will be a process that is uneventful and without unhappy incidents. However, if he can't learn with ease and fails, his frustrations will color his attitude toward himself, and all learning tasks that follow. Thus the experience, and the kind of environment in which he learns, is of prime importance. This is especially significant for the child who appears to be developing more slowly than his peers, or who has had some diagnosable learning dysfunction.

Primary to the teaching of reading is preparing the child through readiness activities. When working on preskills there are a number of suggestions that might be followed:

1) Never assume that the child fully comprehends what is expected of him. Confusion and misunderstanding often occur.

2) Each step in the learning process must be spelled out for the child so that he understands and can follow through independently.

3) Try to limit the number of stimuli, so as to help the child focus on the task. Attention lost through distraction is difficult to regain.

4) Set realistic goals so that a child can accomplish the task. Success is the key to his attitude about himself and the work you ask him to do.

5) Be aware of exactly what you wish your child to learn.

6) Give instant feedback of success, in the form of praise or reward. Children who have failed need tangible evidence of their newfound success.

Readiness activities are not just a question of maturity. Time passes and a child grows older and better able to handle certain jobs by virtue of his growth. However, in dealing with the readiness for reading and other learning tasks, a child may not become more ready just by virtue of being older. He may need to pass through certain prescribed training activities apart from his growth over time.

Readiness activities must be a highly structured instructional program to give a child experiences that provide the training necessary to the development of basic skills.

A good example of this is the tendency to reverse letter forms that are similar in shape but rotated or inverted in their direction in space. Most often the **b–p–d–g–q** are prime examples of this problem. If a child has not yet dealt with his own sense of body directionality successfully, growth alone will not necessarily correct his difficulties. He may need the kind of directional, reversal training techniques mentioned in a previous chapter, Overcoming Reversals, pp. 160–171. Retention in grade three will not necessarily correct the lag in skill development. He will still need the kind of meaningful experiences designed to help him sort out his sensations and put them in spatial and directional order. Without understanding what he sees, hears, touches, smells, and tastes, he cannot integrate these sensations into his information bank for later use. Without organization, his learning is fragmented and confused. Without help he may be willing and able but not ready. Without readiness he cannot do what we ask of him!

Readiness, willingness, and ability are not enough. Your child must be taught basic phonics, or the sounds that letters make. Without these skills, reading each new word becomes a task akin to "reinventing the wheel." Phonics are the basic tools upon which reading skills are built.

MUCH ADO ABOUT PHONICS

How can you help your child to learn phonic skills?

In order to read, your child must be able to make consistent correlation between sounds and symbols. When he sees a letter he must be able to make an instant connection between that letter and a sound that he remembers having heard. We call this process *sound-symbol association*.

For example when he sees **p** as in **p**at, he must be able to pull out the sound of **p** as a separate sound (or phoneme) he has heard.

If he confuses the letter **p** with another letter that looks similar, he may say a **b** = **b**at, **d** = **d**at or a **g** = **g**et.

He cannot sound out new words correctly until he can make a *consistent, automatic association* of single letters and sounds.

The problem becomes more complicated when he tries to associate newly learned groups of letters with sounds. Now he may have to identify patterns of two or more letters with sounds.

An example of this would be:

> **th** as in **th**ing
> **sh** as in **sh**ip
> or
> **ai** as in r**ai**n
> **oa** as in b**oa**t.

Frequently confusion arises for the child who has had some minor perceptual difficulties. If recalling a single sound-symbol association is difficult, then recalling the sound of two or more letter symbols is much more complex.

When he deals with a two-letter pattern, there are two-letter forms that must be correctly identified, for example, a **t** and an **h.** When these letters were found alone they made the sound of

t as in top
and
h as in hat

Now we are telling him that these two sounds are quite different when they are found in a pair.

t as in top
h as in hat
th as in thing

He must remember the shape of each letter. He must make a consistent association of sound-shape. He must remember that the letter sounds different when it is found with a twin **th**. And he must remember the order in which the letters are found: **th** is not the same as **ht**.

The next step in the process becomes more complicated. He must be able to blend the **t, h** or **th** with other sounds to identify words and read them, e.g.,

top,
thing,
hop.

The English language is chaotic. When we try to find rules that will always apply, we see that there are always many exceptions; and many letters change their sounds when found in certain positions or in combinations with other sounds.

For example:

t says **t** as in top
t says another sound in *thing* when combined with **h** (soft sound)
t says a third sound in *this* when combined with **h** (hard sound)

h says **h** as in *hat*
h is silent in *hour*
h says **f** when found with **gh** in *enough*
but
h is silent when found with **gh** as in *thought*
h says **ch** when found in combination with **c** as in *cheese*

---

or

h says **sh** when found in combination with **s** as in *ship*

h says **f** when it is found with **p** as in *phone,* **ph** as in *phonics*

We could go on demonstrating more and more examples of such "orthographic chaos" to you. But it is unnecessary. Reading the English language is confusing for many children. It can only be learned by simplifying the elements and overteaching them.

Complete words are too complicated for many youngsters to absorb. Children need to have the process of *word attack* broken down into its simplest component parts.

Moreover, we must *overteach* each separate sound element, allowing children to overlearn them in a logical step-by-step procedure. Often a classroom teacher cannot devote the necessary time to take each child through such an "overlearning" process unless she is provided with teacher aides, a decrease in class size, and individual training devices.

Schools are hiring more teacher aides, unpaid volunteers, and peer tutors to assist these children. These help fill the gap, but the available number of teacher aides is strictly limited by budget. Teachers must often share aide time. Volunteers must be trained and peer tutors cannot meet the total need.

A parent must *supplement* what is taught at school. Education cannot be a 9 a.m. to 3 p.m. proposition for any child! However, extra assistance is especially necessary for the child who has had difficulty learning to read, write, spell, or perform math computation, whether he has a diagnosed learning disability or not.

If your child has normal visual acuity, normal hearing, and normal intelligence and has no extreme emotional problem, he *can* learn to read and perform other school tasks given:

    a. time and patience,

    b. a simplified approach,

    c. assistance at home as well as at school,

    d. techniques appropriate to his learning style,

    e. a game approach to learning,

    f. a sense of success rather than frustration.

The first step in this home-game approach is the determination of how your child learns best (see pages 81–83 and 87–88, learning style, and checklist).

The second is the making of a simple checklist of the sound patterns that give your child difficulty when he tries to read. Often such a checklist is available at school. Many teachers keep an on-going record of word analysis skills as exhibited by children in their classes. If such a checklist is available, the process is simplified for you. If, however, such a checklist is not available, the following list might be used. Ask your child's teacher to check off the sounds she thinks are giving your child difficulty.

PARENTS INDIVIDUAL PHONICS CHECKLIST — LEVEL I

My child can recognize the following sounds:

Consonants	Can name them from hearing them sounded (1)	Can write them from dictation (2)	Can read them in words (3)
b			
d			
f			
k			
j			
m			
p			
n			
r			
s			
t			

v			
w			
y			
h			
x			
hard c (cat)			
hard g (gun)			
soft c (ice)			
soft g (age)			
qu (quit)			
z			

If the child is having difficulty identifying single consonants, it is helpful to take three-by-five cards and draw one letter on the unlined side of each card so that he has a letter-recognition deck:

b	d	f	k	j	m	p	n	r	s
t	v	w	y	h	x	c	g	z	qu

Keep these cards in the same sequence as the phonics checklist above.

Directions:

(1) sample question: Parent says, "What is the name of
Column 1   the letter that says buh as in 'boy'?"
      Child says "b."

(2) sample question: Parent says, "Write the first letter
Column 2   you hear in the word 'boy.' "

(3) sample question: Parent says, "Can you read this word —
Column 3   'boy'? Can you give me the first sound
      that is in that word?"

To estimate your child's word-attack skills, whether he can identify the sounds that the single consonant makes, you might try the following game of Bingo. Give your child the Bingo card marked child's Test Level I. Use Bingo game chips or tokens. (Circles of cardboard or pennies will serve also as game chips.) The Bingo games that follow are played the way regular Bingo is played, any five spaces in a row constituting a win. Whenever the child has covered five spaces in a row, he must read aloud what is written in those spaces in order to win. If he identifies the letter or words correctly, he wins.

A small prize might provide added motivation to continue playing the game. This prize can be any kind of reward. A reward may be any concrete thing that gives your child a feeling of successful feedback. This can range from raisins and peanuts to a star or smiling face pasted or drawn in a score card or chart.

Step I. Parent says: "We are going to play Bingo. We are going to use words rather than numbers. When I tell you a letter to find, put one of your chips on any word that starts with that letter. When you get five in a row you have Bingo!" (Parent shows the child that five in a row may be gained horizontally, vertically or diagonally by sweeping his finger across a horizontal line on the card, a vertical line and a diagonal line.)

Say: "Let's try one together! Can you find a word that starts with the letter 'b'?" If the child identifies the word "bat" immediately, go on to Step II.

If there is some doubt, show the child where the answer is . . . bat . . . and then try another example.

"Can you find a word that starts with the letter 'f'?"
Give examples until the child has caught on to the idea of the game. It may be necessary to show the child a card with the letter on it the first time the game is played — **b d f** set of letter cards. (See page 224.)

"Here is the letter 'f' — can you find this letter on your card?"
If the child cannot identify the letters even after a stimulus card has been shown, do not go on with the game. It will be too frustrating. Return to games that teach form constancy (pages 155–159). Children need a great deal of practice with form constancy before they can identify letters from a total page of symbols, as required in this Bingo game.

bat	fan	jam	man	van
wig	kick	tip	quick	zip
not	sob	a,i,o,u,e LEVEL I	got	cob
rub	gull	hub	dug	rug
yell	gem	pet	cent	less

TROUBLESHOOTING FROM LEVEL I BINGO

When a child makes certain specific kinds of errors, it is usually indicative of a particular kind of problem. Some problems that arise are:

a) *Difficulty with figure-ground.* If your child seems able to recognize the letters separately when you show them on a card, **b,** but seems confused when looking at the whole Bingo card, he may be having difficulty in separating out specific figures from the many figures in the background. Try to block out all the words except those in one row across. The card will look like this:

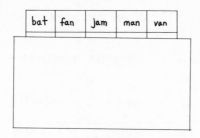

| bat | fan | jam | man | van |

Then let him find the letters without the whole card exposed. If this helps him, he may need uncluttered worksheets; pages cut in half; less work per page; or a window marker to block out too many stimuli. This "uncluttering" of his work pages may help him handle reading more efficiently.

b) *Difficulty with directionality or constancy of forms.* Suppose your child repeatedly identifies letters as their mirror image or inverted forms. For example, he might select

d as in **d**ug for the letter **b**	**d-b**
w as in **w**ig for the letter **m**	**w-m**
q as in **q**uick for the letter **g**	**q-g**
f as in **f**an for the letter **t**	**f-t**

When this occurs repeatedly, it suggests that a child has not fully learned body directionality and the direction of things outside of his own body. This shows up in the constant reversal of the direction of letter forms. He is confused when he must constantly think of look-alike forms and recall their direction.

Such problems are extremely common in younger children and often persist to the end of the first grade. However, if such problems persist beyond the first grade, some further assistance should be given to your child with emphasis upon exercises in form constancy and form direction (pages 155–159).

Do not move on to checklist II or level II until the single consonant sounds have been learned. Return to work in letter and form constancy until the child can consistently identify the letter forms from name and sound, can consistently write the letter forms from name and sound, and can read letter forms from sight stimulus.

When this is completed, you can move on to checklist II and level II in phonics training.

INDIVIDUAL PHONICS CHECKLIST LEVEL II
(Use Bingo card level II)

My child can recognize the following sounds (blends and digraphs)

	Can identify them from hearing them	Can write them from dictation	Can read them in words
sh			
th			
ch			
tch			
wh			
sw			
cr			
br			
dr			
fr			
gr			
pr			
bl			
fl			

cl			
gl			
pl			
sl			
sc			
sk			
sm			
tw			
sn			
spl			

BINGO GAME — TESTING FOR LEVEL II BLENDS AND DIGRAPHS
(Use with individual phonics checklist level II)

ship	thin	chap	match	wheel
swing	creep	bring	drink	free
grim	prom	LEVEL II	blink	flap
clam	gleam	plan	slim	scum
skip	small	twin	snip	split

PARENT'S INDIVIDUAL PHONICS CHECKLIST — LEVEL III
(Use Bingo cards for Testing level I)

My child can recognize the following sounds:

VOWELS	can identify them from hearing them at the beginning of a word	can identify them from hearing them at the middle of a word

Parent dictates the word in parentheses and the child identifies vowel.

a as in apple	(**a**m)	(p**a**t)
i as in indian	(**i**n)	(s**i**p)
o as in ostrich	(**o**n)	(h**o**p)
u as in umbrella	(**u**nder)	(r**u**n)
e as in elephant	(**e**gg)	(g**e**t)

My child can recognize the following sounds:

	can write them from dictation of words	can read them in words (child reads the word)

Parent dictates word and child writes vowel.

a as in mat	(s**a**p)	(r**a**n)
i as in hip	(f**i**g)	(p**i**n)
o as in cop	(l**o**t)	(h**o**p)

u as in rub
  (h**u**m)   (t**u**b)

e as in wed
  (m**e**t)   (r**e**d)

Alternate Words for Vowels: Dictate these words and have child tell you
the vowel he hears, write the vowel he hears, write the complete word

a	i	o	u
cap	fin	rob	muck
rap	slip	crop	club
swap	flit	block	slum

WORDSCOPE

These can be made to learn words and review phonetic patterns.
Some children have trouble separating figure from background
and, therefore, have difficulty reading words from a list. The review list should be given to them through the use of a wordscope
so that they can see only one word at a time. This can be purchased or you can make it yourself.

Instructions for Making a Wordscope

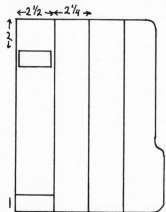

Use a standard manila folder:
1. Measure 2½ inches from the
   folder edge and cut a strip the
   length of the folder.
2. Open flat and cut a window 2
   inches from the top on the right
   half of the strip. It should be
   large enough to expose one
   word at a time. See Illustration
   1.

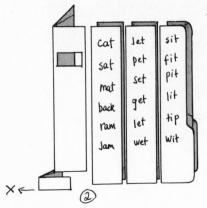

3. Tape the open sides together. Cut 1 inch off the bottom of the scope. The wordscope should be at least 1 inch shorter than the strip. See Illustration 2.

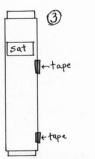

4. Use the rest of the manila folder to cut strips that will pull through the wordscope.
5. Use a pica or large type typewriter to type review lists on these strips. Be sure that the words are double- or triple-spaced so that only one word at a time is exposed through the window. See Illustration 3.

The three-letter words on the preceding list are typed in a primer type on a strip of manila paper or written with thick Magic Marker on a chart for group teaching.

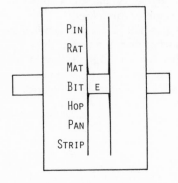

Draw two vertical lines parallel to the list and to the right of it — wide enough for the letter **e** to be inserted. Slit the lines dot to dot as illustrated. Insert the strip to expose the letter **e** printed in the center in red. The child reads the word, pulls the strip to expose the letter **e** next to the word, and then read the new word. First the word is read without the **e**, then with the **e.**

The above item can be bought from the Educators Publishing Service, Inc., or be made as illustrated above.

Sentences for Dictation and Reading — These should depend upon the sounds being taught or reviewed.

E.g.: teaching short vowels   **a** as in **a**pple   **o** as in **o**strich
                                        i as in **i**gloo   **u** as in **u**mbrella
                                        e as in **e**lephant

apple

elephant

igloo

ostrich

umbrella

To review basic sounds level one, two, or three, dictate short sentences of gradually increasing length.

1. Jan got a bit.
2. You can fix the tap with tape.
3. Jan hid and made Jane hide.
4. Did Sam plan to take a plane?
5. The gap in the hill made them gape.
6. Pat got a kit to make a kite.

Try to provide picture cards to associate the sounds that are being learned.

Here is another way to review phonics — it's easy, and fun too!

Making Word Wheels. Materials you will need:

1. Plain white paper plates
2. Brass paper fasteners
3. Scissors
4. Magic Markers — red and black

1) Cut off the border around one of the paper plates (see Figure I).

2) Write a word-family pattern on this plate as shown in Figure I. Sample families are (use red marker for these):

at	it	ot	ut	et
ap	ip	op	up	ep
ag	ig	og	um	em
am	im	om	ug	eg

3) Take a brass fastener and make a hole in the center of the cut paper plate. Now place this plate over the center of a second paper plate. Push the fastener through the center of both plates so that one is directly over the middle of the other. Bend ends of fastener.

4) Rotate the smaller plate or wheel over the outer one. As you rotate it, put letters on the outer or larger (plate) wheel. See Figures II and III. (Use black marker for these outer letters.)

5) Finally draw an arrow under one complete word on the wheel,

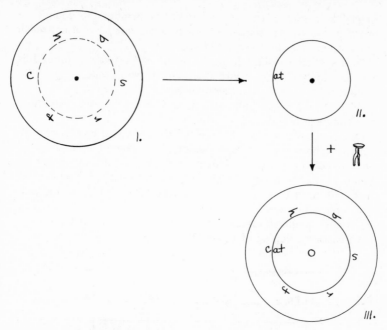

I.

II.

III.

so that your child will know where to start turning his word wheel by lining up the two parts of the arrow. (See Figure III.)

6) The wheel is complete. Now have your child rotate it to practice the words. A special prize upon completion of each wheel is always helpful. (See list of phonics in Figure II for patterns that can be put on wheels.)

When a youngster exhibits a weak memory for sequencing of letters at an early age (often seen as a spelling or word recall problem), the same problem may continue into adolescence. The lag persists and often is called "carelessness" in the older child. It really is more important to analyze the kinds of mistakes he makes rather than the number of mistakes he makes.

Random errors are often indicative of poor memory and poor attention to detail. Errors of letter transposition (*gril* for *girl* or *irrevelant* for *irrelevant*) often indicate a poor memory for sequences, an earlier directional problem. Phonetic respelling of words on the other hand may indicate an auditory-to-visual recall problem. An example of such an error would be the spelling of *special* as *speshull*. The youngster can remember the sounds he heard in the proper sequence, but he does not have visual recall of a pattern of letters to spell that sound.

Poor spellers can take heart, however: Mark Twain is quoted as having said he "never could trust a man who couldn't spell the same word at least three different ways!"

What do we do to help such an adolescent besides decorating his paper with blood-red correction marks?

One suggested approach is the teaching of visual groups of symbols by other than just rote memory. We attempt to give him a structure of recall to help him hold these difficult patterns in his memory. We teach him the six main syllable patterns that he will be called upon to identify within words. When he learns the patterns of syllables and the rules that apply to their use and spelling, the English language assumes some logic for him rather than being just a chaotic grouping of letters.

na____	ra____	sta____	sec____	inspec____
correc____	fac____	trac____	frac____	fric____
dic____	dic____ary	ti-ci-si FREE	Mis____	ces____
fis____	politi____	reac____	na____al	tor____
por____	omis____	na____alism	collec____	commis____

When we examine the illustration above we can see that there are letters omitted from each of the twenty-four spaces for words provided on the Bingo card. The center space (three across and three down) tells the youngster the kind of sound pattern that is missing from each word. The choice is limited to two or three patterns that are especially confusing, visually or phonetically. In this case the sound that is made by all three patterns is the sound of the letters **sh**. It is made by **ti, ci,** and **si.** These three patterns are all nonphonetic, that is, they are not spelled the way they sound.

The parent can actually teach the more difficult spelling patterns with such an activity or game. The parent dictates the twenty-four words on the card. He does this out of sequence, so that the youngster must identify the first syllable of the word from what he hears and then decide how to spell the omitted syllable. Some control over the choices of spelling is obvious. The three nonphonetic patterns are **ti, si,** and **ci** and the final syllables all have the sound of "shun" (spelled "tion," or "sion") and "shan" (spelled "cian").

The game works as follows:

The parent says the following words. After each word is said the child writes the missing letters. After the game all words are read aloud and spelling is corrected. The child should be encouraged to correct his words whenever possible. Making a visual comparison of the word list and his own spelling will give him practice in visual recognition of the word and the correct spelling.

nation	ration	commission	torsion	friction
diction	correction	reaction	national	fission
cession	politician	traction	collection	section
portion	inspection	dictionary	station	fraction
faction	omission	nationalism	mission	

As the student learns to identify the parts of words as logical pieces in the puzzle of language he also is taught the meanings of these parts (prefixes, suffixes, roots) and how these meanings change in usage. He is taught to spell words in groupings in which only one syllable changes at any one time, so that there is less that is unpredictable and changing.

By grouping words into families in this manner, we take away the need to remember unrelated letters in a series. Each new word no longer requires him to "reinvent the wheel" when recalling it.

An example of such word groupings is given below.

Prefix: *sub* (definition: under, from under, or less than normal)

sub tropic	*sub* mit	*sub* order	*sub* scribe
tropical	mission	ordinate	scriber

nation	traction	section	friction	mission
omission	ration	inspection	fraction	cession
politician	station	FREE	diction	fission
portion	fraction	correction	dictionary	national
torsion	collection	reaction	Commission	nationalism

Through grouping we have attempted to give these words some order and organization and therefore the words can be identified more readily, understood more easily, and some similarities observed within the words for spelling purposes.

As spelling rules are taught, language will assume a more orderly structure for a youngster. He is then given tools of understanding to compensate for the lack of good memory.

Complicated words must always be broken down into their component parts so that he can be taught to see small words and word parts that are familiar within unfamiliar words. The youngster who cannot recognize the parts within whole words needs specific help in breaking words down. Sometimes a window marker helps to blot out the extra letters so that he can learn to look for the parts within the word: for example, the word *remember* is better seen when a window marker is used to blot out extra stimuli. Although the student usually protests that he does not need such "aids" to help him, the success they bring speaks for itself. Often the parent sees such a child struggling and needs to step in and show him ways to make his life less complicated when meeting difficult demands.

A simple suggestion that looks much like good common sense may be overlooked by the teacher in the crush of seeing 140 youngsters per day in the secondary school. A parent may need to make concrete suggestions to a subject teacher that will help his own youngster make some headway in a difficult class.

We mulled over the reactions of teachers when we found it necessary to make some specific suggestions concerning modifications for our son Ira. We found the teachers responsive and anxious to make these modifications when they were feasible.

When our son's reading speed was very slow and functionally a few years below level, we suggested that he be given high-interest, less demanding reading than the class, so that he could meet the demands of any assignment. If this was not possible, we asked that he be able to read less per night, or utilize a tape for reading and listening simultaneously.

When Richard could not meet the demands of the math homework within a reasonable time, we asked that he be allowed to do half of the examples required. If he did not keep his numbers in columns we requested that he be given examples on plain lined paper turned sideways to help him structure his work. We also asked that the teacher show him the type of error he had made rather than just marking the example wrong. If the error was one of computation, he would understand where it was made. If, however, it was one of transposing numbers or copying them in the wrong order, he must be helped to recognize it as an error of copying and sequence, not one of multiplication or addition. When he could not remember multiplication facts due to extremely poor retention, we asked that he be allowed to use a 10×10 multiplication square. Teachers may need to be reminded that no architect would work without his graph paper, no engineer would work without his slide rule, no department store allows its employees to add up all purchases with pencil and paper without rechecking on an adding machine.

What appears to a parent to be a simple modification of demands may not be obvious to a teacher who sees so many youngsters in one day. He may need to have the reasons for such modification pointed out to him. Most of these suggestions cost nothing but are priceless in the message that they convey to your child.

They say to him that someone cares enough to make special plans for him, and considers him important enough to allow for his individual needs.

Your child may protest and say: "I can take care of it myself." Despite these protests he knows you will go in to school and fight for his rights, support him when he is wrong, and take the time to go to bat for him whenever necessary. In spite of their initial protests most teenagers respond to this kind of support by saying, "My mom and dad are OK — they understand what I do and they want to help!"

Don't wait for your teenager to tell *you* that he knows you understand him. That may never happen. But he will think it and may say it to others, though never to you. The so-called lack of communication among the generations may just be one of temporary short circuit.

Conclusion

Conclusion is a word that is generally defined as "the end; close; the final part." Is this the end or the beginning for the parent who can recognize, accept, and support his child despite his unique problems? The end must be a new beginning!

As Goethe, the noted eighteenth-century German poet, once wrote: "Treat people as if they were what they ought to be and you help them to become what they are capable of being."

We must treat our learning-disabled youngsters in this way. We must help them feel like whole people, winners despite their individual handicaps. Our friend, ten-year-old Jimmy, a victim of cerebral palsy, saw his crutches as "wings" — while others saw them as impediments.

They pass before us, a parade of youngsters, from four to thirty-four years old; students with whom we have worked as diagnosticians, tutors, consultants, and our own sons to whom we have been parents as well. Their problems varied but many things are the same.

Let us describe just one small freckle-faced, blue-eyed boy who would run and never walk. He might bump into things as he went, breaking treasures, unmindful of the havoc he created. He never seemed to appear the way a proud mother wanted her "special boy" to look. His face and hands were dirty most of the time, and mustard, ketchup, and chocolate stains often decorated his newly washed shirts.

Could any mother communicate approval to this small tornado of arms and legs, screams and cries, torn pants and patches, chaos and disorder?

Could any father praise this son who had repeatedly failed at school? The story was always the same:

"He really must settle down and pay attention."

"In order to learn one must listen."

"To remember one must study."

Could he ever be the success his father had become? Could he pull himself up by his own bootstraps and make it in the real world? Of course he could:

"If only he would try harder!"

"If Mother wouldn't go so easy on him!"

"If only the school would give him more help!"

"If only he would listen to us!"

So it goes. The names and faces are different, but the story is often the same, so reminiscent of our own feelings and frustrations as parents of learning-disabled youngsters.

Time and experience have taught us that these kids were often massively unready for what was expected of them when they entered school. From the very beginning they appeared out of "sync" with the educational environment.

As Ira told us: "I wouldn't sit in the circle when I was in kindergarten and from that time on it seemed as if I was always looked upon as different.

"Even in high school I felt that way. After attending three different schools I didn't have enough credits to graduate with my class. To finish I would have been in high school until I was over twenty. I'd had it and felt that no one treated me as a whole person. There was a school psychologist who understood how I felt. We talked about the High School Equivalency Exam, because he knew that I just wouldn't sit through two more years in that kind of school. I studied for the exam and passed it on the first try and they told me I had passed right away and shook my hand, like they cared. Now I'm beginning to feel like a person."

Kids don't grow out of unreadiness, they just continue to lag behind their age group all along the way. If we could just forget their chronological ages, they might seem on a level with a group of youngsters two to three years younger.

"Truly . . . readiness [for education] is the life experience which a child brings into the classroom." So says Harold Solan in his introduction to *The Psychology of Learning and Reading Difficulties*. If we accept Dr. Solan's definition it follows that parents must help to make these life experiences meaningful and appropriate to education. To do this they need direction.

Question: Where shall a child gain this life experience throughout his growing years?

Answer: In the home.

Question: Who shall guide and direct the experience so that it can be channeled into a supportive educational program?

Answer: The parents.

Question: Who shall give the parents direction to help them make these home experiences educationally meaningful?

Answer: The school personnel whenever possible.

Question: Who shall help the parents if school personnel are not available to them?

Answer: The parent must help himself, by structuring the home so that it becomes a learning environment appropriate to the child's needs.

Question: What should be the role of the parents, schools and the children themselves?

Answer: The child must be "ready, willing and able" to learn. The parent must be supportive, accepting, and tolerant of his child's individual strengths and weaknesses. The school must provide a structure within which attention is paid to alternative programs to satisfy individual needs of children, individual talents of teachers.

In this book we have tried to clarify the basic causes of learning-disability problems and keep parents aware of current medical and educational research. We have tried to organize this information so that a parent can understand it and utilize the information, applying it to his own child's educational style.

In the book *Cradles of Eminence* by Victor and Mildred Goertzel, the suggestion is made that education at home, directed by parents, played a significant role in the lives of many of the outstanding personalities studied. The hand that rocked the cradle was also a source of stimulation and nurture in the growth of these outstanding personalities.

Frequently we are able to observe youngsters during their educational careers. We have noticed that there is a high correlation between a child's success in individualized remedial programs and the degree of direct involvement shown by his parents. This does not necessarily mean direct teaching on the part of the parent. Instead something far less tangible is present in the home environment of these learning-disabled youngsters.

The home environment appears to provide sensitivity to the problems of daily coping experienced by these kids. This sensitivity is coupled with consistent handling. These parents appear to be able to apply predictable penalties to the behavior problems of their children. The penalties appear to be reasonable and appropriate and the youngsters always seem to know what to expect when dealing with their parents. These youngsters seem to sense the support that they are receiving at home, and want to go home for comfort and direction when they are in need of help.

These parents are especially observant of how children learn. They seem able to structure situations so that their children feel less anxious and threatened by new learning. Something as simple as learning how to play checkers can be an encouragement to learning rather than an obstacle if it is handled in a step-by-step way, with successful mastery of each step as a prerequisite to the steps that follow.

These parents indicate a basic understanding of the developmental stages through which each child must pass. This seems to help them gain perspective when dealing with the alternating highs and lows of child rearing. They understand that the child with a history of learning disabilities will often behave in a more extreme manner than their so-called normal children; however, the behavior is often different only in degree and not in its basic character. The crises in the life of a learning-disabled child may seem to occur more frequently, last longer, and appear more profound. However, they are similar to crises experienced by all children when growing up. They treat their learning-disabled children as normal but allow far more toleration of difficult stages of growth.

These are the parents who do not panic and run for cover when their child engages in unacceptable behavior that becomes a social embarrassment to them as adults. They are aware that many learning-disabled children have difficulties in social perceptions as well as academic ones. They have observed that their children learn best by "doing"; unfortunately this may mean "doing" what is wrong as well as "doing" what is right. These youngsters must often experience the real repercussions of their behavior and suffer the unfortunate consequences of punishment before they can understand the significance of what they have done.

They are really learning by doing, not through threats or warnings or in abstraction. Painful though it may be, the parent must stand by and allow his child the right to be wrong despite the social stigma or neighbors' gossip.

The most significant characteristic of these parents is that they treat their children as basically normal, emphasizing their strengths rather than becoming preoccupied with their weaknesses. They see these children as independent beings rather than extensions of themselves and thus do not treat each failure as a tragedy. These parents are usually successful human beings who are satisfied with their own lives and don't seem to need their child's successes to fill the void of a failing marriage, declining career, or their own loneliness.

Such parents are not born, they are made through ongoing personal growth and education and through awareness of the needs of their children. Such parents seem to sense as we do now:

— that children teach us much, if we take the time to listen to them and observe them;
— that children with learning-disability problems teach us even more than their so-called normal peers.

The child with a learning disability is normal. His failure situations may occur more frequently; his temper may flare higher, more often; it may appear that his world is coming to an end, more often; but he can and will make it with constant guidance, understanding and help, and most important — love.

Glossary of Terms

Alexia is . . . the loss of ability to read written or printed language despite normal vision or intelligence. Word blindness is a synonym for alexia.

Anoxia is . . . a deficiency in the supply of oxygen to the brain tissues. It may occur pre- or post-birth, in conjunction with high fever, accident, etc., and is considered one possible cause of diffuse brain damage.

Aphasia is . . . a dysfunction in the sensory area affecting ability to understand words, or causing word blindness. It may also affect motor areas interfering with the ability to speak. It is believed to be a result of brain lesion.

Apperception is . . . prior knowledge that we have and can supply to a new learning situation. If we know that steam coming from a kettle indicates a boiling liquid and we have been burned by a boiling liquid, then we will keep our hand away from steaming liquid in a different container for fear of getting burned.

Articulation is ... a term referring to the quality of speech. Are sounds pronounced so that they can be easily understood by a listener?

Auditory acuity is ... the sensitivity of the ear and the accuracy with which it can discern sound waves.

Auditory discrimination is ... the ability to hear the differences and similarities among and between sounds. Poor discrimination often decreases ability to receive spoken language.

Auditory dyslexia is ... a dysfunction in which the child has learned and can recall what letters look like but has not learned their sound associations. He can remember that the name of "b" is "bee," but cannot correctly associate it with "bee" sound.

Auditory retention span is ... the ability to retain auditory material presented over time. It can be short-term or long-term, depending upon the length of time required for memory.

Auditory sequencing is ... the ability to remember things we hear in the correct sequence: recalling a phone number after someone has told it to us or recalling the first stanza of a poem or a song.

Autonomic is ... a term meaning self-controlling or functionally independent activities of the body or organism.

Body image is ... an awareness of one's own body and the relationship of the body parts to each other and to the outside environment. The ability to identify parts of the body correctly and to locate them on oneself or another person would be a good test of body image. This is often tested through the use of the "draw a man" (House-Tree-Person Test).

Catastrophic behavior is ... an excessive reaction to stress. Frequently a learning-disabled child overreacts with fear and anxiety to what is apparently a minor causation.

Central nervous system is ... the brain and spinal cord sectors of the nervous system. Thought to be where information received is processed, stored, and retrieved. It is the main computer of the human body through which all messages are transmitted.

Cerebral dominance is ... the development of sidedness and consistent preference for the use of a hand, ear, foot, and eye (right or left). When a person has not established a one-sided preference, we say he exhibits mixed cerebral dominance. This is frequently manifested in youngsters exhibiting learning lags; however, no causal relationship has been found as of this writing.

Cognition is ... a generic term for any process whereby a person obtains knowledge of an object. Includes perceiving, conceiving, judging, reasoning.

Development is ... a hierarchy of expected performance related to chronological age. The rate at which a child develops is dependent upon his central nervous system which is in turn affected by inherited traits and by physical and emotional factors in the environment.

Distractibility is ... a characteristic of a person whose attention is easily drawn to outside stimuli. The highly distractible child is constantly affected by sights and/or noises in his environment. This must be considered when planning a good learning situati~ ˉ for him.

Dyscalculia is ... a lack of ability to perform   hematical skills, usually associated with neurological dysfunction. It is often a specific disability that may or may not occur along with other problems. Thus a child can appear to be experiencing difficulties *only* in math. This is puzzling to the adults around him.

Dysgraphia is . . . the inability to perform the motor movements required for handwriting, resulting in extremely poor handwriting. The condition is often associated with neurological dysfunction, or neurological soft signs. Sometimes it is a function of slower development of fine motor controls.

Dyslexia is . . . a *partial* word blindness or an inability to read with understanding. It is not related to general intelligence. It often exists concurrently with symptoms of hyperactivity, difficulties in directionality, and poor integration skills.

Echolalia is . . . the parrotlike repetition of words, phrases, sentences spoken by another person, without understanding the meaning of what is being repeated.

EEG is . . . the abbreviation for an electroencephalogram. It is a graphic record of the wavelike changes in electric potential within the brain, observed when electrodes are placed on the skull. It is one method of determining existence of brain damage.

Etiology is . . . the theory of the causation of any disease or dysfunction: the sum of knowledge regarding causes of any condition or disorder. When trying to determine the origin of a learning problem, medical history, emotional factors, and educational information give clues to etiology.

Expressive language skills are . . . the skills that help us communicate with each other. Speaking and writing are expressive language skills. A marked discrepancy between writing and speaking skills may indicate a learning disability.

Eye-hand coordination is . . . the ability to synchronize the working of eye and hand in motor activities. This skill is necessary to many gross and fine motor tasks, such as: sports, walking, eating, slicing food and mechanical operations. The hand usually leads the eye; seeing is first, then doing.

Feedback is . . . the way we receive a report from our own body telling us the speed or degree of movement. It is also the response we get from others as a result of our own behavior.

Fine motor skills are . . . those skills necessary to perform precision tasks such as manipulating a pencil properly or, when fingers begin to work smoothly, enabling the child to grasp small objects, operate tiny buttons and knobs. The child's fingers respond efficiently to his brain's command.

Form constancy is . . . the ability to recognize a letter form in various places or contexts despite slight differences in color, size, or angle.

Hyperactivity is . . . also a highly active behavior level. However, this must be differentiated from hyperkinetic behavior. Hyperactivity is excessive activity, but does not necessarily interfere with learning or behavior.

Hyperkinetic behavior is . . . the tendency to be overactive when compared to averages of expected activity level for age group, behavior characterized by excessive restlessness and constant mobility. It often inter-feres with learning activities. It is sometimes medicated.

Hypokinetic behavior is . . . a tendency to be underactive and lethargic when compared to average for age group.

Image of body in space is . . . knowledge on the part of the child as to where he is in relation to the objects around him. Thus he can avoid bumping into things and appearing awkward in managing motion in space.

Inner language is . . . how we internalize and organize our inner experi-ences without speaking. It is the language of our thoughts.

Intelligence is . . . the aggregate capacity to act purposefully, think ra-tionally, and deal effectively with the environment (according to David Wechsler, Ph.D., author of WISC).

Kinesthetic is . . . the body sense in which we get feedback concerning body part or body movement. Pertaining to motion, position, etc. Kines-thetic dysfunction in a child tends to cause distortions in perceptions and learning and possible emotional side effects.

Kinesthetic method is . . . an approach to remediate disability via tracing symbols in the air or on paper before writing or using body movement to learn abstract concepts.

Kinetic is . . . the physical act of movement. Also refers to high level of activity in a person or matter in environment.

Language is . . . a learned behavior involving the use of symbols (words and numbers). Language involves four functions: (1) spelling; (2) writing; (3) reading; and (4) listening.

Latent condition is . . . a subtle hidden condition that cannot be found on the surface but has the potential of developing.

Laterality is . . . the process by which the person develops an awareness of the existence of two sides of his body, and the ability to recognize these two sides as right and left.

Learning disability is . . . defined in many ways. Public Law 91–230 (dated April 13, 1970) states: "The term 'children with specific learning dis-abilities' means those children who have disorder in one or more of the basic psychological processes involved in understanding or in using lan-guage, spoken or written, which disorder may manifest itself in im-perfect ability to listen, think, speak, read, write, spell, or do mathe-matical calculations. Such disorders include such conditions as per-ceptual handicaps, brain injury, minimal brain dysfunction, dyslexia, and developmental aphasia. Such term does not include children who have learning problems which are primarily the result of visual, hearing, or motor handicaps, of mental retardation, of emotional disturbance, or of environmental disadvantage."

Learning lag is . . . a poor development of skills in selected academic areas. It is often a result of poor teaching or lack of readiness on the part of the child to retain certain skills.

Learning style or mode is . . . the way a child is best able to understand and retain academic learning. We all learn best through one or more channels, visual, auditory, motor, or a combination of these (experien-tial).

Maturational lag is . . . a slower rate of development in certain specialized aspects of neurological readiness (see Development).

Modality is . . . a pathway by which one receives information and learning. Among these are vision, hearing, touch, taste, and smell.

Multisensory (interneurosensory) learning is . . . learning resulting from two or more combined channels or modalities rather than only one. For example, reading words and listening to them on tape combines the visual and auditory modalities and is multisensory.

Ocular pursuit is . . . any eye movement that is the result of visually tracking a moving target. It is necessary for many visual functions. The child who chronically swings at a ball with a bat but misses may be experiencing difficulties in ocular pursuit.

Perception is . . . how one receives impressions via the senses. How we understand what we see, hear and smell. It is a highly complex system involving the central nervous system for relay of impulses. Any slight imperfection in the system can cause the whole process of integration to break down. (It is comparable to a phone switchboard with crossed wires.) Learning is based on the smooth integration of perceptions, processing, and well-developed modes of expression.

Perseveration is . . . the tendency to repeat words or actions in order to make the ones learned previously appear more secure and predictable. The dysfunctional child often perseverates to a degree which annoys and puzzles adults. Such a child also may have difficulty in shifting to a new activity. Example: The child who is writing letters of the alphabet but continues to make enlarged circles over the original or florid designs around each letter and seems unable to turn it off and shift to a new letter form.

Phoneme is . . . the smallest unit of sound in any particular language. For example, the sound made by the letter *t* is a phoneme. A *phoneme* becomes a *grapheme* when it is written down.

Phonic skills or **phonetics** is . . . learning to associate sounds or *phonemes* with letters or combinations of letters (graphemes). *Phonetics* is the overall study of the sounds of speech and language and how these sounds are produced.

Receptive language is . . . language that is spoken or written by others and received by the individual. The receptive language skills are listening and reading. Example: The child with a poor understanding of what he hears or reads may be a child with poor receptive language skills.

Retardation is . . . an overall or global lag in the acquisition of educational skills. Very slow in development when compared to chronological age norms.

Reversals are . . . errors appearing in reading and writing, reversal of single letters (b or d); of the order of letters within a word (pat for tap); or of the order of a whole line. Most common, however, are reversals of single letters and words. When we refer to reversals of words, we also call it a transposition of letters.

Sensorimotor is . . . pertaining to the neural transmission of messages from a sense organ to a muscle. Example: When a foul smell is sensed by the nose, it causes the nose to wrinkle up. (Sense leads to muscle response.)

Slow-learning child is . . . one who requires more teaching to acquire abstract concepts. He may require many concrete experiences in order to learn and much time, patience and overteaching. He is not necessarily a specifically learning-disabled child, who may learn concepts with ease but have difficulty in technical reading.

Social perception is . . . the ability to interpret stimuli in the social environment and appropriately relate such interpretations to the social situation. Socially inappropriate behavior and lack of social perception are often associated with learning problems.

Soft neurological signs are . . . neurological abnormalities that are mild or slight and *difficult* to detect in contrast to the gross or obvious neurological abnormalities. Most youngsters exhibiting learning problems exhibit soft neurological signs rather than any gross discernible symptoms.

Space relations is . . . the relationship among objects in space that takes their three-dimensional (length, width and height) attributes into consideration within the relationship.

Speech is . . . a motor act involving the lips, tongue, jaw, vocal cords, etc., in which an audible sound is produced.

Syndrome is . . . a set of symptoms that usually occur together and make a discernible pattern.

Tactile sense is . . . the ability to touch and feel objects, to sense the similarities and differences between them in texture, shape, and size.

Transposition is . . . reversal of the order of a sequence of letters, a common symptom of dyslexia (see Reversals).

Trauma is . . . any injury, wound, or shock to the body or its parts. Trauma can be both physical and emotional and is often considered a causal factor in learning disability problems.

Visual tracking (see Ocular pursuit).

Vocabulary is . . . the level of knowledge we have of word symbols and their meanings and usage. *Receptive vocabulary* is that which we understand when others speak. *Expressive vocabulary* is our level of spoken language. *Reading vocabulary* is that level of understanding we have of words we can decode or read. Tests measuring vocabulary levels are often included in tests of intelligence, but only measure specific kinds of skills.

Notes

Chapter 2
1. NINDS Monograph No. 9, Department of Health, Education and Welfare, 1970.
2. Clyde Hawley and Robert Buckley, "Food Dyes and Hyperkinetic Children," *Academic Therapy*, Volume X, No. 1 (Fall 1974), 27.
3. Domeena C. Renshaw, M.D., *The Hyperactive Child* (Chicago: Nelson-Hall, 1974).
4. Theodore Reik, *Listening with the Third Ear* (New York: Pyramid Books, 1948).
5. Advice from one of our mothers, Esther Ginandes.

Chapter 3
1. "Two Doctors Offer Dyslexia Theory," New York *Times*, April 29, 1974, p. 29.

2. Macdonald Critchley, M.D., *Developmental Dyslexia* (London: William Heineman Medical Books and C. C. Thomas, 1964).
3. Samuel T. Orton, M.D., *Familial Occurrence of Disorders in the Acquisition of Language* (1930).
4. Dirk Bakker, "Hemispheric Specialization and Stages in the Learning to Read Process," *Bulletin of the Orton Society,* Volume XXIII (1975).
5. Sidney Carter, M.D., and Arnold Gold, M.D., "The Nervous System — Diagnosis of Neurologic Diseases," reprinted in Sapir, Selma, *Children with Learning Problems* (New York: Brunner-Mazel, 1973), p. 569.
6. Annemarie P. Weil, M.D., "Children with Minimal Brain Dysfunction," from "Psychosocial Process," *Journal of Jewish Board of Guardians,* Volume 1, No. 2 (1970), 89–97.
7. Macdonald Critchley, M.D., *Developmental Dyslexia* (London: William Heineman and C. C. Thomas, 1964).
8. Macdonald Critchley, M.D., "Some Problems of the Ex-Dyslexic," *Bulletin of the Orton Society,* Volume XXIII (1975), 7–14.
9. Keogh, *Academic Therapy,* Volume VII, No. 1 (September 1971), 47–50.
10. F. Speer, M.D., *Allergies of the Nervous System* (New York: Charles C. Thomas, 1970).
11. Ben Feingold, M.D., *Why Your Child Is Hyperactive* (New York: Random House, 1974).
12. K. E. Moyer, M.D., *The Psychobiology of Aggression* (New York: Harper & Row, 1975).
13. Dr. Herbert Rie, from an address at the American Medical Association Convention, Chicago, Illinois, June 25, 1974.
14. Sidney Walker, M.D., "Blood, Sugar and Emotional Storms," *Psychology Today,* June 1973, pp. 69–74.
15. Marilyn Fergusen, *The Brain Revolution* (New York: Taplinger Press, 1973), p. 212.
16. Robert Atkins, M.D., *Dr. Atkins Diet Revolution* (New York: David McKay & Co., 1972), p. 70.
17. Kolvisto, Sequetos, and Krause, "Developmental Medicine and Child Neurology," London, *Spastics International Medical Publication,* October 1972, reprinted in *Journal of Learning Disabilities,* Volume 14, No. 5, pp. 603–614.
18. Marilyn Fergusen, *The Brain Revolution* (New York: Taplinger Press, 1973), p. 212.

Chapter 4
1. Anna Freud, *Psychoanalytic Study of the Child* (New York: International Universities Press, 1958).
2. Doreen Kronick, *A Word or Two About Learning Disabilities* (San Rafael: Academic Therapy Publications, 1973), p. 14.
3. Haim G. Ginott, *Between Parent and Teenager* (New York: Macmillan Co., 1969).
4. DeHirsch, Jansky, and Langford, *Predicting Reading Failure* (New York: Harper & Row, 1966), p. 57.
5. Facetious wall plaque in office of Headmaster Samuel Ross, Green Chimneys School, Brewster, New York.

6. Stella Chess, M.D., *How to Help Your Child Get the Most out of School* (New York: Doubleday, 1975).
7. Peanuts characters, United Features Syndicate, Inc. (Greenwich: Fawcett, 1973).
8. Jules Henry, *Pathway to Madness* (New York: Random House, 1971), p. 240.
9. Haim G. Ginott, *Between Parent and Teenager* (New York: Macmillan Co., 1969).
10. Anna Freud, *Psychoanalytic Study of the Child* (New York: International Universities Press, 1958).

Chapter 5
1. Jerome Brunner, M.D., *Toward a Theory of Instruction* (Cambridge, Mass.: Belknap Press, 1966).

Chapter 6
1. See *Project Cope* by Helen and Martin Weiss, © 1975, Treehouse Associates, P.O. Box 568, Great Barrington, Mass.

Chapter 7
1. Lawrence Silver, M.D., Chief, Division of Youth Services, Professor of Psychiatry, Rutgers University Medical School, at a speech for the Orton Society, Biltmore Hotel, March 1975.

Chapter 9
1. Educational Interpretation of the Wechsler Intelligence Scale for Children. Remediation Associates, Box 318, Linden, N.J. (William E. Ferinden, Jr., and Sherman Jacobson.)
2. Wechsler Adult Intelligence Scale, Psychological Corporation, New York.
3. Wechsler Pre-Primary Scale of Intelligence, Psychological Corporation, New York.
4. Detroit Test of Learning Aptitude, Bobbs Merrill Co., Inc., Indianapolis, Indiana.
5. Terman and Merrill, Stanford Binet Intelligence Scale form LM (Boston: Houghton Mifflin, 1960.)
6. G. N. Getman, E. R. Kane, M. R. Halgren, and G. W. McKee, *The Physiology of Readiness Programs* (Chicago: Lyons & Carnahan, 1966).
7. Slingerland Screening Tests for Specific Language Disabilities and Malcomesius Screening Test for Specific Language Disability, Educators Publishing Service, Cambridge, Massachusetts.
8. Malcomesius Test for Specific Language Disability, Educators Publishing Service, Cambridge, Massachusetts.
9. Peabody Individual Achievement Test, Dunn & Markwarat, American Guidance Service, Inc., Circle Pines, Minnesota.
10. Massachusetts Association for Children with Learning Disabilities.

Chapter 10
1. Stella Chess, M.D., *How to Help Your Child Get the Most out of School* (New York, Doubleday, 1975).

2. Laura Schreibman and Robert J. Koegel, "How Parents Can Treat Their Troubled Children," *Psychology Today,* March 1975, pp. 61–66.
3. *Ibid.*

Chapter 11
1. Second Step Reading Program, College of St. Rose, Albany, N.Y. 12203.

Chapter 12
1. Sullivan-Webster, McGraw Hill, New York.
2. World Book, Field Educational Enterprises, Chicago.

Chapter 13
1. Newell C. Kephart, *The Slow Learner in the Classroom* (Columbus: Charles E. Merrill, 1960).

Chapter 14
1. Robert E. Valett, *Handbook of Psychoeducational Resource Programs* (Palo Alto: Fearon Publishers, 1967).
2. Newell C. Kephart, *Motoric Aids to Learning* (Columbus: Charles E. Merrill Publishing Co., 1968).
3. MKM, 809 Kansas City Street, Rapid City, S.D.

Chapter 15
1. This particular approach to multisensory learning was developed by Mrs. Beth Slingerland. It is spelled out in her book *A Multisensory Approach to Language Arts for Specific Language Disability Children* (Cambridge, Mass.: Educators Publishing Service, 1972).

Chapter 18
1. Doris Johnson, "The Language Continuum," in *Children with Learning Problems, Readings in a Developmental-Interaction Approach,* ed. Selma Sapir and Ann C. Nitzburg (New York: Brunner Mazel, 1974), pp. 366–7.

Chapter 19
1. Boehm Test of Concepts, Psychological Corporation, New York, New York.

Bibliography

Books

Arena, John I., editor. *Building Handwriting Skills in Dyslexic Children.* California: Academic Therapy Publications, 1970.

Behrman, Polly. *Activities for Developing Visual Perception.* California: Academic Therapy Publications, 1970.

Bettelheim, Bruno. *Dialogues with Mothers.* New York: Avon Publishers, 1971.

Bird, Caroline. *The Case Against College.* New York: David McKay Co. Inc., 1975.

Bott, R., et al. *The Teaching of Young Children.* New York: Shocken Books, 1971.

Bradfield, Robert H., editor. *Behavior Modification of Learning Disabilities.* California: Academic Therapy, 1971.

Bruner, Jerome. *Toward a Theory of Instruction.* Cambridge, Mass.: Belknap Press, 1966.

Brutten, M., et al. *Something's Wrong with My Child.* New York: Harcourt Brace, 1973.

Byler, Ruth, editor, et al. *Teach Us What We Want to Know.* New York: Mental Health Materials Center, 1969.

Chess, Dr. Stella. *How to Help Your Child Get the Most out of School.* New York: Doubleday, 1975.

Clark, Louise. *Can't Read, Can't Write, Can't Talk Too Good Either.* Walken Co., 1973.

Cohen, Dorothy H. *Observing and Recording the Behavior of Young Children.* New York: Teachers College Press, 1965.

DeHirsch, Katrina; Jansky, Jeanette Jefferson; and Langford, William S. *Predicting Reading Failure.* New York, Evanston, and London: Harper & Row, 1966.

Fader, Daniel, et al. *Hooked on Books Program and Proof.* New York: Berkley Publishing Co., 1972.

Featherstone, Joseph. *Schools Where Children Learn.* New York: Avon Books, 1973.

Ferguson, Marilyn. *The Brain Revolution.* New York: Taplinger Publishing Co., 1973.

Gesell, A., and Ilg, F. *The Child from Five to Ten.* New York: Harper & Row, 1946.

Ginandes, Shepard. *The School We Have.* New York: Delacorte Press, 1973.

Ginott, Haim G., M.D. *Between Parent and Child.* New York: Avon Books, 1973.

Ginott, Haim, G., M.D. *Between Teacher and Child.* New York: Hearst Corp., 1975.

Golic, M. *A Parent's Guide to Learning Problems.* Quebec, Canada: Quebec Association for Children with Learning Disabilities, 6338 Victoria Avenue, Montreal 252, Quebec, Canada.

Gordon, Dr. Thomas. *Parent Effectiveness Training.* New York: Peter H. Wyden, 1970.

Hechinger, G. and F. *Teen-Age Tyrant.* Greenwich, Conn.: Fawcett, 1964.

Henry, Jules. *Pathways to Madness.* New York: Random House, 1971.

Keats, John. *The Sheepskin Psychosis.* New York: Dell Publishing Co., 1966.

Kirk, Gordon, et al. *Progress and Parent Information.* California: Professional Growth and Academic Therapy.

Koppitz, Elizabeth Munsterberg. *Children with Learning Disabilities.* New York: Grune & Stratton, 1971.

Kronick, Doreen. *A Word or Two About Learning Disabilities.* San Rafael, Cal.: Academic Therapy, 1973.

L'Engle, Madeleine. *A Circle of Quiet.* Greenwich, Conn.: Fawcett, 1975.

Lerner, Janet W. *Children with Learning Disabilities.* Boston: Houghton Mifflin, 1971.

Lewis, Harold R., and Streetfeld, Dr. Harold S. *Growth Games.* New York: Harcourt Brace Jovanovich, 1971.

Lewis, Harry, Ed.D. *Second Step Reading Program.* Albany: Center for Developmental Studies, College of St. Rose, 1975.

McCarthy, J., and McCarthy, J. *Learning Disabilities*. Boston: Allyn & Bacon Inc., 1972.

McKee, William. *A Primer for Parents*. Revised. Boston: Houghton Mifflin.

Redl, Fritz. *When We Deal with Children*. New York: Free Press, 1966.

Reik, Theodore. *Listening with the Third Ear*. New York: Pyramid Pub. Inc., 1964.

Richette, Lisa Aversa. *The Throwaway Children*. New York: Dell Publ. Company, 1973.

Sapir, Selma, editor. *Children with Learning Problems*. New York: Bruner Mazel Inc., 1973.

Schulz, Charles. *The Wisdom of Linus*. United Features Syndicate, Inc., 1971.

Shrieber, David, editor. *Profile of the School Dropout*. New York: Vintage Books, 1968.

Stevenson, Nancy. *The Natural Way to Reading*. Boston: Little, Brown and Co., 1974.

Stott, D. H., M.D. *The Parent as Teacher: A Guide for Parents of Children with Learning Disabilities*. Toronto: New Press, 1972.

Weiss, Helen and Martin. *Parents' and Teachers' Guide to Learning Disabilities*. Treehouse Associates, P.O. Box 568, Great Barrington, Mass., 1973.

Weiss, Helen and Martin. *Survival Manual: Case Studies & Suggestions for the Learning Disabled Teenager*. Treehouse Associates, P.O. Box 568, Great Barrington, Mass., 1974.

White, Marian, editor. *High Interest Easy Reading*. New York: Citation Press, 1972.

Periodicals

Bakker, Dirk J. "Hemispheric Specialization and Stages in the Learning to Read Process." *Bulletin of the Orton Society*, Frederick, Md., Vol. XXIII (1973), 15–27.

Critchley, Macdonald, M.D. "Some Problems of the Ex-Dyslexic." *Bulletin of the Orton Society*, Frederick, Md., Vol. XXIII (1973), 7–14.

Gomez, Manuel, R., M.D. "Neurologic Approach to Specific Language Disability." *Bulletin of the Orton Society*, Frederick, Md., Vol. XX (1970), 17–29.

Keogh, Barbara K. "Hyperactivity and Learning Problems — Implication for Teachers." *Academic Therapy Magazine*, Volume VII, No. 1 (Fall 1971) 47–58.

Yudkovitz, E. Mancy Lewison, and Rottersman, J. "Communication Therapy in Childhood Schizophrenia." From *Psychosocial Process, Journal Jewish Board of Guardians, Issues in Mental Health*, Vol. IV, No. 1 (Spring 1975).

Titles of interest in the area of Special Education from Little, Brown

The Hyperactive Child
  Domeena C. Renshaw, M.D.

The Natural Way to Reading: A How-To Method for Parents of Slow
  Learners, Dyslexic; and Learning Disabled Children
  Nancy Stevenson

The Siege: The First Eight Years of an Autistic Child
  Clara Claiborne Park

Square Pegs, Round Holes: The Learning-Disabled Child in the Classroom and at Home
  Harold B. Levy, M.D.